MEN & INTIMACY

*Personal Accounts Exploring the
Dilemmas of Modern Male Sexuality*

Edited
by
Franklin Abbott

The Crossing Press
Freedom, CA 95019

Cover art and interior illustration by Mark Johnson
Cover design by Betsy Bayley
Typesetting by Archetype Publishing & Design

Printed in the U.S.A.

Library of Congress Cataloging-in-Publication Data

Men & intimacy : personal accounts exploring the dilemmas of modern
male sexuality / edited by Franklin Abbott.
      p.   cm.
  ISBN 0-89594-408-1. — ISBN 0-89594-407-3 (pbk.)
  1. Men—Psychology. 2. Intimacy (Psychology) 3. Love 4. Sex
(Psychology) I. Abbott, Franklin. II. Title: Men and intimacy.
  HQ1090.M427   1990
  306.7'081—dc20
                                  89-78362
                                  CIP

CONTENTS

PART II: UNDERSTANDING INTIMACY

PART III: ON OUR OWN

Acknowledgements

The assistance I have received in editing this anthology has been both practical and inspirational. On the practical side I wish to thank the editors of a number of small journals who recommended contributors either directly or by publishing their work. Michael Biernbaum and Rick Cote with *Changing Men*, Sy Safransky with *The Sun*, John Nierenberg with *The Men's Report* and David Barstow with *Pilgrimage*. Also, thanks to Carl Morse and Will Roscoe for their assistance and to Gerritt Wilson and Shepherd Bliss for their help with the title.

I am grateful to Christina Ishtar and George Baker who struggled to turn my handwritten pages into typewritten ones, and to Linda Bryant, Sherry Emery and Carolyn Mobley, partners at Charis Books, who created a men's section in their women's bookstore where I located chapbooks containing the writings by David Mura and Bruce Kokopeli and George Lakey. I want to acknowledge the support of Mary Mehl and my Venezuelan family — Alejandro, Alex, Ramon, Jorge, and Oscar — who gave me space to work on this book.

For inspiration I am indebted to my men friends in Atlanta and around the world whose trust in sharing the intimate details of our lives has left me with a desire to share even further. I want to acknowledge the support of my friends and colleagues Neil Adams, Roger Bailey, Martha Lou Brock, Russell Brooker, Jane DeMore, Edith Kelman, Cal Gough, Luis Montenegro, Elaine Mueller, John Speaks, Sharon Sanders, Illene Schroeder, Bill Thompson, and Raven Wolfdancer. Special thanks is due my advisor, Kay Harrison. I also feel deep gratitude toward my teacher and mentor, Earl Brown, whose authenticity has made it possible for me to plumb my own depths, to the wizard of poetry James Broughton, whose celebration of Eros approaches eight decades, to my friend Lanier Clance who has taught me something of erotic possibilities beyond the cultural programming, and to Charles Haver, my lover and partner, who has steadfastly loved me because of and in spite of who I am. Finally, I offer thanks to John Gill and Elaine Goldman Gill for taking another chance with me on a book that suggests that men can change.

I dedicate this volume to the memory of two friends who taught me a great deal about intimacy: Mike Richey (1948-1972) and Michael Mason (1954-1989).

Franklin Abbott

Introduction

Franklin Abbott

In *New Men, New Minds: Breaking Male Tradition*, I published an essay of my own on androgyny. In it I told of a magical journey I took one spring by train from Atlanta to Birmingham to visit my grandparents. I am going again tomorrow. It is likely the last time I will see my grandfather. A stroke has devastated him, leaving him unable to speak or walk, just four months short of his eighty-ninth birthday. When I spoke with my grandmother last night, she told me that their doctor of twenty years advised her that she had to let him go. She said my grandfather didn't want tubes or machines to keep him alive, so there are none. As his strength ebbs his family gathers, watches and waits. Though he became increasingly flexible toward the end of his sixty-plus-year marriage with my grandmother, he is still our family's last patriarch. He is also the only member of my family I have been afraid to share my homosexuality with. Perhaps he would have been accepting, putting aside his strong, long-held beliefs about right and wrong. He accepted all the "friends" I've brought to visit, and I have brought them all. Unless some grim miracle occurs, he will be dead by the time this book is published, and I am relieved that he will not chance to see it. It is not his disapproval that I fear, it is the loss of his affection. I have always known that he loves me, and at times his love was the only man's love that I have been sure of. In a sense his death will spare us both the possibility that because our minds differ so radically, our hearts must close off one to the other. There are times when death can be a healer.

My friend Susan Smithers was a big, loving, playful, depressed woman I'd known since I was eighteen. She was one of a few from college that I maintained contact with. Four years ago she wrote to me that she had been raped in broad daylight as she walked from her apartment to the corner store in her nice neighborhood north of L.A. She seemed to recover with support groups, therapy and California-style spirituality. Two years later her mother left a message on my answering machine saying that Susan had taken her own life. Susan was unhappy for a number of reasons, but I can't help speculate that that rape tipped the scales and as a result, she succumbed to her despair. There are times when death can be an answer to the pain of living. Who am I to judge her way out of pain? Who am I to judge her rapist and the society in which so many men rape that no woman is ever really safe?

Over the first six months of this year I sat week after week with one of my psychotherapy clients who was dying from AIDS. I had seen Eric for almost four years prior to his diagnosis. We had begun our work expecting he would conquer his demons and live life more freely and fully. Our expectations were shattered after his diagnosis with AIDS. Eric fought AIDS for two and a half years. As his suffering intensified Eric was often despondent and angry. He put his family, friends and doctors through many a rigorous test. Eric was also loving, curious, vulnerable, and kept his sly sense of humor. He accepted his decline from youth to old age in barely two years, finding a wisdom at thirty-one that put me often in awe. Eric's courage and his mother's courage and his lover's courage to keep on loving right up until the end taught me something I hadn't known: that the human heart can stay open, no matter what. This time, at least for me, death was a teacher.

If you're asking exactly what these stories have to do with a book about men and intimacy, I'll do my best to try to explain. I believe that patriarchy is dying and that its demise is healing the wounds between genders, between women and women, and between men and men. The older generation is dying literally. Their ideas about sex and sex roles lose weight with the passing of each true believer. Feminism and gay liberation are gaining strength world-wide. These strong social movements challenge misogyny and homophobia, the cornerstones of patriarchy.

I believe that the pain of women and homosexuals has reached a critical mass. My friend, Susan, could not live with her pain and we can no longer live with ours. That does not mean mass suicide. It means massive resistance, overt and covert, highly organized and deeply personal. The slogan used by the AIDS activist group ACT UP, *Silence = Death*, sums up our sentiment succinctly. We will not be raped and beaten back into a silence that will cost us our lives. There will be victims, like my friend, who are destroyed by patriarchal violence. There will be many others who will recover and fight back with a strength that we are just beginning to fathom.

AIDS has been another crack in the code of patriarchy. What

some patriarchs have proclaimed as God's revenge on perverts has necessitated an open discussion of sex in our society, a society in which silence about sex, real sex, has been a strictly maintained taboo. Psychologist James Hillman says that men, at least heterosexual men, don't talk to each other about sex. He says "dumb sex" is part of our American culture. Dumb sex has become deadly sex, and we are all beginning to talk about sex because to refrain from doing so is a threat to our survival. My client, Eric, never apologized for having AIDS. He told everyone of significance in his life the truth. He volunteered his time to help train doctors and wrote letters to politicians. He did not die quietly or ashamed.

This anthology about men and intimacy is by no means definitive. Few of the writers, if any, would call themselves experts. There are obvious gaps in discussing the sexuality of young boys and adolescents, and that of older men. There is plenty of room to expand upon what the men of color herein have to tell us. Neither is this book a sex manual. There are no prescriptions for better orgasms, no recipes for sexual nirvanas. What is talked about is the terrible pain, sometimes fierce, sometimes numb, that men feel about their sexuality and about intimacy. As perpetrators and victims of sexual violence, as sex addicts and erotophobes, men are often in bondage to their implicit, war-oriented, boyhood-deep indoctrination in sexual politics. The authors in the first section address this in their writings about male privilege, homophobia, rape, child sexual abuse, circumcision, pornography and AIDS. It is painful but essential reading for any man who wants to understand his sexuality and the obstacles to emotional closeness.

The second section on understanding intimacy is grounded in the logic that men cannot overcome the legacy of their sexual violence alone. We need the insights of women and other men translated into real relationships to begin the process of sexual and emotional healing. The authors in this section write about the healing that love brings to men and women, and men and men who dare to open themselves to it. The final section, "On Our Own," deals with what men are beginning to do with what we are learning about love, how we are better able to love ourselves.

The writings in this book come to you largely as they came to me. As editor I've solicited, selected, and arranged but little else. Consequently, some of the writings are raw and some you may find flawed. They are all, as best as I can determine, sincere. I wanted to share this with the readers, because it is the closest thing to the truth I can tell you about men, sex, and intimacy. We, as men, must dialogue through our disagreements. We must challenge, support and educate each other. We must do better, far better, by the women we share this planet with. Shame and silence are not the answers, but *it is* hard to talk, and there is so much about sex and intimacy that is confusing and painful to look at. This is an invitation from the writers of this book to begin an honest examination of our relationship as men with our own sexual and intimate capacities. I invite those who read this to approach it with both a critical mind and an open heart.

Franklin Abbott
October, 13, 1989
Atlanta, Georgia, U.S.A.

Part I: *Overcoming Violence*

Triad

Edward Field

A temple sculpture: Two Warriors in Combat.
Down between their knees a Female
with one of their stone pricks up her cunt,
at the same time, bending over backwards
to take the other's cock in her mouth,
while the men cross swords above her.
Even confronting each other with sharp steel,
according to this ancient mystery
something tender bridges them,
a goddess joining the warriors in her body—
for she has to be a goddess
and this is obviously her function:
But is she consoling, neutralizing,
trying to bring peace about,
or delivering the charge that sets the swords a-clashing?
Or do they only appear to fight
to deny the sexual connection below?
But no one seems to be hiding anything—
it's open as a diagram, illustrative,
rather than a daisy chain like The Three Graces.
When we say men are "joined" in battle
do we too mean like this,
opposition at one pole, concord at the other,
and in the contest both at once?
Beyond the fierce worldly display,
the glitter of rivalry, the squiring of women,
a secret brotherhood?
And this goddess created out of mutual need?
As if maleness cannot mate without a medium—
and only by a female principle can men unite . . . or fight.

More Power Than We Want: Masculine Sexuality and Violence

by Bruce Kokopeli and George Lakey

Masculine sexuality involves the oppression of women, competition among men, and homophobia (fear of homosexuality). Patriarchy, the systematic domination of women by men through unequal opportunities, rewards, punishments, and the internalization of unequal expectations through sex role differentiation, is the institution which organizes these behaviors. Patriarchy is men having more power, both personally and politically, than women of the same rank. This imbalance of power is the core of patriarchy, but definitely not the extent of it.

Sex inequality cannot be routinely enforced through open violence or even blatant discriminatory agreements—patriarchy also needs its values accepted in the minds of people. If as many young *women* wanted to be physicians as men, and as many young men *wanted* to be nurses as women, the medical schools and the hospitals would be hard put to maintain the masculine domination of health care; open struggle and the naked exercise of power would be necessary. Little girls, therefore, are encouraged to think "nurse" and boys to think "doctor."

Patriarchy assigns a list of human characteristics according to gender: women should be nurturant, gentle, in touch with their feelings, etc.; men should be productive, competitive, super-rational, etc. Occupations are valued according to these gender-linked characteristics, so social work, teaching, housework, and nursing are of lower status than business executive, judge, or professional football player.

When men do enter "feminine" professions they disproportionately rise to the top and become chefs, principals of schools, directors of ballet, and teachers of social work. A man is somewhat excused from his sex role deviation if he at least dominates within the deviation. Domination, after all, is what patriarchy is all about.

Access to powerful positions by women (i.e., those positions formerly limited to men) is contingent on the women adopting some masculine characteristics, such as competitiveness. They feel pressure to give up qualities assigned to females (such as gentleness) because those qualities are considered inherently weak by patriarchal culture. The existence, therefore, of a woman like Indira Gandhi in the position of a dictator in no way undermines the basic sexist structure which allocates power to those with masculine characteristics.

Patriarchy also shapes men's sexuality so it expresses the theme of domination. Notice the masculine preoccupation with size. The size of a man's body has a lot to say about his clout or his vulnerability, as any junior high boy can tell you. Many of these schoolyard fights are settled by who is bigger than whom, and we experience in our adult lives the echoes of intimidation and deference produced by our habitual "sizing up" of the situation.

Penis size is part of this masculine preoccupation, this time directed toward women. Men want to have larger penises because size equals power, the ability to make a woman "really feel it." The imagery of violence is close to the surface here, since women find penis size irrelevant to sexual genital pleasure. "Fucking" is a highly ambiguous word, meaning both intercourse and exploitation/assault.

It is this confusion that we need to untangle and understand. Patriarchy tells men that their need for love and respect can only be met by being masculine, powerful, and ultimately violent. As men come to accept this, their sexuality begins to reflect it. Violence and sexuality combine to support masculinity as a character ideal. To love a woman is to have power over her and to treat her violently if need be. The Beatles' song "Happiness Is A Warm Gun" is but one example of how sexuality gets confused with violence and power. We know one man who was discussing another man who seemed to be highly fertile—he had made several women pregnant. "That guy," he said, "doesn't shoot any blanks."

Rape is the end logic of masculine sexuality. Rape is not so much a sexual act as an act of violence expressed in a sexual way. The rapist's mind-set—that violence and sexuality *can* go together—is actually a product of patriarchal conditioning, for most of us men understand the same, however abhorrent rape may be to us personally.

In war, rape is astonishingly prevalent even among men who "back home" would never do it. In the following description by a marine sergeant who witnessed a gang rape in Vietnam, notice that nearly all the nine-man squad participated:

> They were supposed to go after what they called a Viet Cong whore.
> They went into her village and instead of capturing her, they raped
> her—every man raped her. As a matter of fact, one man said to me
> later that it was the first time he had ever made love to a woman with
> his boots on. The man who led the platoon, or the squad, was
> actually a private. The squad leader was a sergeant but he was a
> useless person and he let the private take over his squad. Later he
> said he took no part in the raid. It was against his morals. So instead
> of telling his squad not to do it, because they wouldn't listen to him
> anyway, the sergeant went into another side of the village and just
> sat and stared bleakly at the ground, feeling sorry for himself. But
> at any rate, they raped the girl, and then, the last man to make love
> to her, shot her in the head. [Vietnam Veterans Against the War,
> statement by Michael McClusker in The Winter Soldier Investiga-
> tion: An Inquiry Into American War Crimes.]

Psychologist James Prescott adds to this account:

> What is it in the American psyche that permits the use of the word
> "love" to describe rape? And where the act of love is completed with
> a bullet in the head! [Bulletin of the Atomic Scientists, November
> 1975, p. 17.]

Masculinity Against Men:
The Militarization of Everyday Life

Patriarchy benefits men by giving us a class of people (women) to
dominate and exploit. Patriarchy also oppresses men, by setting us
at odds with each other and shrinking our life space.

The pressure to win starts early and never stops. Working class
gangs fight over turf: rich people's sons are pushed to compete on the
sports field. British military officers, it is said, learned to win on the
playing fields of Eton.

Competition is conflict held within a framework of rules. When
the stakes are really high, the rules may not be obeyed; fighting
breaks out. We men mostly relate through competition, but we know
what is waiting in the wings. John Wayne is not a cultural hero by
accident.

Men compete with each other for status as masculine males.
Because masculinity equals power, this means we are competing for
power. The ultimate proof of power/masculinity is violence. A man
may fail to "measure up" to the macho stereotype in important ways,
but if he can fight successfully with the person who challenges him
on his deviance, he is still all right. The television policeman Baretta

is strange in some ways: he is gentle with women and he cried when a man he loved was killed. However, he has what are probably the largest biceps in television and he proves weekly that he can beat up the toughs who come his way.

The close relationship between violence and masculinity does not need much demonstration. War used to be justified partly because it promoted "manly virtue" in a nation. Those millions of people in the woods hunting deer, in the National Rifle Association, and cheering on the bloodiest hockey teams are overwhelmingly men.

The world situation is so much defined by patriarchy that what we see in the wars of today is competition between various patriarchal ruling classes and governments breaking into open conflict. Violence is the accepted masculine form of conflict resolution. Women at this time are not powerful enough in the world situation for us to see mass overt violence being waged on them. But the violence is in fact there; it is hidden through its legitimization by the state and by culture.

In everyday middle-class life, open violence between men is of course rare. The defining characteristics of masculinity, however, are only a few steps removed from violence. Wealth, productivity, or rank in the firm or institution translate into power—the capacity (whether or not exercised) to dominate. The holders of power in even polite institutions seem to know that violence is at their fingertips, judging from the reactions of college presidents to student protest in the 1960s. We know of one urban "pacifist" man, the head of a theological seminary, who was barely talked out of calling the police to deal with a nonviolent student sit-in at "his" seminary!

Patriarchy teaches us at very deep levels that we can never be safe with other men (or perhaps with anyone!), for the guard must be kept up lest our vulnerability be exposed and we be taken advantage of. At a Quaker conference in Philadelphia, a discussion group considered the value of personal sharing and openness in the Quaker Meeting. In almost every case the women advocated more sharing and the men opposed it. Dividing by gender on that issue was predictable; men are conditioned by our life experience of masculinity to distrust settings where personal exposure will happen, especially if men are present. Most men find emotional intimacy possible only with women; many with only one woman; some men cannot be emotionally intimate with anyone.

Patriarchy creates a character ideal—we call it masculinity—and measures everyone against it. Many men as well as women fail the test and even men who are passing the test today are carrying a heavy load of anxiety about tomorrow. Because masculinity is a form of domination, no one can really rest secure. The striving goes on forever unless you are actually willing to give up and find a more secure basis for identity.

Masculinity Against Gay Men:
Patriarchy Fights a Rear Guard Action

Homophobia is the measure of masculinity. The degree to which a man is thought to have gay feelings is the degree of his unmanliness. Because patriarchy presents sexuality as men over women (part of the general dominance theme), men are conditioned to have only that in mind as a model of sexual expression. Sex with another man must mean being dominated, which is very scary. A non-patriarchal model of sexual expression as the mutuality of equals doesn't seem possible; the transfer of the heterosexual model to same-sex relations can at best be "queer," at worst, "perverted."

In the book *Blue Collar Aristocrats*, by E.E. LeMasters, a working class tavern is described in which the topic of homosexuality comes up. Gayness is never defended. In fact, the worst thing you can call a man is homosexual. A man so attacked must either fight or leave the bar.

Notice the importance of violence in defending yourself against the charge of being a "pansy." Referring to your income or academic degrees or size of your car is no defense against such a charge. Only fighting will re-establish your respect as a masculine male. Because "gay" appears to mean "powerless," one needs to go to the masculine source of power—violence—for adequate defense.

In the documentary film *Men's Lives*, a high school boy is interviewed on what it is like to be a dancer. While the interview is conducted, we see him working out, with a very demanding set of acrobatic exercises. The boy mentions that other boys think he must be gay. "Why is that?" the interviewer asks. "Dancers are free and loose," he replies; they are not like big football players; and "you're not trying to kill anybody."

Different kinds of homosexual behavior bring out different amounts of hostility, curiously enough. That fact gives us further clues to violence and female oppression. In prisons, for example, men can be respected if they fuck other men, but not if they are themselves fucked. (We use the word "fucked" intentionally for its ambiguity.) Often prison rapes are done by men who identify as heterosexual; one hole substitutes for another in this scene, for sex is in either case an expression of domination for the masculine mystique.

But for a man to be entered sexually, or to use effeminate gestures and actions, is to invite attack in prison and hostility outside. Effeminate gay men are at the bottom of the totem pole because they are *most like women*, which is nothing less than treachery to the Masculine Cause. Even many gay men shudder at drag queens and vigilantly guard against certain mannerisms because they, too, have internalized the masculinist dread of effeminacy.

John Braxton's report of prison life as a draft resister is revealing on this score. The other inmates knew immediately that John was a conscientious objector because he did not act tough. They also assumed he was gay for the same reason. (If you are not masculine, you must be a pacifist and gay, for masculinity is a package which includes both violence and heterosexuality.)

A ticket of admission to masculinity, then, is sex with women, and bisexuals can at least get that ticket even if they deviate through having gay feelings as well. This may be why bisexuality is not feared as much as exclusive gayness among men. Exclusively gay men let down the Masculine Cause in a very important way—those gays do not participate in the control of women through sexuality. Control through sexuality matters because it is flexible; it usually is mixed with love and dependency so that it becomes quite subtle. (Women often testify to years of confusion and only the faintest uneasiness at their submissive role in traditional heterosexual relationships and the role sex plays in that.)

Now we better understand why women are in general so much more supportive of gay men than non-gay men are. Part of it of course is that heterosexual men are often paralyzed by fear. Never very trusting, such men find gayness one more reason to keep up the defenses. But heterosexual women are drawn to active support for the struggles of gay men because there is a common enemy—patriarchy and its definition of sexuality as domination. Both heterosexual women and gay men have experienced firsthand the violence of sexism; we all have experienced its less open forms such as put-downs and discrimination, and we all fear its open forms such as rape and assault.

Patriarchy, which links characteristics (gentleness, aggressiveness, etc.) to gender, shapes sexuality as well, in such a way as to maintain male power. The Masculine Cause draws strength from homophobia and resorts habitually to violence in its battles on the field of sexual politics. It provides psychological support for the military state and is in turn stimulated by it.

Patriarchy and the Military State

The parallels between these two powerful institutions are striking. Both prefer more subtle means of domination but insist on violence as a last resort. Both institutions provide role models for socialization: the masculine man, the feminine woman, the patriotic citizen. Both are aided by other institutions in maintaining their legitimacy—religion, education, business, sport.

The sexual politics of the family provides the psychological model for the power politics of the state. The oft-deplored breakdown of the family may, from this point of view, have positive effects. Future Vietnams may be ruled out by the growing unmasculinity of soldiers and unfeminine impatience of women.

The business allies of the military are no doubt appalled. The patriarchal family gets constant bolstering from that camp: family services are traditionally the best funded of the private social work agencies; business promotes the Feminine Mystique quite consciously.

The interplay at the top levels of the state between violence and masculinity is becoming clearer. Political scientist Richard Barnet refers to the "hairy chest syndrome" among National Security Managers in government agencies:

> *The man who is ready to recommend using violence against foreigners, even where he is overruled, does not damage his reputation for prudence, soundness, or imagination, but the man who recommends putting an issue to the UN, seeking negotiations or—horror of horrors—"doing nothing" quickly becomes known as "soft." To be "soft"—that is, unbelligerent, compassionate, willing to settle for less—or simply to be repelled by homicide, is to be "irresponsible." It means walking out of the club.* [Men and Masculinity, by Joseph Pleck and Jack Sawyer, p. 136]

The Mayaguez incident, in which the U.S. bombed Cambodia with no real effort at negotiations or other steps, was a clear example. In fact, it was so clear that Henry Kissinger felt impelled to deny that the U.S. response was to "prove our manhood."

The struggle for a world without war must also be a struggle against patriarchy with its masculine character ideal and its oppression of women and gays. Pacifist men, by rejecting violence, have taken a healthy first step in dropping out of masculinity. Some have sought to compensate for that by being more rigorously "tough" in other ways and by participating in the oppression of women and gays. This must stop. The feminist and gay struggles are other dimensions of the same cause: an end to violence.

It seems equally obvious that feminists and gays must include, in our list of patriarchal enemies, the military state. The sexual politics of domination/submission is so reinforced by militarism that one cannot be eliminated without the other. Masculinity and violence are so intimately related that one cannot be defeated by itself.

Androgyny: New People for the New Society

If the masculine character ideal supports militarism, what can support peace? Feminity? No, for that character ideal also has been shaped by patriarchy, and includes, along with virtues such as gentleness and nurturance, a kind of dependency which breeds the passive-aggressive syndrome of curdled violence.

We are encouraged by the vision of androgyny, which includes a blend of the best characteristics now allocated to the two genders. Courage. Awareness of feelings. Cooperativeness. Rooting one's sense of identity in being as well as doing, and not tying it to ownership of people or things. Initiative. Befriending persons rather than physical characteristics. Sensuality, with appreciation for the erotic dimension of everyday life.

Many of these characteristics are now allocated to the feminine role, which has led some men to conclude that the essential liberating task is to become effeminate. We don't agree, since to us some desirable characteristics are now allocated to the masculine role (for example, initiative, intelligence). Further, some desirable characteristics are not assigned to *either* gender in this culture: having an identity independent of ownership of people and things, for example. Women are expected to be as jealous as men, and as absorbed in material accumulation or consumerism.

We invite people to continue the exploration of what a peaceful and sexually liberated society will be like and what kind of people will inhabit it. Let us allow our creativity to flow beyond the definitions patriarchy has given us.

Also needed are strategies for moving toward the androgynous vision, which will show us how to change our organizations, campaigns, and lifestyles. The authors are already clear that all of us in this struggle have a lot to be proud of, and none of us needs to be guilt-tripped into changing. Let's all find the support we need to keep on growing. The future is ours if we only claim it.

The Myth of the Sexual Athlete

Don Sabo

The phrase "sexual athlete" commonly refers to male heterosexual virtuosity in the bedroom. Images of potency, agility, technical expertise and an ability to attract and satisfy women come to mind. In contrast, the few former athletes like Dave Meggyesy and Jim Bouton who have seriously written on the subject, and films such as *Raging Bull* and *North Dallas Forty*, depict the male athlete as sexually uptight, fixated on early adolescent sexual antics and exploitative of women. The former image of athletic virility, however, remains fixed within the popular imagination and, partly for this reason, there has been very little said about the *real* connections between sport and male sexuality.

Locker Room Sex Talk

I played organized sports for 15 years and they were as much a part of my "growing up" as Cheerios, television, and homework. My sexuality unfolded within this all-male social world of sport where sex was always a major focus. I remember, for example, when we as prepubertal boys used the old "buying baseball cards" routine as a cover to sneak peeks at *Playboy* and *Swank* magazines at the newsstand. We would talk endlessly after practices about "boobs" and what it must feel like to kiss and neck. Later, in junior high, we teased one another in the locker room about "jerking off" or being virgins, and there were endless interrogations about "how far" everybody was getting with their girlfriends.

Eventually, boyish anticipation spilled into *real* sexual relationships with girls which, to my delight and confusion, turned out to be a lot more complex than I ever imagined. While sex (kissing, necking, and petting) got more exciting, it also got more difficult to figure out and talk about. Inside, most of the boys, like myself, needed to love and be loved. We were awkwardly reaching out for intimacy. Yet publicly, the message that got imparted was to "catch feels," be cool, connect with girls but don't allow yourself to depend on them. Once when I was a high school junior, the gang in the weight room accused me of being wrapped around my girlfriend's finger. Nothing could be further from the truth, I assured them, and in order to prove it, I broke up with her. I felt miserable about this at the time and I still feel bad about it.

Within the college jock subculture, men's public protests against intimacy sometimes became exaggerated and ugly. I remember two teammates, drunk and rowdy, ripping girls' blouses off at a mixer and crawling on their bellies across the dance floor to look up skirts. Then there were the Sunday morning late breakfasts in the dorm. We jocks would usually all sit at one table and be forced to listen to one braggart or another describe his sexual exploits of the night before. Though a lot of us were turned off by such kiss-and-tell, ego-boosting tactics, we never openly criticized them. Real or fabricated, displays of raunchy sex were also assumed to "win points." A junior full-back claimed to have defecated on a girl's chest after she passed out during intercourse. There were also some laughing reports of "gang-bangs."

When sexual relationships *were* "serious," that is, tempered by love and commitment, the unspoken rule was silence. It was rare when we young men shared our feelings about women, misgivings about sexual performance or disdain for the crudeness and insensitivity of some of our teammates. I now see the tragic irony in this: we could talk about superficial sex and anything that used, trivialized or debased women, but frank discussions about sexuality that unfolded within a loving relationship were taboo. Within the locker room subculture, sex and love were seldom allowed to mix. There was a terrible split between inner needs and outer appearances, between our desire for the love of women and our feigned indifference toward them.

Sex As Sport

Sport is a social setting in which gender learning melds with sexual learning. Our sense of "femaleness" or "maleness" influences the ways we see ourselves as sexual beings. Indeed, as we develop, *sexual* identity emerges as an extension of an already-formed *gender* identity, and sexual behavior becomes "scripted" by cultural meanings. The prevailing script for manhood in sport is basically traditional; it emphasizes competition, success (winning), domination, aggression, emotional stoicism, goal-directedness and physical strength. Many athletes buy into this hypermasculine image and it affects their relationships with women. Dating becomes a "sport" in itself and "scoring," or seeking sex with little or no regard for emotions, is regarded as a mark of masculine achievement. Sexual relationships get defined as "games" in which women are seen as "opponents," and "winners" and "losers" vie for dominance. Too often, women get used as pawns in men's quests for acceptance among peers and status within the male pecking order. I believe that for many of us jocks, these lessons somehow got translated into a "man-as-hunter/woman-as-prey" approach to sexual relationships.

How did this happen? What transformed us from boys who needed and depended on women to men who misunderstood, felt separated from, and sometimes mistreated women? One part of the problem is the expectation that we are supposed to act as though we want to be alone, like the cowboy who always rides off into the sunset alone. In sport, there is only one "most valuable player" on the team.

Too often this prevents male athletes from understanding women and their life experiences. Though women's voices may reach men's ears from the sidelines and grandstands, they remain distant and garbled by the clamor of male competition. In sport, communication gaps between the sexes are due in part to women's historical exclusion from sport, the failure to create coed athletic programs, and coaching practices which quarantine boys from the "feminizing" taint of female influence. One result of this isolation is that sexual myths flourish. Boys end up learning about girls and female sexuality *from other males*, and the information that gets transmitted within the male network is often inaccurate and downright sexist. I can see in retrospect that as boys we lacked a vocabulary of intimacy which would have enabled us to better share sexual experiences with others. The locker room language that filled our adolescent heads did not exactly foster insights into the true nature of women's sexuality—or our own, for that matter.

Performance and Patriarchy

Traditional gender learning and locker room sexual myths can also shape men's lovemaking behavior. Taught to be "achievement machines," many athletes organize their energies and perceptions around a performance ethic which influences sexual relations. The goal-directedness and preoccupation with performance and technique enters into male scripts of lovemaking. In the movie *Joe*, a sexually liberated woman tells her hardhat lover that "making love isn't like running a 50 yard dash."

When intercourse becomes the chief goal of sex, it bolsters men's performance inclinations and limits their ability to enjoy other aspects of sexual experiences. It can also create problems for both men and their partners. Since coitus requires an erection, men are under pressure to get and maintain erections. If erections do not occur, or men ejaculate "too quickly," their self-esteem as lovers and men can be impaired. In fact, sex therapists tell us that men's preoccupation and anxieties about erectile potency and performance can cause the very sexual dysfunctions they fear.

It is important to emphasize that it is not only jocks who swallow this limiting model of male sexuality. Sport is not the only social setting which promotes an androcentric, eroticism-without-intimacy value system. Consider how male sexuality gets socially constructed in fraternities, motorcycle gangs, the armed forces, urban gangs, pornography, corporate advertising, MTV, magazines like *Playboy* or *Penthouse*, and the movies—to name but a few examples. These are not random and unrelated sources of traditional masculine values. They all originate in patriarchy.

Sexual relations between men and women in western societies have been conducted under the panoply of patriarchal power. The sexual values which derive from patriarchy emphasize male dominance and the purely erotic dimensions of the sex act while reducing women to delectable but expendable objects. An alternative conception of human sexuality, however, is also gaining ascendancy within the culture. Flowing out of women's experiences and based on egalitarian values, it seeks to integrate eroticism with love and commitment. It is deeply critical of the social forces which reduce women (and men) to sex objects, depersonalize relationships and turn human sexuality into an advertising gimmick or commodity to be purchased. This is the sexual ethos proffered by the women's movement.

Today's young athletes don't seem as hooked on the hypermasculine image that traditional sport has proffered. Perhaps it is because alternative forms of masculinity and sexuality have begun to enter the locker room subculture. Sex segregation in sport is not as pronounced as it was when I was a young man in the mid-sixties. More girls are playing sports than ever before, and coed athletic experiences are more common. As more women enter the traditionally male environments of sport, business, factories or government, men are finding it more difficult to perceive women in one-dimensional terms. Perhaps we are becoming better able to see them for what they really are and, in the process, we are beginning to search for alternative modes of being men.

What Do Men Really Want . . . Need?

Most of us do not really know what it is we want from our sexual lives. Men seem torn between yearning for excitement and longing for love and intimacy. On one side, we feel titillated by the glitter of contemporary cosmetics and corporate advertising. Eroticism jolts our minds and bodies. We're sporadically turned on by the simple hedonism of the so-called sexual revolution and the sometimes-sleek-sometimes-sleazy veil of soft- and hard-pornography. Many of us fantasize about pursuing eroticism without commitment; some actually live the fantasy. On the other side, more men are recently becoming aware of genuine needs for intimate relationships. We are beginning to recognize that being independent, always on the make and emotionally controlled, are not meeting our needs. Furthermore, the traditional masculine script is certainly not meeting women's expectations or satisfying their emotional needs. More and more men are starting to wonder if sexuality can be a vehicle for expressing and experiencing love.

In our culture many men are suffering from "sexual schizophrenia." Their minds lead them toward eroticism while their hearts pull them toward emotional intimacy. What they want rarely coincides with what they need. Perhaps the uneasiness and the ambivalence which permeates male sexuality is due to this root fact: the traditional certainties which men used to define their manhood and sexuality no longer fit the realities of their lives, and until equality between the sexes becomes more of a social reality, no new model of a more humane sexuality will take hold.

As for me, I am still exploring and redefining my sexuality. While I don't have all the answers yet, I do have direction. I am listening more closely to women's voices, turning my head away from the sexist legacy of the locker room and pursuing a pro-feminist vision of sexuality. It feels good to stop pretending that I enjoy being alone. I never did like feeling alone.

The Masks of Rape

Lawrence J. Cohen

I was riding an exercise bike in a gym one day, and the man next to me nodded towards a woman across the room. "She's really fine," he said, and then added, "I hope she's not your wife or anything."

It took me two years to figure out what bothered me so much about this comment. Two years of reading, research and clinical work in the areas of rape, incest, sexual stereotypes and male-female interactions. What I finally figured out was that the second part of this man's statement made it clear that the first part was not a compliment to the woman or even an observation on her physical attractiveness. Rather, his comment was hostile, an insult, a "petty rape," a statement of possession and control. The fact that he had to clear the statement with me, so as not to trespass on another man's possession, was the tip-off that we were both (he by his comment, I by my silence) participating in rape-supportive behavior.

The comment by the man in the gym was hard to recognize for what it was because it was disguised as a compliment. Similarly, but less convincingly, catcalls and pinches and leers wear the mask of compliment. Underneath the mask is a rather hideous face of domination and control of women, of hatred and fear of women.

Male domination and women-hating wear other masks as well. All of these masks serve to make invisible the face behind the mask. This invisibility succeeds because of the rigidity of our beliefs about the world. Anything that does not fit the cultural stereotype automatically becomes invisible. Rape, for instance, is seen as something that is perpetrated by crazed psychopaths in back alleys against women who somehow provoke the attack through provocative dress or being in a dangerous place. Rapes that violate these sacred stereotypes (as almost all do) are invisible because they are not recognized as rape.

For example, when a woman is raped by her boyfriend in her own apartment with only enough force to keep her pinned down, neither the victim nor the perpetrator are likely to think that a rape has occurred. In fact, in Diana Russell's research, many women who reported that they had been forced to engage in sex against their will said they had never been raped, especially when the perpetrator was a husband or date.[1] When even the victim is unable to penetrate the disguise, the insidious effectiveness of these masks becomes apparent.

Just as rape becomes invisible, so do rapists. According to the popular image, rapists are either lunatics or not really rapists at all, just redblooded Americans with a strong sex drive (presumably driven to frustration by prudish, frigid women). The research on rapists reveals that a few are lunatics and virtually none are simply sexually frustrated. Nicholas Groth has found that rapists are motivated by power, anger or sadism.[2] While a few are clearly insane, the vast majority are normal men, even "pillars of the community"—and hence invisible.

The invisibility of male violence can also be accomplished through cultural acceptability. Since coerced sex among intimate couples is socially sanctioned, many people believe rape cannot exist in the context of a romantic relationship or marriage. The basic mechanism for this mask is the idea of consent in advance. The marriage vows are often taken as a contract for sex at any time it is desired by the husband. Finkelhor and Yllo describe the "license to rape" that husbands are given in our society, and the liberty that men are given to enforce this right with violence and threats of violence. Nevertheless, when most people think of marital rape they imagine a masterful husband with his shy virgin bride. In the fantasy, he awakens her dormant sexuality; in the reality, he enforces his male power and her eternal submission.

With date rape, the scenario is slightly different. Here, although no marriage vows are involved, the woman is seen to have given her consent for sex in advance when she agreed to go on the date, agreed to have a drink with the rapist or agreed to kiss him. In these cases, the sexual exploitation of women is disguised by the semblance of normal social interaction. The recent innovation of "dating contracts," promoted by some so-called men's rights groups, seeks to formalize this process of dating. In these pseudo-contracts, the person who pays for the date (note the illusion of sexual equality) has the right to demand sex.

There are numerous other masks which hide men's hatred and fear of women, and which allow us to deny responsibility for rape and other forms of violence. The mask of non-violence works by pretending that the only form of coercion is explicit violence. But men who obtain sex by appealing to marital obligations, threatening to leave or have an affair, withholding money or affection, or accusing their partner of frigidity all have powerful means of "non-violent" coercion at their disposal.

Like compliments and unsolicited touches, pornography is frequently used as a means of possessing and degrading women. The illusion of innocence is maintained by the masks of eroticism, or freedom of expression, or the celebration of sexuality. Pornography also gives us the clearest expression of the theme of the overpowering woman, a theme which is echoed by men trying to defend themselves against accusations of rape. From Eve onward, women's sexual power has been blamed for the evil of the world, including the evils of rape and the enslavement of women. This incredible reversal is aided by the fact that virtually any behavior by a woman will be interpreted as sexually provocative, if such an interpretation is convenient for a man who wants to hide his fear of losing power over women, especially those women who might think they control their own sexuality.

Besides all of the masks and disguises, there is another technique that our rape-prone culture uses to achieve its ends. This is an elegantly simple technique: leave the mask off, and no one will want to look too closely or point out the ugliness to anyone else. This situation applies best to childhood sexual assault. The overwhelming majority of sexual assaults of children are committed by fathers, stepfathers or other close male relatives, yet we still warn children about perverts hanging around the playground. The real danger is too ugly, too horrible to even contemplate, so we lull ourselves with a created boogie-man. The logic is quite striking: it would be horrible if that were true, therefore it cannot be true.

But it is true. The hatred and fear of women is there, not far under the surface, beneath the "she's really fine looking" and the "he couldn't be a rapist, he's a pillar of the community" and the "I never laid a hand on her." To tear off the masks, even to recognize them for what they are, does not make life simpler or easier. When I was riding my exercise bike, remaining silent was safer than confronting the violence behind the compliment. Like women, men have learned to be afraid of other men's aggression and ashamed of our own helplessness. But as women have done, we can act in spite of fear and shame. We can build strength by relinquishing power and build equality by relinquishing violence.

NOTES
1. Diana E.H. Russell, *Rape in Marriage* (Macmillan, 1982).
2. Nicholas Groth, *Men Who Rape* (Plenum Press, 1980).

Rape: Prisoner of My Fantasies

Anonymous

You see, I know what Charles Whitman felt like. And Jack the Ripper. Their inner conflicts, the years of frustration, the knotted guts, the holding back, and finally the explosion. Psychologists and sociologists have compiled intellectual studies of disturbed criminals, and much of their information is correct. This account, however, is different; it is visceral. I nearly raped a woman once.

Twenty-four years old. Going to a university in Illinois. It was a very lonely year for me. All the women on campus seemed to be either Chicago suburb Barbie Dolls or god-fearing farmers' daughters. There was a small alternative community, but my floundering attempts to penetrate it were failures. It wasn't that they were elitist hippies, though that's what I told myself then (it eased the pain), but that I was a lost soul, afraid to show my need for companionship.

The whole year I had about two dates. No women friends at all. And only one male friend. Mike was a Catholic revolutionary. I became a radical that year, half from tagging along behind Mike and half because I believed in what we were doing. I remember the two of us, alone, the dead of winter, standing in front of a supermarket. We were urging people to shop elsewhere because of the farm workers' boycott. Looking at him through the huge falling snowflakes, I asked, "Mike, what in the hell are we doing here?" I was there because he was there. I loved Mike, but I didn't know how to tell him.

After four years in the Navy I got into school. It took me two years and hindsight to see that my chief interest in college was finding a woman. Oh well, nothing wrong with that, I was just lonely. I went to school one year in Idaho and then because my dreams were unfulfilled, seized an opportunity to go to school in Illinois.

Shortly before getting out of the Navy I tried to take my own life. There seemed no hope left, no reason to go on. When things weren't working out my first year of college I got depressed and went as far as buying a couple bottles of pills. Never used them. My projected flight to Illinois kept me going.

A new school, new people, a chance to start over again! Or so I thought . . . Actually, it *was* a chance for a fresh start. Everything was fresh except for me. I wanted someone to care for me, to care about me. I craved intimacy (sex). But I was a bundle of need, too tied up inside to ask for what I wanted. Macho. It wasn't that I was a swaggering chauvinist, quite the opposite, I was timid and introverted. The other side of the macho coin that is often overlooked is the denial of need, the suppression of one's humanity. In order not to show the way I really felt I had to deaden myself and act hard. That is where I was at two years ago. This piece of writing recounts how my suppressed need almost burst out of me in the form of violent rape.

I started masturbating when I was 14 or 15. I thought I had discovered something no one else knew about. My earth-shaking find was to be shared with the world in a book titled something like *Paradise is Within an Armslength* or *Handful of Pleasure*. This says a lot about what I was told about puberty and sex—zilch.

Masturbation is not harmful, say the scientists. When beating off is part of a healthy sex life, no, it isn't harmful. But for me there was no other sexual release. Girls were unapproachable, fearsome, and yet desirable. My attitude toward the opposite sex was perverted by my mother's taunting sing-song, "Tony's got a girlfriend." Do you remember that one from the third grade playground? She did that to me during my adolescence. Was it bad to have a girlfriend? I didn't know. Much of my attitude toward sexual morality and male/female relations was taken from television in lieu of parental guidance.

Beating off combined with my fantasies and absolutely no contact with women had me twisted like a pretzel by the time I was 19. Then I joined the Navy and added the aberration of screwing whores to my neurosis. Did you see *The Last Detail*? A very accurate portrayal of Navy life. Till the last year of my hitch I was still too scared to seek out women other than prostitutes.

Mine were never rape fantasies. Rather, the most important feature of them was that I was tremendously desirable, sought after. In one fantasy every man in the world except me died off overnight. No more did I have to worry about finding women and making them like me. They threw themselves at me! And they were always beautiful and sexy. These Playboy-shaped females, whom I felt most ignored and put down by, were the same ones I dallied with in dreams.   Play

I want you to understand that I was a prisoner of my fantasies. There *was* no reality for me because I had not yet started to live a sexual reality. I actually expected the real world to conform to my illusions. This is why my first year in college gave me suicidal depressions.

So, off I went to Illinois with renewed hope. My fantasy world had a new lease on life. Now if only those women would see what a stud I was everything would be alright.

My first attempt at meeting a female there was at an outdoor beer bust. She wore impeccable white pants, painted nails, and a haughty, bored expression. The kind of woman that I *knew* was barely concealing her lust for me. I tried to be cool as I stumbled along conversationally. Ten minutes later I withdrew, ready to cry from my painful encounter with reality. And thus it went. In history class and econ class and at the bookstore. Nothing.

Through Mike I came in contact with "liberated" women. Their being more or less in touch with their sexuality scared the shit out of me. So eventually I dealt with them only as political allies in whatever cause we were championing at the moment.

At that time I never told anyone that I was a whoremonger in the Navy nor that I had tried to kill myself. This and much more I kept inside. I defended it. I lied to protect the truth from being known. No one penetrated my shell and I felt secure. It was safer to be alone. I opened up to no one, not even Mike. The day before leaving for Austin I told him about everything. And he understood. Dear man! He didn't condemn me for being crazy. I was too scared to open up to my best friend. What a tragic loss.

My dad didn't like me to show weakness. He was ashamed of me when I got scared and cried. He still thinks it was silly for me to have been frightened by thunder when I was little. When I was 13 we were climbing a mountain and I got scared of the height. He ignored me. He wanted me to act like a man (whatever that was). That is what I tried to do; for years I tried.

The women I fantasized about passed me by and the ones who were open scared me stiff. I had no women friends. In my mind opening up to other males was an act of weakness. And I was programmed not to be weak. So I was alone. It was a dilemma that bound me up in a knot. The more frustration and loneliness, the harder I swallowed my feelings. Tension cannot be maintained forever; there must be a release.

• • •

I was idly reading the bulletin board in the Student Union. It was a warm spring day, late afternoon. I hung around the Union a lot, acting busy and actually ogling women.

From behind me . . . clip, clop, clip, clop, clip clop . . . I knew what it was. My head swung around automatically. She was average height, cute, short skirt, tight sweater. Usually I didn't stare at women, not wanting them to know what I was doing. Normally, I would glance back at the bulletin board, or my book, or hamburger, then sneak another look seconds later.

But she was smiling. Eyes on someone behind me. Over by the door where she was heading. I turned to see who it was. Her boyfriend? There was no one there. My heart jumped . . . clip, clop, clip, clop . . . She was nearing me, still smiling at someone by the door. What the fuck? She didn't even glance at me as she passed ten feet away . . . clip, clop, clip, clop . . . What the fuck! . . . *Bitch* . . . Who are you smiling at? There's no one in this lobby but you and me . . . *Look at me!* . . . clip, clop . . . *Cunt* . . . My mouth was hanging half open, my eyes riveted on her swaying ass, heart beating faster. The clip, clop was deafening. The only sound. She reached for the door . . . and I started after her. Her loose skirt swung back and forth with the clip, clop, clip, clop.

My heart was pounding with the adrenalin of impending physical violence. I stayed twenty feet behind her. Each snap of her skirt was a taunt . . . *You can't have me . . . Fool . . . Sissy . . . You're not a man* . . . clip, clop . . . *I wasn't smiling at you* . . . *Turkey* . . . *I didn't even see you* . . . . clip, clop, clip, clop . . . I screamed back at her . . . *Look at me!* . . . *Bitch* . . . *Cunt* . . . *Mommy, look at me* . . . *please* . . . Hypnotic and rhythmical, clip, clop. Skirt snapping, hips undulating, insulting me in defiant cadence . . . *Act like a man* . . . *Pansy* . . . *You can't fuck me, you're not good enough* . . . . *Chicken* . . . clip, clop, clip, clop . . . *Daddy help me.*

There must have been other people around. But all I could see was her backside as she walked into the setting sun . . . *Fucking cunt, I'll make her notice me.* My breath was shallow. My hands clammy. *Just go over to the history building* . . . clip, clop . . . I'll shove her in the restroom and then she'll notice. *Goddamn it! Then you'll notice, won't you cunt.* My mommy watched soap operas and not me. *Look at me, Mommy!* I smiled bitterly, savagely, *Yeah, you'll notice when I rip your fucking clothes off and climb all over you and beat the shit outta you. You'll notice!!*

Come on, just across the street. At the intersection I stood two feet from her. Holding my breath, I hoped she didn't hear my heart thundering. Little did she know . . . *Cunt* . . . *Temptress* . . . Across the street. Good. She turned left . . . clip, clop . . . Now, baby, if you turn into the history building . . . Mind racing. Should I shove her into the men's room or the women's? Get a wad of paper and try to stick it in her mouth so she won't scream . . . clip, clop, clip . . . I don't want to be caught, of course. Where to go when I get through with her? *Daddy, I don't really want to do this, but I have to. Please understand* . . . clip, clop.

OK. This is it . . . *Turn* . . . I knew she would turn, she had to . . . *Turn!* . . . clip, clop, clip, clop, clip, clop . . . *Turn!!!* . . . She didn't turn . . . clip, clop, around the corner and out of sight. Stunned; I couldn't believe she didn't turn. I looked where she should have gone, and went there . . .

Wandered into the men's room. I glanced in the mirror. Went in a toilet stall and took a deep breath. My hands trembled, knees quivered. Would I have done it? If it were dark I probably would have. If she had turned? . . . I don't know. I sat down and cried, head in hands.

● ● ●

Two years later my life is vastly changed. The pressures that nearly made me a rapist have been permanently relieved through therapy. I have learned that my aggression toward women sprang from my mother's indifference. Perverse mores, transmitted through the mass media, shaped my problems with the opposite sex. Parental neglect of my sexual education forced me to fend for myself. Sadly, the best I could do was to fantasize and masturbate; reality was too monstrous to deal with. I sometimes marvel at how I survived long enough to start undoing the pains of my life.

And finally the big question in your mind, "Could he do it again?" No.

Now I know what my father never told me—that it is not shameful to be scared and lonely. I don't have to act like an island unto myself anymore.

Now I know who my mother is. Before, all women were symbols of her—aloof, unattainable, but life-giving. For me violence and vengeful words can never change the past—my past. And that is the end of the story.

And I must live with it.

Afterword
In the 14 years since I wrote this I have continued to strip away the layers of hurt that made me the person I am today and was then.

A year and a half before the incident described I made two suicide attempts. When I got myself in the door to the therapy room it was like a great emotional dam bursting. Session after session I screamed, cried, and pounded the punching bag. Nine months later a great cloud of sorrow and despair had lifted; I knew that I wanted to live. Periods of depression came to visit for another seven or eight years, but never have I had even a fleeting thought of suicide.

After another year with the same therapy group I wrote the article you have just read. Shortly after that I met Sydney. At age 27 for the first time I felt loved by another human being. I poured so much of my stored-up need onto her that inevitably our affair ended after a steamy two months. It took me two and a half years to start to recover from my first foray beyond my world of sexual fantasies. Renewed political activism with a more healthy ability to deal with people brought me into lots of social interactions. The month that Reagan took office I started counseling again. More layers were stripped away. There were some brief sexual encounters. There were a few short relationships the best of which I destroyed in a spectacular incident of drunkenness. I stopped drinking.

I became a leader in our local political group. I lived in the real world more and more. The layers peeled back like one might peel an onion.

Finally, two years ago peeling layers brought me to the core. The memory emerged, a piece at a time swirling in a fog. My father had fondled me and violated my anus with his finger. Oh, God, how I didn't want it to be true! I was very small, he was drunk, at first his touch was soothing, loving, and I pretended to be asleep. Then it all became very weird. I lay there horrified, but unmoving lest I be killed for resisting.

Needless to say this is the issue I deal with in counseling these days. It is slow going; I still don't want to believe it. Once the counselor said something to me matter-of-factly about how I was a rape victim. Raped! Me? It was shattering to think of myself in this light. No, I was not taken by an erect penis, but, yes, I was violated against my will. I was overpowered, but there was no struggle.

And now knowing of my own victimization I understand my actions at college in Illinois in a different light. Nothing could have ever excused or justified the rape I almost committed. But now I know that I was a ticking time bomb from a young age. I was implanted with the seeds of rage and powerlessness. For me—and,

I believe, for millions of other men and boys—victimization, even far below conscious memory, sent me on the search for a victim.

Boys and adolescent males are socialized to accept violence. We are spanked, threatened, harassed, corporally punished at school, beat up and told to shut up. We are also raped, fondled, sodomized, and humiliated to a vastly greater degree than anyone imagines. When this male legacy is combined with permission from our sexist society to dominate women, then the result is rape and woman battering in the amounts that they occur.

Statistics tell us that about 70 percent of battering men either witnessed violence between their parents or were brutalized themselves. I can't prove it, but I know viscerally that most, if not all rapists have been raped themselves.

Prison Rape: Torture in the American Gulag

Tom Cahill

U.S. taxpayers are funding a criminal justice industry that is mass-producing rapists among other criminals. More than 26,000 adult males are raped *daily* in U.S. jails and prisons and even more boys are sexually abused in reform school. And the by-products of prison rape are murder, suicide, AIDS, psychosis and a cycle of violence that is spilling over walls of "correctional" institutions.

The overwhelming majority of males raped behind bars are heterosexual and many victims become rapists themselves in a demented attempt to regain what they consider their "lost manhood." If they continue the cycle of violence upon release, they are mostly likely to victimize women as preferred and easier prey. Thus sexual assault behind bars may be a major root cause for the increasing rape rate of women in free society. It may be the quickest, most cost-effective way of producing a sociopath or even a psychopath.

While some women prisoners also rape vulnerable cellmates, it is less a problem for females because they tend to be less violent than males and constitute only four percent of the prisoner population nationwide. When women prisoners are raped, it is often by guards.

Terry Lynn Watters, 28, was repeatedly raped by a male guard at the California Institution for Women. Her charges were ignored until three female correctional officers were also sexually assaulted by Jesse Harris, who pled guilty in early 1989. In a more sensational case in North Carolina a decade ago, Joan Little stabbed to death a jailer who she claimed raped her.

But guards also rape male prisoners. In Somerset County, Pennsylvania, Sheriff Guy H. Davis was convicted in March 1987 of raping a prisoner, Roy J. Duke, who accepted an out-of-court settlement of $5,000. "I didn't sue for a great amount, like a million dollars, because I just wanted to let the system know you can't look the other way," Duke told the media.

Yet most of those who make, interpret and enforce the law in the U.S. have long ignored prison rape. "You shut your mind to it," Judge Vincent Femia of Prince George's County, Maryland, told Loretta Tofani of *The Washington Post* in 1982. For her series on rape in a detention center not far from the nation's capital, Tofani won a special Pulitzer prize in 1983, making it more difficult for careerists in the U.S. criminal justice system to plead ignorance of this brutality.

In violating the most basic human rights, rape in confinement also violates two amendments of the U.S. Constitution: the Eighth, forbidding cruel and unusual punishment, and the Thirteenth, forbidding slavery. Once raped, most prisoners become sexual slaves—called "punks" in prison lingo—and are often prostituted to other prisoners by their "masters" for contraband, including drugs.

Dennis M. Dee in the Southern Ohio Correctional Facility wrote to friends that he was forced to shave his legs and chest and was repeatedly gang-raped. Another prisoner on the East Coast related that before some punks were sexually assaulted, they had to model women's lingerie that was simply mailed into the prison while most books and other goods were carefully scrutinized and often arbitrarily refused by prison staff.

Once "turned-out"—prison parlance for raped—a survivor is caught in a bind. If an inmate reports a sexual assault, even without naming the assailant, he will be labeled a "snitch," a contract will automatically be placed on him, and his life expectancy will be measured in minutes from then.

Or the victim can report the assault and request protective custody. But of course protection is not guaranteed and "PC" is like extra punishment. In this jail within a jail, an inmate is deprived of even the few amenities provided the general population.

Under these circumstances, it is not surprising that few prison rapes are reported. Ron Sable, a physician at Cermak Health Services in Chicago, estimates that only one in ten prison rapes are reported. My estimate of the reporting rate, based on personal experience, is one in a hundred. But one in a thousand might be more accurate.

Remaining silent almost guarantees further assaults or even virtual enslavement. Rather than endure continued humiliation, some prisoners try to escape. For others, murder is the only honorable response to rape. Victims who go this route may have years added to their terms whether successful or not.

Suicide is the final option. Speakers at the 1985 National Conference on Correctional Healthcare indicated that most prison violence results from rape or sexual harassment. So AIDS may be a blessing for some prisoners; a respite from daily sexual torture. The controversy over condoms for convicts may eventually reveal that the overwhelming majority of sex behind bars is *non*-consensual and between *heterosexuals*. Very few prisoners have conjugal visits and the percentage of gays in confinement is small.

And what else besides AIDS and rape could be increasing the suicide rate among prisoners? California, followed by New York, Michigan, and Texas leads the nation in inmate suicides, according to Bruce Krasnow of the *Florida Times Union* in Jacksonville.

One horror story after another about brutal sexual assault behind bars was related to Senator Edward Kennedy of Massachusetts and others investigating prison conditions more than a decade and a half ago when reform was in the air because of so many bloody prison riots. Today the senior senator as well as his close associate and fellow liberal Senator Alan Cranston of California, among others in government, have ignored pleas and even demonstrations for help from activists trying to stop prison rape.

Stephen Donaldson believes prison rape is a "management tool" used by guards to blackmail prisoners into becoming informers, divide and conquer the prison population, destroy leaders, and discipline troublemakers.

Donaldson was a Quaker activist and journalist at the time he was arrested during a "pray-in" at the White House in 1973. Refusing to post $10 bond on grounds that bail discriminates against the poor, he was jailed. Donaldson, who is white, was placed in an all-black cellblock and ended up torn and bleeding in a hospital after being raped some sixty times in two days.

I was also an activist and journalist when I was arrested for civil disobedience in San Antonio, Texas, in 1968, and placed in Bexar County Jail's "gorilla cage"—a cell deliberately overcrowded and racially mixed to create a tinderbox.

"Fresh meat," announced a burly, young prisoner as the grinning guard opened the cell. The prisoners then beat, tortured, and gang-raped me for twenty-four hours until an ex-convict I knew got word into our cell that I wasn't a child molester as the inmates had been told.

Stephen Donaldson and I are survivors of prison rape. We are victims of a system in which those who are dominated and humiliated come to dominate and humiliate others.

• • •

Rape is less an act of sex than one of domination by violence and humiliation.

"How does one man assert his power over another, Winston?" O'Brien asks in Orwell's *1984*.

"By making him suffer," Winston replies.

"Exactly," says O'Brien. "Power is in inflicting pain and humiliation. Power is in tearing human minds to pieces and putting them together again in new shapes of your own choosing."

Prison rape is torture, the infliction of severe physical and/or emotional pain as punishment and/or coercion. It is also menticide, the murder of one's ego or self-esteem. Because rape may be considered the ultimate humiliation, a strong sense of stigma is attached. Stigma can be described as the situation of an individual whose identity has been spoiled because of a degradation that disqualifies him or her from full social acceptance.

Rape is a major life crisis starting with feelings of disbelief, terror, and vulnerability occurring during or immediately after the initial assault. Blocking out the experience is common and makes it more difficult to heal. This denial phase often leaves the survivor feeling emotionally numb. Shame, guilt, depression, disorientation, flashbacks, the inability to concentrate, misdirected anger and claustrophobia often overwhelm the victims of most types of rape. These emotions are common for men survivors as well as women. Above all the survivor—only when ready—needs to be *heard, understood, believed,* and *accepted.*

In the advanced stages of rape trauma syndrome, which is a form of post traumatic stress disorder, depression becomes the major symptom often replaced by extreme anger or outright rage. Sometimes there is a fluctuation between the two with periods of malaise between. Close loved ones are often secondary victims, often suffering similar emotions, especially misdirected anger. This type of anger deserves much more study since it could be a key to much of the violence in our society.

"I have nightmares about it. It makes you lose your mind," eighteen-year-old Ronald Fridge told *The Washington Post,* describing his rape while in jail for breaking a window, a charge that was dropped a week later.

Male victims of rape often suffer sexual dysfunction and confusion regarding sexual preference, confusion about their own masculine identity. Other emotional problems are substance abuse, a history of revictimization, chaotic relationships, inability to express emotions clearly, fear of intimacy, a sense of powerlessness. The list of aftereffects of rape could go on and on. Often there is a delayed reaction to the trauma akin to the post traumatic stress suffered by Vietnam vets, victims of torture in Central America, and other survivors of violent horror. Laurie Thompson, a California researcher, claims 97 percent of the people who develop multiple personalities have suffered sexual abuse.

And *everyone* in society is a potential rape victim. Older men as well as older women have been raped. A few years ago in Jackson Prison in Michigan, Thomas Spaulding, in his fifties, was raped by a much younger prisoner. The rape of a two-year-old has been recorded. Burly, macho men have been raped. A Marine was raped by his drunken buddies in Vallejo, California, in 1982. A few years earlier, a "Green Beret" was raped in Southern California. The true-life drama of the rape of a police officer, Richard Beck, was aired on ABC-TV in June 1985. "He was a tough cop. Maybe too tough. Until it happened to him," read the advertisement in *TV Guide*.

T.E. Lawrence (of Arabia) was without doubt raped while a prisoner of the Turks in November 1917 and showed definite signs of rape trauma syndrome in his last years. And Mohandas "Mahatma" Gandhi *may* have been raped while a prisoner in Pretoria, South Africa, in February 1909, according to one of his biographers, Geoffrey Ashe.

Many of us who have survived prison rape become living time bombs, without clocks to program our explosions. Our rage can end up misdirected, even self-destructive. Donaldson, for example, has exploded unexpectedly several times and despite being a former instructor at Columbia University and member of Mensa, has spent much time behind bars since his rape in 1973.

In 1984, I fasted two months trying to bring media attention to prison rape. When a reporter for *The San Francisco Chronicle* rudely hung up the telephone on me, I smashed a plate glass door to his office building and ended up naked and cold in solitary confinement.

Now Donaldson and I, along with other prison rape survivors, are trying to channel our rage in a constructive manner to alleviate the senseless suffering in U.S. reformatories, jails and prisons. Donaldson is president and I am director of People Organized To Stop Rape of Imprisoned Persons. POSRIP was established in 1979 by Russell D. Smith, a black prisoner who had been raped throughout his life in reform school and later in prison. We are a support group for victims and loved ones as well as a lobby attempting to demonstrate to the public how our taxes are being not only wasted but misused to make crime pay for the judges, attorneys, law officers, guards and everyone else in the criminal justice business. For as Clarence Darrow, the famous American attorney, once said, "The failure of justice may be more detrimental to society than crime itself." And before Darrow, it was Anatole France who said, "Justice is the means by which established injustices are sanctioned."

POSRIP is also gathering names of prisoners and former prisoners raped behind bars for a class action suit against the U.S. Federal Bureau of Prisons which at least partially subsidizes most correctional institutions in the country. Perhaps when the cost of prison rape in tax dollars and lost revenue is finally tallied, something will be done in earnest to stop this barbarism. And in 1992, we hope to send a representative to the human rights convention in Moscow to tell the world about this torture in the American gulag.

Prison rape *can* be stopped or at least minimized. In the San Francisco County Jail, prisoners are screened by a nurse so the obviously vulnerable ones are segregated from the obviously violent ones at little extra cost to taxpayers.

Increasing numbers of lawsuits may enlighten other correctional officials and legislators. Most prison rape cases are settled out-of-court at a cost to taxpayers of up to $100,000 so far. In response to such suits, a bill was introduced in the Delaware Legislature by Senator Herman M. Holloway Sr. providing terms of up to seven years for prison guards and health care workers who allow individuals in their custody to be sexually assaulted.

As for repairing the damage done by rape, feminists have long pointed the way with rape crisis centers, support groups, seminars, media campaigns and other methods of raising the survivor's and the public's awareness about the debilitating effects of rape on the victim as well as all of society.

Meanwhile the sentiment of Pearl Buck—Nobel prize-winning author—will continue to haunt America's halls of justice everywhere: "A civilization can best by judged by the way it treats its least fortunate citizens." Or more succinctly as Dostoyevsky once wrote, "A civilization can best be judged by entering its prisons."

The Loss

Billy Ray Boyd

> "The maltreatment of children has existed since recorded time, and has taken many forms . . . Children were mutilated for a variety of reasons. Circumcision, foot and head binding, and castration were all accepted at various times in history."
> —Norman S. Ellerstein, M.D.
> *Child Abuse and Neglect: A Medical Reference*

Lying leisurely in bed, relaxing from a hectic life, I find myself slipping delightfully into sexual arousal. I reach for the personal lubricant and start to caress and stroke my penis. Then, watching as it swells in size, I realize—for the very first time, amazingly, and with considerable shock—that it's *mutilated*. Whittled on. Scar tissue, right there.

In just moments in a hospital long ago, I lost a piece of skin the size of a quarter containing more than three million cells, twelve feet of nerves, one hundred sweat glands, fifty nerve endings, three feet of blood vessels, . . . and my penis's own personal lubrication. An essentially internal organ now made permanently external, with the drying out and desensitization that accompanies any moist, sensitive skin adapting itself to frequent contact with an often abrasive world. My erotic feelings quickly subside as my penis shrinks back, attempting a vain retreat into the protective covering of the foreskin sliced off so long ago. I am, like so many others, a victim of vivisection, of genital mutilation.

The shock of my realization helps me understand why a few years previously I'd been overwhelmed with nausea when reading an account of circumcision practices, male and female, around the world. More recently, my work has brought me to editing a book by the director of the National Organization of Circumcision Information Resource Centers (NOCIRC). Here's some of what I've learned:

• Many men circumcised in adulthood report a lessening of sensitivity soon afterward or commencing up to two or three years later. Such loss is probably even greater with infant circumcision, due to the ripping apart of the foreskin and glans prior to the surgery (in adults, they have already naturally separated). In terms of sexual functioning, the decrease in sensitivity frequently becomes more of a problem with advancing age.

• Infants' penises have been lost in the slip of a knife or the neglect of electric current—two in in Georgia hospital in a single year, 1985. One baby was subsequently converted into a baby girl, with the necessity of taking hormones for the rest of his/her life.

• Estimates of rates of complications from circumcision vary widely from less than one-tenth of 1 percent to well over 50 percent. Whatever the frequency, documented infections and complications have led to impotence, to quadraplegia, and to death. Even pro-circumcision writers admit to to three U.S. deaths per year, with other estimates ranging as high as two hundred.

• Done without the consent of the patient, infant circumcision is the most commonly performed surgery in the United States—over a million each year.

• At a cost of between $100 million and $200 million a year, about 58 percent of baby boys born in the U.S. are currently being circumcised, down from about 90 percent as recently as the 1960s. In the western states, intact baby boys are now in the majority. It's the circumcised boys who will be different in the locker rooms of the future.

In the Beginning

No one knows for sure how male or female circumcision began in various cultures. It may have been a way to squelch divisiveness in a tribe to to clearly establish power over subjects through forcing them to yield up their children for genital mutilation, or it might have been a humane reform from a previous practice of child sacrifice. Male circumcision may have been an imitation of the mysterious power of women, the menstruating bearers of children, or a branding for slaves (as for the Jews in Egyptian bondage). It may have even been a perceived medical necessity for desert nomads with little water to keep clean—though we now know that, since urine is sterile, an effective means of cleaning is to pinch the foreskin shut, urinate, then release. In many cultures, it developed—and is still practiced—

as a puberty rite for teens or preteens.

"For thousands of years, in many different cultures, the genitals have fallen victim to an amazing variety of mutilations and restrictions. For organs that are capable of giving us an immense amount of pleasure, they have been given an inordinate amount of pain."
—Desmond Morris
Body Watching

Health and Disease

It wasn't until the last century that circumcision took on a distinctly medical rationale: to lessen sensitivity and thereby discourage masturbation, which was thought by some doctors to cause a host of problems, from asthma to insanity. Sensitivity it lessened, but as it became apparent that circumcised men were wheezing and going crazy at the same rates as intact men and that nothing short of coma, castration, or death would interfere with masturbation, a sad parade of medical rationales for circumcision began, each successively discredited only to be replaced by another. In 1987, the California Medical Association continued this shameful tradition by declaring—in a resolution adopted against the advice of their own Scientific Board—that circumcision is "an effective public health measure." The medical professions in Britain, Australia, and New Zealand have led the move *away* from such folly, and their current circumcision rates are now down to 1 percent, 18 percent, and 2 percent, respectively. No reputable medical organizations abroad support routine circumcision. In the words of Australia's National Health and Medical Research Council:

"There are no medical indications for undertaking routine circumcision on newborn male infants, as the hazards of the operation at this age outweigh any possible advantages."

Only in the U.S. have so many doctors continued to support the practice. We're now the only country in the world to practice mass secular circumcision. Medical arguments in vogue at present include urinary tract infections, penile cancer, phimosis, and AIDS.

Circumcisionists claim that urinary tract infections occur in about 1 percent of intact men, compared with one-tenth of 1 percent of uncircumcised men. Even if this statistic is true (and it is contested), still, there is no other medical condition for which a highly sensitive, functioning body part (such as the foreskin) is cut off to *prevent* such a low chance (1 percent) of future problems. Good penile hygiene goes a long way (perhaps all the way) toward preventing urinary tract infections.

Penile cancer is extremely rare; when it does occur in the U.S. it's usually in an intact man. Studies of other cultures which do and don't circumcise yield a confusing and contradictory tangle of implications, so that both pro- and anti-circumcision activists can find fuel for their arguments if they look hard enough. Hygiene seems to be crucial. And again, with the chances of occurrence so remote, even if intact men are more likely to contract this rare disease, that's no reason to circumcise as a preventive measure, and to do so simply shows our cultural bias in favor of the practice. The very real risks of circumcision itself would seem to mitigate against this argument.

Phimosis, or unretractability of the foreskin, usually calls forth a complete circumcision from American doctors, though it's usually remediable with gentle stretching with warm, soapy water and cremes. In some cases, a simple surgical slitting may be necessary. In rare cases, the tip of an inelastic foreskin may need to be removed—but a full circumcision is almost never necessary.

AIDS is the latest scare, with an African study of men who visited prostitutes in Kenya reportedly showing a higher contagion rate among intact men than among circumcised ones. Yet the Centers for Disease Control in Atlanta has rejected the claim that circumcision protects against AIDS. In fact, circumcision can *increase* our susceptibility to some sexually transmitted diseases. A recent Army study found that circumcised men are twice as likely to contract the venereal disease *nongonococcal urethritis*. Pediatrician Robert W. Enzenauer, M.D., wrote in the *New England Journal of Medicine* (11 June 1987), "Circumcision removes the protection normally provided by the foreskin. The absence of circumcision may actually protect against the transmission of AIDS by protecting the urethral mucosa."

Media in *any* society tend to report more favorably and extensively information which supports the culture's values and practices; this can be seen in the way our newspapers and magazines report research findings for and against circumcision. And we who are circumcised and who have circumcised our children tend to more readily accept studies whose results support the practice than those whose results cast doubt on its legitimacy. We question neither the data nor its reporting, and we tend not to consider other, less drastic measures short of foreskin amputation. Specifically, *teaching a boy about penile hygiene and safe sex will serve him far better than cutting off a functional, highly sensitive part of his penis.* The Ad Hoc Committee on Circumcision of the Academy of Pediatrics in 1975 put it a bit more conservatively:

A program of eduation leading to continuing good personal hygiene
would offer all the advantages of routine circumcision without the
surgical risks.

Even if a boy or a man should foolishly decide to have insertive
vaginal or anal intercourse with a possibly infected person, use of a
nonoxynol-9 personal lubricant will provide *some* protection.[1] If a
condom should break or a supposedly safe partner confesses after
the act that they're not safe, a cleaning immediately afterward with
a disposable nonoxynol-9 towelette, perhaps followed by coating the
glans with a nonoxynol-9 personal lubricant, while being no guaran-
tee, would be a prudent measure *as far as the presumed under-the-
foreskin risk goes*, though the risk from direct transmission (blood to
blood through minor tears in the skin) of course remains. We should
also remember that the virus concentrates in semen as well as blood,
and, because usually much more semen flows than blood, it is the
receptive partner, not the insertive one, who is at far greater risk of
HIV infection in unprotected vaginal or anal intercourse. If a condom
should break during intercourse, nonoxynol-9 contraceptive gel
with applicator should be used to get generous amounts of the gel—
and therefore nonoxynol-9—into the vagina or anus. Nonoxynol-9
lubricant and contraceptive jel should be part of our bedside safe-
sex paraphernalia in this age of AIDS. Speaking from personal experience of safe sex, unsafe sex, and being circumcised, I'd far rather
be intact and take safe sex precautions than to be circumcised and
still have to take safe sex precautions.

Since circumcision seems to generally reduce sexual sensitivity—wearing a condom on a circumcised penis has been compared
to wearing two on an intact one—making the procedure routine may
actually have set this country up for the AIDS epidemic by increasing the natural resistance to use condoms. In addition, to get a
circumcision and still engage in unsafe sex with a potentially infected
person would be to play a distinctly American version of Russian
Roulette, and the illusion of safety based on this argument could well
make the epidemic worse. I can hear the conversations now in
bedrooms, bars, and backseats across the country: "It's o.k., honey,
we don't need the condom—I'm circumcised."

Ludicrous? Of course. But it's only a slight parody of the extent
to which we'll go to avoid coming to terms with AIDS. Circumcision
simply isn't a "protective shield" against HIV any more than Star
Wars is against incoming nuclear warheads, and anyone trying to
protect themself—or their kid—with a circumcision instead of a
condom needs to have more than their blood examined. Yet some
doctors—who in the last century might have prescribed it for

asthma—are now encouraging circumcision as a preventive measure against AIDS.

The foreskin doesn't only keep the glans moist and sensitive (a function that should be appreciated by anyone familiar with the pleasures of sloppy kissing). When the penis becomes erect it pushes out of this nerve-loaded sleeve of skin, so that what in the flaccid state is the sensitive *inside* of the foreskin becomes *outside* skin of the lengthened penis, covering up to a third or more of the entire shaft. While it may be impossible for us circumcised men to *know* what we're missing, there *is* a way to get a very strong hint. Here's how. Wet your finger and lightly run it, moving it back and forth a little, from the tip of the penis up over the corona, into the neck of the glans, across the circumcision scar—what's left of your foreskin, the stump—is much more sensitive than the rest, even than the glans itself. It is such tissue as this, with its capacity for sensual communication and pleasure in contact with a partner's similar tissues, that circumcision removes forever.

Violence Against Men

At least in some cultures, circumcision started out as an adolescent puberty ritual, and in fact is still done to teen-age or pre-teen boys (and girls) in many African and Islamic cultures.

It's quite sobering to realize that if what is routinely done to baby boys were ever done to even a few baby girls in the U.S., there would be a public outcry and very legitimate charges of child abuse. But the force of tradition has shut out our cries at our own violation, our mutilation, and we've adapted to the silent denial. At my first venture into the men's movement—at the 13th Annual Conference on Men and Masculinity (Seattle, 1988)—men in the activist caucus were planning a demonstration at a nearby porno theater to protest the violence depicted against women. There in Seattle on the day of that demonstration—on any day, in any city or town—a great number of baby boys were strapped down on molded plastic boards called Circumstraints, designed specifically to hold them immobile while their most sensitive tissues were efficiently and traumatically amputated, with who knows what psychological and social repercussions. Yet the group was largely unreceptive to concerning themselves with this issue and a conference workshop on circumcision was attended by only a handful of the hundreds present.

What's clearly a men's issue also has definite implications for heterosexual women in terms of physical sensation during love-making. (Sadly, quite a few American women, though sexually experienced, have never even seen an uncut penis, while a few, unaccustomed to intact penises, find the natural lubrication repugnant.) Most Americans, men and women, are as unaware of the negative consequences of male circumcision as people in Arabic and Central African countries are that female circumcision is an abomination.The increasing public understanding about the implications of widespread sexual abuse—one in four girls, one in six boys—contrasts with our bland acceptance of the fact that *a full 58 percent of U.S. infant males, over a fourth of all children, experience extreme genital violence in the form of circumcision* during the totally vulnerable pre-verbal period of infancy. Custom and ritual help those who perpetrate the violence avoid the full impact of what they're doing, but does it help the victims? Or is the social acceptance of this mutilation, sometimes even a pride in it, a profound disempowerment of the violated, a discounting of our experience?

Just as members of any historically violated or oppressed group—women, slaves, industrial workers—must adapt to and in many cases wind up identifying with the very system responsible for their pain and their limitations, so have we as men come to perpetrate our own mutilation on our sons: as noted earlier, the most common reason given by parents for circumcising their sons is so the kid will look like Dad. Denial is widespread—what man wants to admit even to himself what he's lost, much less to proclaim it, to risk scorn or ridicule? What parent wants to admit what they've allowed their precious sons to endure?[2] And just as male rapists in therapy are often surprised to learn that their victims actually suffered, that the women really did mean "no," doctors are numbed to the babies' only way of attempting to withhold their consent—with their struggles and their screams.

The Loss

Despite the identification of male circumcision with Judaism, in the United States, where only 3 percent of the population is Jewish, circumcision is overwhelmingly a secular, not a religious, phenomena. Or, more accurately, it's an issue for all American men. Not only do we get socialized into being cannon fodder, working ourselves to death at an early age, and generally denying our softer, more nurturing sides. We also, most of us in the U.S., get our penises quite literally whittled on as our welcome into life, followed by days of sometimes intense burning as urine and feces irritate the exposed, raw *glans* and unhealed surgical wound. I can now remember my post-surgery wailing, the pain of my loss, age eight—"Oh, my penis!

Oh, my penis!" My cries, wave after wave of hurt and pain, filled the corridors of the entire small-town hospital. And I was relatively lucky, mind you: because of being past infancy, I'd had the benefit of general anesthesia during the surgery itself. My foreskin had repeatedly grown to the glans, perhaps because they'd been prematurely forced apart, as doctors frequently and ignorantly do or advise parents to do. A circumcision was recommended to solve the problem once and for all. My mother says that hearing me was heart-rending. "You thought you were ruined, for sure!" she now recalls, laughing.

Ruined?—No. Unlike some circumcision victims, I'm sexually functional. Robbed, violated, assaulted, ripped off?—Most certainly.

Recognizing the sexual role of the foreskin, the great eleventh-century rabbi Moses Maimonides quite succinctly stated that the effect—indeed, the purpose—of circumcision was

> ... to limit sexual intercourse, and to weaken the organ of generation as far as possible, and thus cause man to be moderate.... for there is no doubt that circumcision weakens the power of sexual excitement, and sometimes lessens the natural enjoyment; the organ necessarily becomes weak when ... deprived of its covering from the beginning. Our sages say distinctly: It is hard for a woman, with whom an uncircumcised [man] had sexual intercourse, to separate from him.[3]

One man I talked with underwent surgical foreskin restoration to regain sensitivity. Having experienced ridicule in his search for a competent and sympathetic surgeon, he compared the psychological implications of foreskin loss with what a woman experiences after a mastectomy. "No one today would tell a woman she shouldn't be emotionally traumatized by the loss of part of her body," he says. "It's a natural reaction. So how *dare* they tell me I shouldn't mourn *my* loss and want my foreskin back?"

Another example of the sensitive issue of sensitivity is excerpted from a letter to NOCIRC by a British man who, while studying at UCLA, developed a skin disorder around his glans. Medical student friends informed him that he required "minor surgery." Circumcision was never mentioned.

> An operation was performed, and I recovered clear consciousness to discover that I had been circumcised. My newly naked, sensitive *glans penis* was protected from irritation with bandages and such. Slowly the area lost sensitivity, and as it did I realized I had lost something rather vital. Stimuli that had previously aroused ecstasy had relatively little effect. There was a short period of depression, but acceptance of the situation developed, as it had to.

> The acute sensitivity never returned; something rather precious to a sensual hedonist had been lost forever.
>
> So it is that I hope you will do what you can to discourage circumcision. My experience and reading indicate that the operation is not only medically unnecessary in the great majority of cases, but also that circumcision destroys a very joyful aspect of the human experience for both males and females.[4]

As with the man above, my circumcision happened after infancy. My parents never even considered circumcision when I was born, for which I'm grateful. It was because of what seemed to be medical necessity that they later consented—not just so I'd look like my father or because they thought God told them to do it—and my mother now regrets not exploring other alternatives. Yet unlike the British student and like the great majority of American men my age—including doctors who circumcise and judges who preside over legal challenges to the practice—I don't know what I'm missing. I can't. Gone forever are those three million cells, twelve feet of nerves, one hundred sweat glands, fifty nerve endings, and three feet of blood vessels. Gone is my penis's own personal lubrication, since a permanently exposed glans dries up and develops, in the body's wisdom, a layer of nerveless skin, a *corneum*, that tries to perform the protective function of a foreskin. (Still, even such a partly desensitized naked glans is much more easily irritated than a foreskin is by rubbing against clothes.) According to nationally syndicated TV medical advisor Dr. Dean Edell, the *corneum* is twelve to fifteen cell layers thick, compared with one or two layers in a glans constantly cuddled and protected by a moist foreskin. How much sensitivity remains also depends on how much of the frenulum, or frenum, was cut away or left. This is the web of skin on the underside of the penis that keeps the foreskin from going back too far when retracted, and is loaded with nerves. One intact married man wrote of his childhood:

> I am *not* cut and *all* of my friends were, so I was very different. . . Even when I was very little . . . and I learned about circumcision, I wondered why something should be cut off that felt so good . . . after puberty . . . during circle jerks with my friends (all cut) I could make myself come by just rubbing my frenum between my thumb and index finger, so the sensitivity is unquestionable.[5]

Varying degrees of the frenulum are cut away in circumcision. Many babies under the knife lose it all, some a chunk or two of their glans as well, and a few their sexual functionality, their penises, their health, even their lives.

Coming Out: The Healing Begins

With an understanding lover, I've cried over my loss. My sadness is now being transformed into political action, into a demand: Don't do unto others as was done unto me. Let the violence stop with us, let the healing begin. I've helped found "The Victims Speak," a group of men, friends and loved ones victimized in various ways and degrees by circumcision and dedicated to using nonviolent action, both symbolic and direct, to end the violence of genital mutilation. The medical debate goes on and on, just as the arguments went on and on in my native South about whether blacks had the same mental capacity as whites and whether segregated black schools were academically equivalent to their white counterparts. While it was necessary for progressive people to engage in such debate in order to undermine the rationalizations that supported institutionalized violence and oppression, it was black people (and white allies) finally standing up (and sitting-in) and saying "No more!" that sent Jim Crow reeling. It was Stonewall that launched gay rights into the political agenda, and street demonstrations, draft card burnings, and the choice of jail over genocide that helped extract us from Vietnam. Action, in short, speaks louder than words. Those of us victimized in various ways and to varying degrees by circumcision have a unique power to make parents understand that it's not just an academic debate, that their own sons may well come to resent having their genitals mutilated, regardless of the parents' motivation in having it done. Here is one man's lament over his loss, expressed as a desire for radical political action:

> . . . the greatest disadvantage of circumcision, in my view, is the awful loss of sensitivity when the foreskin is removed . . . I was deprived of my foreskin when I was 26; I had had ample experience in the sexual area, and I was quite happy (delirious, in fact) with what pleasure I could experience—beginning with foreplay and continuing—as an intact male. After my circumcision, that pleasure was utterly gone. Let me put it this way: on a scale of 10, the uncircumcised penis experiences pleasure that is at least 11 or 12; the circumcised penis is lucky to get to 3. Really—and I mean this in all seriousness—if American men who were circumcised at birth could know that deprivation of pleasure that they would experience, they would storm the hospitals and not permit their sons to undergo this unnecessary loss.[6]

The groundwork for "storming the hospitals" began to be laid with demonstrations at the annual meetings of the American Academy of Pediatrics (October 1988) and the California Medical Association (March 1989). The AAP had maintained a neutral position on circumcision for sixteen years, stating there was "no absolute medical necessity" for it, while pro-circumcision forces in the organization had been pressing to weaken this stand. The CMA, against the advice of its own Scientific Board, had declared circumcision to be "an effective public health measure" in a resolution authored and pushed through by circumcisionist Dr. Aaron Fink; concerned CMA members had subsequently prepared a resolution to rescind the pro-circumcision one.

We've also developed an informed consent questionnaire for administering to new and expectant parents on the street, in childbirth education classes, or in "guerilla raids" into hospital maternity wards, to see if doctors are fulfilling their duty to fully inform parents about the nature and implications of circumcision before asking them to sign the consent form. (Doctors and hospitals more often than not simply hand parents the form at the last minute and essentially say, "Sign here, it's standard procedure.") The answers on the back of our questionnaire educate the parents. While we are abolitionist—no parent has the right to slice off part of "their" child's body—the area of informed consent is one in which useful work can be done, both in reducing the circumcision rate and in raising public consciousness. We also refer people to written materials, workshops, and resource people dealing with strategizing nonviolent social change; unlearning racism, sexism, and anti-semitism; getting in touch with repressed feelings in order to work through them in a way that leads to empowerment through social action; and nonviolence training for direct action.

Organizing around the issue of circumcision is difficult, because few men have any idea of what's been done to them. Those who do know are understandably reluctant to admit their violation and their loss, much less to stand up in public and declare it. One man recently asked to be removed from our contact list for anti-circumcisionists because "It's too painful to me to be reminded of circumcision in any way." At least this man is aware of his trauma; most Americans are in a state of either ignorance or profound denial.

Awareness seems much higher among gay and bisexual men, probably because they experience other men's penises and can compare. Heterosexual men—to the extent that we're too homophobic to curiously look or ask about, much less feel, other men's genitals—never get that opportunity. And so we muddle through our sex lives not knowing what we're missing, with no idea that it could ever be better, that we've been ripped off. The biggest educational problem, then, is among heterosexual men (and among women). Had

I not met and become friends with an anti-circumcisionist activist, I would have stayed like the overwhelming majority of Americans—ignorant or in denial.

Hearts and Minds

As I was working on this article and at the same time editing the book *Circumcision: Whose Decision?*, I one day found the latter's author, head of the National Organization of Circumcision Information Resource Centers, weeping at her phone. She had just retrieved messages from her answering machine. A brand-new father had called twice, saying that he and his wife had considered the pros and cons, including a piece of NOCIRC literature they'd somehow come across, and had decided to circumcise. The deciding factor, he said, was that the NOCIRC literature was "emotional," and so his infant son was set to become, thirty minutes after the last call and in the father's words, "civilized."

We suffer from a tyranny of the intellect over the emotions. A dictatorship of the head over the heart instead of an integration of these complementary aspects of our being. Tradition dictating to, not being informed by, protective and nurturing instinct. A separation of ourselves from nature, from nonhuman animals, from "uncivilized" peoples. This seems to me a fundamental dis-ease that lies at the root of many of our problems—from widespread genital mutilation to class exploitation, sexual violence, and Armageddon overkill in drag as national defense.

Like so many of the crucial issues we face today, circumcision *is* emotional as well as requiring clear-headed thinking and analysis. We need to bring all that both our heads and our hearts have to offer to transform our pain, our loss, into action for an intact world.

The Journey Begun

I've only begun the process of getting in touch with the long-suppressed, long-denied trauma, the grief, the loss that most men of my generation have experienced. Like many other men with this suppressed terror, I still can't bring myself to watch a video of a circumcision from beginning to end—the pain is simply too great. I've started foreskin restoration through sustained gentle stretching of what's left, and am delighted to report it seems to be working—I'm surprised at the psychological lift I've experienced from my genitalia starting to be whole again, and as more and more of us try to get back what we've lost, we create a powerful statement against mutilation.

I'm interested in but wary of surgical techniques; though some insurance companies will pay for the procedure, I have little trust in the profession that cut it off to put it back. I speak openly about the issue with friends and colleagues, and find sympathetic understanding as frequently as laughter, joking, aversion, and retreat into tradition—which after all are only ways of initially dealing with uncomfortable new information. I enjoy the lightness that humor brings to the subject, and am helping organize political action against routine circumcision, for an intact world.

One foot in front of the other, this unexpected journey has begun. I don't know where it will lead. I only know I have to go.

NOTES

1. Nonoxynol-9 is a gentle detergent that in .5 to 1% concentrations effectively destroys viruses, including HIV (far less concentrations kill sperm and bacteria). It is now routinely added to many personal and condom lubricants and contraceptive gels and creams as a back-up safety factor. Most brands of moist "baby wipe" towelettes, easily available in baby-care sections of supermarkets and pharmacies, are impregnated with nonoxynol-9 (check labels).

2. The unstudied implications are broad, with many unanswered questions: What about our resistance as men to admitting our sensitivities, part of which we've physically lost? How much guilt do we have around the penis, rather than feeling wholesome and good about it? Penises (both cut and uncut) are not infrequently used as weapons, as instruments of domination and control. How does circumcision affect our potential to love and respect our penises, our bodies, and our partners?

3. Maimonides, Moses, *Guide for the Perplexed*, Part III, Chapter XLIX.

4. Letter received by the National Organization of Circumcision Information Resource Centers, dated 21 April 1987.

5. Letter received by The Victims Speak dated 19 October 1988.

6. Letter received January 1989 by the National Organization of Circumcision Information Resource Centers.

Sexual Abuse of Young Males: Removing the Secret

Robert J. Timms and Patrick Connors

THE SECRET: A personal statement from Robert

I remember many things from my childhood years: I remember feeling isolated from others much of the time; I remember being afraid much of the time; and I remember feeling "different" much of the time. Now I know these three things which I remembered were all the consequences of one thing which I forgot: I "forgot," for nearly 40 years, that when I was six years old I was attacked and raped by my favorite uncle.

How amazed I was to learn at the age of 46 that I had repressed all conscious memory of this event, even though unconsciously it had controlled my life. The powerful sense of isolation was a direct consequence of being attacked and then being left alone afterwards, following my uncle's threat that he would kill me if I ever told anyone what had happened. Sitting all alone in the loft of my uncle's barn, I cried without any consolation, and swore to myself that I would never, ever, tell anybody what happened. This was my secret and I was alone with it.

From the attack came my fear: both a fear of being hurt again and a fear of all men. In particular I was afraid of any man older than I or in a position of authority. I trusted none of them. To me, every man was a potential attacker, especially if he liked me or wanted to be friends with me.

Today I know that confusion and fear are consequences for most boys that are sexually abused in childhood. Then, however, I had no such reassurance and I was too afraid to discuss my fears with anyone. I did not know such things happened to other males. The fear was the basis of my feeling so different from all other men. In turn, the sense of being "different" from other men led to my strong feeling of isolation. I was isolated because I kept a secret about my abuse. Now

I know that I was raped by my uncle, that it hurt and terrified me, and that I blocked out all conscious awareness of that event for forty years. At this point in my recovery, I know I am not different from the millions of other men who were sexually abused in childhood.

With therapy, I have learned much about the impact on my life of holding my secret for forty years. I know, now, that my journey is not yet over and that some scars will always remain. However, I will not return to my old isolation from other people. I feel loving encouragement of others, and that gives me courage to continue my growth. I still have fears on occasion, but I continue to work toward keeping my heart open to life, love, and the future. It helps when I remember that the word "courage" comes from a word meaning heart.[1]

Removing the Secret of Abuse

In 1984 psychologist Ed Tick wrote an article for a psychotherapy journal describing his childhood abuse and his efforts as an adult to get professional help with his abuse issues. Basically, he found it almost impossible to find a therapist to work with him, since at that time so few professionals knew anything about the sexual abuse of males or how to treat it. Tick concluded his article by summarizing the information then available about male abuse in hopes of helping others deal with this problem. He referred to the sexual abuse of young boys in America as "The Best Kept Secret." Though we know considerably more today than in 1984, sexual abuse of males is still a "secret" for most men (and women) in our country. Today educators believe that as many as one in three females will experience some form of sexual abuse before age eighteen; the current estimate of young boys who are abused is about one in five. This implies that at least twenty percent of all adult males in our country have experienced some form of sexual abuse in their childhood years—and yet most people are still not willing to look seriously at this problem.

One reason is given in the personal statement above: many men who experienced sexual abuse in childhood are not able as adults to remember the experience(s). Amnesia for some or all of the abuse probably happens to about 20 to 25 percent of abuse survivors. Denial that abuse occurred, or that the experiences were really abusive, is widespread, both by the public and by health professionals.

What constitutes sexual abuse of boys? Who are the persons who abuse young boys? Why do so many men deny they were abused, or become amnesiac about the abuse? The answers to these questions are all interconnected, and have implications for treatment and prevention.

Most definitions of childhood sexual abuse say that any use of a boy under 16 for the sexual pleasure of another person at least five years older than the boy is abusive. These behaviors may range from inappropriate touching, or fondling of genitals, to masturbation, to oral and anal contact. About 85 percent of all sex abusers are male. For young boys, the abuser is a family member about 50 percent of the time.

Often sexual behaviors may be forced on the child, either by coercion or violence. However, in many other cases the child in some way is tricked into thinking that the experience is mutual and is a sign of love or affection from the older person. An example would be an older relative who tells the child, "I am the only one in the family who really loves you; I am the only person who will protect you and take care of you. We are really special to each other." One of the most frequently used arguments by pedophiles is that they are merely trying to teach the young boy to love and be a healthy person, and that the sexual experience is only for the child's benefit, not for the adult's pleasure.

The most extreme forms of male sexual abuse involve using the boy for pornography and/or prostitution. Though rare in occurrence compared to other forms of abuse, these do occur more often that most people would think. Though child pornography is illegal in the United States, it is available to anyone willing to search and pay the price for it (in New York City, actual photographs of young boys in sex acts with adult men may cost $100 each). In large cities boys as young as seven or eight are on the streets, controlled by pimps, for the sexual use of older men. Sometimes these children are physically tortured; occasionally, they are killed.

Though the extreme forms of abuse are more dramatic, all cause great harm to children and lead to problems in adult life. Before we identify these problems and show ways of solving them, we need to look in detail at why sexual abuse of males is so denied and ignored in our country.

Denial is a widespread, almost universal occurrence among men. We see it as having three parts: 1. We deny our own feelings ("I don't hurt," "Men don't cry,"), 2. we deny the feelings of others, and 3. we deny the reality and impact of our behaviors. All of us have the potential in us for abusive behavior, and most of us do abuse someone at some point in our lives, either ourselves (through drug, alcohol, or food abuse) or others, either verbally or physically.

These three parts set the stage for denial as follows. We grow up in a world full of expectations of how a male is "supposed" to behave and feel. Males, in our culture, are expected to be strong and to be in control. Thus, if sex is forced upon a young boy, he feels weak and out of control—and our culture sees these feelings as feminine. Most boys are terrified of feeling "feminine," so they will either deny that anything happened to them, or, if they admit it happened, they will rationalize that they wanted it and caused it to happen. Either way, the denial of the experience (and the feelings) is based on a need to be in control and to be strong—a "man" as our culture defines it.

If the behavior is not forced on the child, but rather the child is tricked into thinking it is mutual, the second part of denial comes into play: the boy will think he is "special" to the older person and deny that he is merely an object of sexual satisfaction for the older person. We often find this type of denial in males who were sexually abused by their fathers or by special family friends.

Finally, the third type of denial is also based upon cultural expectations. Boys are supposed to "experiment" and become sexually active at an early age. They are supposed to want and seek sex. If the abuse is from an older female, society tends to see the experience as "good luck" for the young male—and the young man will start to deny his feelings and look at the experience that way, too. For example: Think of a thirteen-year-old boy who has intercourse with a twenty-nine-year-old woman. Does that seem different to you than the reverse, a thirteen-year-old girl who has intercourse with a twenty-nine-year-old man?

A special type of denial often found in adult male abuse survivors is based on this thought: "I enjoyed it, so it couldn't have been abuse." It is amazing how many bright men fail to see the flaw in this logic. This same type of faulty thinking is often applied to women in rape cases: "She enjoyed it, therefore it wasn't rape." It's time we all realize that just because our genitals respond with pleasure to certain friction does not mean we have given consent to the act.

Two aspects of denial deserve special attention. One is denial of the abuse because the child was threatened by his abuser. Young boys usually take such threats very seriously. Here are some examples from men we have worked with: One young boy was held down and masturbated by his older brother and friends. Afterwards, the brother told the boy, "If you tell Mom or Dad, we'll beat you up." A man having sex with his son told the boy, "Don't tell your mother, it would get her upset and she would leave us." A co-worker forced his business partner's son, at gun-point, to perform oral sex, then told the boy that the father would be shot if the boy were to tell. Threats such as these cause long term consequences in adult life, such as chronic anxiety, distrust of others, constant vigilance, and a heightened sense of needing to protect others. Second, an extreme form of denial is amnesia for the abuse. This usually happens following extremely traumatic events, such as rape, or when there is repeated severe abuse which causes the child both physical and emotional pain. We then forget the bad things that happened to us (analysts call this repression) to protect ourselves from further pain.

Strong denial usually causes many problems in adult life; amnesia always does. What is not remembered or confronted by the conscious mind is constantly gnawing away at a person's health and happiness in unconscious ways. In our work with abused men, we find a pattern of reactions common to many abuse survivors. While not all of these will apply to any particular man, survivors usually show many of these in their life. These problems include feeling depressed and unhappy, lowered energy, and feelings of not being good enough. Many of these men have felt suicidal at some point about their abuse. Many abused men report physical symptoms of frequent headaches, chest pains, and high blood pressure. Alcohol and drug abuse, or other out of control behavior, such as gambling, excessive spending, eating problems, or sexual promiscuity may be present.

Many men who were sexually abused as children find themselves as adults confused over their sexual orientation. Some may be uncertain whether they are gay or straight. Sexual difficulties are often found; these may include impotence, difficulty reaching orgasm, and what is often called the "bashful bladder" syndrome: difficulty in starting to urinate in a public restroom when another man is present. Many male survivors end up in relationships with partners who were also sexually and/or physically abused in childhood. Often this latter fact has never been talked about in the relationship.

One of the most pervasive and problematic behaviors we find in adult male survivors is passivity in personal behavior and relationships. The man often finds it difficult to assert himself in a healthy, appropriate way, and instead either lets people walk over him, or overreacts in a hostile, belligerent way that is not effective.

The above problems can be very debilitating to some men. However, it often takes strong problems or extreme unhappiness before most men will seek professional counseling or therapy. When help is sought, it is usually from a physician for some of the health problems above. Our experience shows that careful questioning and good listening by the physician will help bring out the abuse history. Unfortunately, so far, most physicians either do not know about sexual abuse of boys, or do not want to recognize it and treat the problems it presents. This is probably because most physicians in our country are men and have their own denial about abuse. Professionally, we work to educate professionals about abuse and their reactions to it.

Ministers, too, are usually male, and filled with both societal and religious denial. So far, they do not have a good track record of helping abused men. They have tended to add more problems by arousing guilt based on advice to immediately forgive the abuser or else saying "just forget about it and put it in the past where it belongs." To their credit, more clergy are seeking training and guidance to help people with these painful problems.

Fortunately, more and more therapists and counselors are trained in recognizing the indications of abuse and in helping survivors work through the reactions and feelings. Therapy can help reduce the depression and pain over the abuse, and helps remove confusion about sexual issues. Body therapy, in the form of massage or other appropriate hands-on work, has been shown to be a valuable part of therapy with abuse survivors, helping many recover their full memory of the abuse and then to heal more rapidly from the effects of their abuse. As a result of therapy, most men show improvement in their health and become more appropriately active. Therapy groups composed of male abuse survivors are very powerful and are recommended as an integral part of recovery from abuse in child-hood. Groups help men express safely and work through their anger and depression. Groups also help develop normal close emotional contact with other men and define the true experience of intimacy with another male. We see this intimacy as being a natural state of being alive, and different from closeness. Intimacy means being truly yourself with others, and relating honestly with another person in a relationship. The "sharing out loud" with another person the thoughts and feelings you often kept to yourself bridges the gap between two people and promotes true intimacy. This intimate sharing is what makes group therapy work and what leads to such deep growth for abuse survivors in recovery groups. Since the abuse was originally tolerated in silence, it broke off intimacy; reopening to being truly yourself with others brings profound healing. Most men have been accustomed to having this type of intimacy only with a woman, and thus often, incorrectly, confuse intimacy with sexuality. This confu-sion blocks true emotional intimacy with other males.

In recovering from abuse, this growth toward greater intimacy, and the decrease of the personal passivity referred to above, both have major impact on the man's relationship with his primary partner in life. The wife or partner may be confused, hurt or even angry. One common complaint at this point from the partner is "You have changed so much I don't know you any more." Many partners want the man to be the way he was before—and few survivors are willing to go back to their original fearful, passive way of being. This does strain relationships for a while, sometimes to the breaking point. However, counseling and the opportunity for the partner to grow and change also, and accept the new changes in the man's life, can lead to greater growth and happiness for both.

We want to remind all the men who have suffered from childhood abuse that there also are millions of women who were abused in childhood. Many of their issues and needs are the same as those of men. All are looking for healing, and all of us must work together to change society so that boys and girls in the future will never have to experience the pain and anguish, both in childhood and later in adult life, which results from childhood sexual abuse.

So far, most of the workers in the field of child abuse treatment, education, and prevention have been women. Men must now join them in taking a strong stand against sexual abuse. Volunteer agencies that work against child abuse always need male volunteers. Here is one area where you can directly get involved, and where your efforts will make a difference immediately. Since most abuse is committed by men, and since most of the judicial system in our country is still controlled by men, males need to assume appropriate roles in speaking out about their own abuse, rather than continuing to deny. As men, we must also defend and support all who have been abused. In our old cultural stereotypes of gender roles, women have been expected to be nurturers and men protectors. This stereotype needs to be changed into a reality in which both men and women are expected to nurture and protect. Men and women must respect themselves and others and work *together* to protect the children. Such responsible protective behavior will help put an end to the anguish of childhood sexual abuse.

NOTES

1. An expanded version of this personal statement is in the May-June, 1989 issue of *Pilgrimage*, Volume 15, Number 3, pages 2-6.)

Fast-Forwarding to Intimacy:
An Honest Look at Love

John M.

I am a recovering sex addict. As an adult, my sex life has ranged from periods of sexual prudishness to compulsive promiscuity and almost everything in between. Over the years, I've done hundreds of one-night stands; orgies; multiple partners; committed, monogamous relationships; and now I find myself, for the most part pretty content, predominantly celibate and dating. I have spent many, many years preoccupied with sex. I still am.

I was fifteen when I discovered dirty bookstores, and sexual fantasies have been my fix ever since. I have been using various forms of pornography as masturbatory stimulation for over twenty years.

Jacking off with porn has been the greater part of my sex life since my adolescence. I grew up in a very dysfunctional Catholic family and sex was such a mysterious, sinful taboo it became compelling. Since my family had more than our share of tragedies, sexual fantasies were a great escape. I also got really hooked on the good feelings I found in my body at an early age as the pleasure helped to ease what seemed like insurmountable pain and helped me through some very hard times. It still does.

At the onset of the AIDS crisis, I joined a 12-step program for people who were sexually out of control. I was sick of compulsively making unhealthy choices about sexuality and I knew that if I didn't change drastically and fast, I was going to kill myself and maybe others by getting or spreading the HIV virus. I had also reached the point where I felt like I wasn't having sex, it was having me.

I didn't realize it at the time, but I was terribly lonely, with very low self-esteem and the excitement of multiple sexual contacts interrupted the overwhelming emptiness that was eating away at me. Anonymous sex helped me believe I was wanted in a society that made me feel undesirable.

Ultimately, I was looking for love, which is a noble pursuit. The problem was I was looking for it in all the wrong places. What I failed to realize was that hunting for immediate gratification was compounding my lack of self worth. It was a very hurtful syndrome. Essentially, my sexual hunger was really a search for intimacy but the only way I had learned to meet that need was costing me my dignity.

What was it that led me to believe that I could find the answers to my questions about love and affection amidst a sea of darting glances from fellow desperados in those nasty smelling places I ran red lights trying to get to night after night?

I was in so much pain that eventually even orgasm, my ultimate solace in a cruel world, became ineffective. I tried having more sex to prove to myself that it could still bandage my emotional wounds as it had done all of my life, but, I was insatiable and more and more sex brought less and less gratification. I was really hurting and terribly depressed, caught up with trying to heal my emotional pain with physical pleasure, and it just wasn't working. Eventually, this charade could no longer disguise the truth.

I wanted more for myself. Deep down inside I knew, even amidst the delirium, that I deserved better. I always believed sex was precious, even sacred, and here I was running around trying to get my erotic needs met in the street. I wanted to make love at home, not in seedy places after dark. I wanted clean sheets, long walks and close talk. I wanted bacon and eggs the morning after. I wanted a committed, intimate relationship with one special friend that could grow, not fleeting moments with a parade of strangers.

At the same time I started going to Sexaholics Anonymous meetings, I bought a VCR and masturbating to porno films has been a survival technique for me ever since AIDS became epidemic. It keeps me off the streets and it's safe. Presently, I am too frightened to get tested so I don't know my HIV status and it's better to watch porno stars have sex on TV than to put myself or others at risk. Infrequently, I still do have sex but it is always safe and in bed at home. My sexuality has been confusing enough without riddling it with the fear of death and murder.

As much as I depend on my pornographic escapades, I am bugged by some of the scenes that are acted out in these gay male videos. It looks to me like some of these porno stars are in a lot of pain while they are supposed to be making love. It also appears that the top man's sexual gratification comes at the cost of his partner's physical discomfort. I often perceive the top man as angry and working out his hostile aggressions on the bottom man's ass; no rubbers, no lube, just a hard, fast and inconsiderate fuck inter-spersed with intense spanking.

I always grab my remote and fast forward through these scenes. I can't stand watching them. It looks painful. The top man is slapping the bottom man's butt really hard as he pounds his dick in and out of his ass. It appears he has contempt for his partner. It seems to me that in a same sex coupling, this could be interpreted as his own self hate projected onto his unwilling victim.

Often, the facial expressions on these porno stars do not connote pleasure or ectasy. Their faces are contorted. They are gritting their teeth. They don't smile, they sneer. It seems like some kind of fight or struggle where someone is being held prisoner and their bed is their battleground. Often, the implications of the way the top man handles his partner alludes to ownership as in a master/slave relationship and to me, it looks and sounds like a hurtful exercise in eroticized punishment or a trial by fire of masculine sexual endurance and it does not make me cum, it deeply upsets me.

I get so unnerved that I have to admit that in some way these porno scenes must remind me of myself; otherwise I wouldn't be so affected. It's taken me years to see the connection.

And sex in lots of porno flicks is not gentle or tender, it's often brutal. The bottom men in these sado-masochistic scenes remind me of that part of myself that believes I deserve to be punished for being who I am; for wanting to be loved by another man both physically and emotionally; for wanting to hold another man inside of me and take in his essence.

Then there's the spanking which adds an air of violence to the affair. Spanking on the butt reminds me of the humiliation and punishment children receive from their parents at impressionable ages when they do something their parents think is wrong and a bad boy gets spanked harder than a bad girl. Allegedly, we can take it harder because we're male.

The top men in these videos and their demeaning anger and contempt for their partners remind me of my own self hatred and internalized homophobia. Then, of course, the general feeling of what I see on the TV is like a mirror for me because I can never forget the years I spent on the streets, trying to assuage my deep emotional hurt by getting myself into endless, unhealthy sexual encounters that, in the long run, wound up hurting me even more. These porno scenes reflect the syndrome which is more than figuratively a dead-end.

It has taken years of self-examination to understand what I was really doing to myself then and I know I am not the only gay man who has used sex to punish himself or others, but why?

I am not naive. I am sure that these erotic productions are sensationalized, but pornography is a multi-million dollar industry in this country and around the world. It must meet a need. I know I buy and rent videos on a regular basis and presently, I have no intention of stopping.

I am also aware that my history of sexual encounters and the sexual encounters in these videos involve consenting adults. I also know that my fantasies and the scenes in these videos I chose to watch are pretty lightweight considering all of the violence I know is enmeshed in gay male sexuality. I have heard plenty of horror stories about men hanging from the ceiling by their scrotum or nipples, anal hemorrhaging and the disabling results of certain sexual punishment practices.

I also know that pornography shapes a lot of male sexual behavior. It's shaped mine. Using porno is a way I entertain my fantasies and, in the past, I have spent years running the streets trying to make them a reality. I cannot deny that it has unmistakably influenced my sexual relationships over the years and because of my 12-Step meetings, I know I am not alone.

I was visiting an old friend in L.A. a while back. We hadn't seen each other in a couple of years and got to talking about all kinds of things; our careers, future plans and mutual friends. Then the conversation shifted to our sex lives and fantasies and current crushes. I didn't know too much about what was going on for him. I remembered that when we were in college, we were both in and out of gay relationships and it all seemed pretty normal. Then all of a sudden this dear old friend says something that gave me the feeling that I was talking to a complete stranger. I was dumbfounded when he looked me in the eye with a cocky smile on his face and said, "Oh, but I enjoy getting whipped."

Seven years ago, I was in New York and having dinner in the East Village with another college chum. His best friend had recently died and his mother was in a near fatal accident about six weeks previous to that. After bringing each other up to date and eating seconds of all the Cantonese food on our table, I nonchalantly asked him, "What did you do last night?"

Just as nonchalantly, he was pleased to report that he went to a bar and got picked up by a big, burly guy who took him home, handcuffed his hands behind his back, tied up his feet, blindfolded and gagged him. "Then," my friend said enthusiastically, "he fucked my brains out! It was great! I'm a little sore, but it was worth it."

I freaked out and tried not to show it as I quickly asked the waiter for the check. I desperately needed some fresh air. It was obvious that my friend was grieving but he wasn't shedding a tear, he was out sexing. I'll never forget the fortune cookie he got which said, "IF EVERYBODY IS JUMPING OUT OF WINDOWS, THERE MUST BE A REASON."

In my day, I had also had several one-night stands where the men I was with wanted to be fucked. On each occasion, we greased up and I entered them as slowly and as considerately as I would want to be entered. At some point, both of these guys winced a little and I, trying to be a sensitive lover, immediately asked if I was going too fast or if I should pull out and they all had very similar responses that basically boiled down to, "Yes, it hurts. But it's okay, go ahead and do whatever you have to do."

What led these guys to believe that their physical discomfort would get me off?

Now, regardless of the effects of pornography, I am well aware of the sexual hell I've been through. Then a good friend tells me he enjoys getting whipped and another good friend tells me that there was only a little rectal bleeding that had stopped the morning after he spent the night getting his brains fucked out by some sadistic stranger; no rubbers, no lube. Then I recall the faces of those men who gave me permission to cause them physical pain so that I could get off fucking them in the ass and I can't help but wonder why. I intuitively feel all this adds up and even though it is very complex, difficult and terrifying to put into words . . . THERE MUST BE A REASON.

This is scary to me because I am sincerely not interesting in offending anyone, especially my gay brothers. We have enough trouble battling straight society's homophobia without giving each other a hard time, particularly during this AIDS crisis. And, regardless of how questionable I may find anyone's behavior, it is only questionable when I consider adopting the behavior for myself. I am not interested in intervening with anyone's right to do whatever they want to do and I am in no position to be casting stones.

I just have a hunch that maybe some of us are participating in our own victimization and it really hurts me because of my commitment and love for myself and my community. I don't blame the victim. I only question why some of us make the choices we make because I believe that they are not in our best interest as gay people.

Is it possible that as gay people we are still punishing ourselves for being who we are because no matter how hard we try, we cannot get our parents' (or society's) approval or acceptance? Because we are oppressed as gay people, have we possibly learned to deny or anesthetize our unidentified and our unexpressed pain as a survival technique in a holier-than-thou hetero society? I know I have. Have we subconsciously internalized the judgement of our oppressors to such an extent that we are condemning ourselves and acting out strict sentences in our lives with self-destructive behaviors? Is it affecting our immune systems? Then finally, what is our ultimate punishment?

Recently, I was informed that one out of every three gay people is addicted to drugs or alcohol or both. Without even considering sexual addiction, which I dare say is rampant in the gay male community, that is a lot of brothers and sisters with compulsive addictive personalities. But we are not alone.

Substance abuse is also high in other minority communities. It makes sense. Minorities are systematically oppressed by the majority culture. Oppression hurts us, we get stressed out and we find some way to overcompensate; to deal with the pain the best way we know how. We survive.

Gay bars are typically the places where we gather to meet and have a good time but the proprietors of these establishments want to make money, and they do that by selling us booze. Meanwhile, if we are using drugs, alcohol and sex to feel better or get high, what does that imply about how we feel when we are sober?

Drugs and alcohol are toxic poisons that kill brain cells. Poisoning our bodies in this way interferes with the functioning of our brains, which release enzymes and hormones in order to develop the T-cells that make up our immune system. We require excessive vitamins to detox and to rebuild our immunity functions, but alcoholics and drug addicts often lack nutrition because of poor appetites and diets. The THC content in marijuana has been clinically proven to be immuno-suppressive. Blood vessels constricted by poppers suppress blood flow to the brain. Cocaine and IV drugs are highly addictive with even greater destructive effects. Basically, the use of drugs and alcohol causes damaged or dead brain cells and what's left is a compromised immune system.

Psycho-neuro-immunology is a field that is just beginning to receive some attention during this AIDS epidemic. It is by far more profitable for drug companies to develop a new drug that will be the magic cure. Funding and research tends to go in that direction. However, the notion that there is healing power in self-esteem and personal contentment is becoming more popular as we seriously consider the many aspects and implications of how human beings combat disease. There is a shortage of hard evidence to prove recent findings, but a developing trend of thought suggests that people who feel good about themselves have stronger immune systems than those who don't.

Maybe laughter really is good medicine after all. In one experiment, immediately following a funny movie, a test group of people had a high concentration of antibodies in their saliva. A second group watched a depressing movie and immediately after their saliva tested immuno-suppressed. It makes sense to me but how does it relate?

As gay people, we often grow up aware that we are somehow different. We also grow up without positive role models. Then, for the rest of our developmental years through adulthood, our families, the mass media, society, and organized religions most often lead us to believe there is something bad or even evil about our homosexual tendencies. Not to mention the fact that because, as gay people, we feel condemned by modern religions, we wind up throwing out the baby with the bath water and deny ourselves any form of spiritual exercise or expression. I'd be willing to bet that it affects our self-image, how we treat ourselves and each other and the health of our immune system.

Add it up! First you have alcohol and drug abuse and their associated lack of morality or clear thinking. Couple this with a historic and often unidentified reservoir of pain, lack of self-respect and spiritual abandonment. Add other unhealthy and unsafe choices around sexual behavior like getting fucked hard, without protection, causing rectal bleeding which may go unnoticed. Even when the bleeding is microscopic, which is typical, it is nonetheless sufficient to transmit the HIV virus. What you more than likely get is a wide range of people very susceptible to infection and a memorial quilt honoring the thousands and thousands who have died. I've heard it said that we are just at the tip of the iceberg.

And why? Because we're too proud to admit that we hurt? Because, as males, we're forced to stop crying at an early age and have forgotten how? Because we are too macho to shed our tears? Because we're terrified that expressing our rage and despair will kill us? Because we're deluded and think ourselves immune? Because we don't have the courage to face our histories and confront the source of our pain so that we may regain our lives and our health?

Denial and avoidance don't make pain disappear, they just postpone our healing. Better to heal now before it's too late.

Maybe if we faced our pain, shed our tears and felt the relief that comes from this built-in, natural healing mechanism in our bodies we would be able to get over it and appreciate the good feelings in our bodies and in our lives.

I'll never forget meeting a little four-year-old boy named David at a gay men's gathering in the Blue Ridge Mountains of North Carolina. Sixty men were indoors, sitting in a silent circle meditating during a massive thunderstorm, while David and a few other boys were running from the porch to the kitchen, up the ladder to the bedroom loft and back to the veranda, reeling on the porch swing in the pouring rain. I'll never forget the boys' faces, as bright as the lightning. And their laughter, just as loud as the thunder.

Suddenly, David fell about twelve feet from the top of the ladder to the floor below. He let out a blood-curdling scream and cried as hard as I have ever seen anyone cry in my entire life. Only his father comforted him while the rest of us gave him our undivided attention and wouldn't you know, within a minute or two, that kid wiped away his tears and was running back out to the porch to enjoy the storm.

Little David was one of the greatest teachers I have ever had. I learned so much about healing from this little tyke. He made it look so simple, so natural. He taught me that if you get some good attention and really feel your pain, you can let it go and get to the important things in life, like swinging with laughter.

For over a year, I have been very involved in learning how to be a caregiver for People Living With AIDS. My best friend has recently recovered from his first bout with Pneumocystis Carinii Pneumonia. He and a lot of people I have met have deeply affected me. Many of them are now dead and the sense of loss in my life and in the gay community is tremendous. We don't have time to grieve all of those brothers and sisters that have died because of the growing numbers that are requiring the support to stay alive.

And that's what it's all about. Staying alive. Because I certainly don't deserve punishment, and I certainly do not deserve to die, regardless of my history or my choices around sex and love, and neither does anyone else. We are not guilty of anything. If more men learned from us how to love one another, we wouldn't have to live our lives shrouded in the fear of war and nuclear destruction. More intimacy between men could save this planet.

Still, our first step towards healing has got to be with ourselves. And for me, the key is forgiveness, especially self-forgiveness. I cannot take one step forward without going back and doing that. It's hard and it can hurt but it's worth it.

Too many of us have already died. From them I have received and learned so much about what's important about being fully alive. I owe it to them to try, in a committed way, to heal myself and be available to my community. To honor them, I'll stay healthy. They've left us no greater legacy than this: life is not without its rainstorms but they pass and you can laugh just as loud as the thunder.

A Male Grief:
Notes on Pornography and Addiction

by David Mura

I PREMISES

1

Start with the premise that a person—generally a male—may be addicted to pornography, and that this addiction may be part of a larger addiction to any number of other sexual "highs"—affairs, visits to prostitutes, anonymous sex, exhibitionism, voyeurism, etc. See where this premise leads.

2

A man wishes to believe there is a beautiful body with no soul attached. Because of this wish he takes the surface for truth. There are no depths. Because of this wish, he begins to worship an image. But when this image enters the future, it loses what the man has given it—momentary devotion. The man wishes for another body, another face, another moment. He discards the image like a painting. It is no longer to his taste. Only the surface can be known and loved, and this is why the image is so easily exhausted, why there must be another.

What is this danger that lies beneath the surface? How can it hurt him? *It* reminds him of the depths he has lost in himself.

3

At the essence of pornography is the image of flesh used as a drug, a way of numbing psychic pain. But this drug lasts only as long as the man stares at the image. Then his pain reasserts itself, reveals the promised power as an illusion.

What is it to worship an image? It is to pray for a gift you will never receive.

4

There are certain states of mind that the closer one understands them, the closer one comes to experiencing evil. This is certainly true with the world of pornography. The experience of those who view a pornographic work dispassionately, without a strong sexual response, is not pornographic, though they may capture some flickerings of that world. For in pornographic perception, each gesture, each word, each image, is read first and foremost through sexuality. Love or tenderness, pity or compassion, become subsumed by, and are made subservient to, a "greater" deity, a more powerful force. In short, the world is reduced to a single common denominator.

5

Such a simplistic world, of course, does not exist. But the addict to pornography desires to be blinded, to live in a dream. Any element which questions the illusion that sexuality is all encompassing, the very basis of human activity, must be denied. The addict can become enraged by any evidence, such as an inadvertent microphone, that the people on the screen are actors or less than perfectly tuned sexual beings. On a wider scale, those in the thrall of pornography try to eliminate from their consciousness the world outside pornography, and this includes everything from their family and friends to their business deals or last Sunday's sermon to the political situation in the Middle East. In engaging in such elimination the viewer or reader reduces himself. He becomes stupid.

6

Although the pornographic viewpoint attempts to numb any psychic urge but sexuality, such numbing can never be complete. We might envision those who engage in it as attempting to attack a Hydra, constantly cutting off what will appear again, only doubled.

7

Those who are addicted to pornography attempt to erase the distinction between art and life. On the one hand the addict knows, at some level of consciousness, that the world of pornography is unreal. To block out this knowledge, the addict tries to convince himself that all the world is pornographic, and that other people are too timid to see this truth. Thus the addict does not view or read pornography in the same way a scholar might read a poem about shepherds. While the latter acknowledges the fictional nature of the bucolic, the addict wants to deny pornography's fictional nature. In refusing the symbolic nature of art, the addict wishes to destroy the indestructible gulf between the sign and its referent.

8

Like all addicts, the addict to pornography dreams then of ultimate power and control. When reality invades this dream and causes doubts, the addict thinks: I have nothing else. I have, all my life, done my best to deny and destroy through my addiction whatever would replace this.

Thus, the addict returns to the inertia of the dream.

9

The addiction to pornography is not fun. Underneath all the assertions of liberty and "healthy fun" lie the desperation and anxiety, the shame and fear, the loneliness and sadness, that fuel the endless consumption of magazines and strip shows, x-rated films, visits to prostitutes. If addicts portray themselves as hedonists or carefree, this portrayal is belied in those moments and feelings they do not let anyone else see. Like all actors, they mistake their life on stage as being truest and most real. What happens offstage cannot possibly have a bearing on who they are.

10

In pornographic perception, the addict experiences a type of vertigo, a fearful exhilaration, a moment when all the addict's ties to the outside world do indeed seem to be cut or numbed. That sense of endless falling, that rush, is what the addict seeks again and again. Its power comes from a wild forgetting, a surrender to entropy, to what he knows is evil.

Those who stand back from the world of pornography cannot experience this falling, this rush. They cannot understand the attraction it holds. But for the addict the rush is more than an attraction. He is helpless before it. Completely out of control.

II THE ETIOLOGY OF ADDICTION

1

One defense of pornography is that it defies repression and therefore represents an act of freedom. Such a defense ignores the repression that takes place within the world of pornography, for the pornographic world is so limited that to list what it leaves out would require an endless encyclopedia.

The libertarian defense of pornography also misconstrues the nature of freedom. The defense argues that freedom is the liberty to do anything to anybody. But this defense ignores the fact that nowhere in this world can such liberty exist for everyone. In particular, certain acts require an abuser and a victim, and in such acts, to possess the liberty to play the abuser, one must deny another the freedom to be anything but a victim. A hierarchy is set up which denies freedom. Sade's prisoners do not have a choice.

But is pornography an act which requires an abuser and a victim? And what if, of one's own free will one chooses to be the victim? In examining these questions, feminist writers have, I think, convincingly argued that women are abused in pornography and are coerced into the victim role, and I will not go over their arguments here. Instead, what I want to show is that the person engaged in viewing the world pornographically is abusing himself, as well as women. In doing so, he becomes his own victim.

2

To start with, addiction is a learned behavior. Usually this behavior is learned as a child, and is reinforced and supported by a set of beliefs or ideology which is also learned by the child. The method of instruction is what is commonly called abuse, and this abuse can be sexual, physical or emotional, or any combination of these three.

But to decide precisely what constitutes abuse is problematic. We can say that it is obvious that a father who has intercourse with his seven-year-old daughter, or a mother who whips her infant with a hanger, has abused the child. But this argument is merely tautological and does not answer the defense offered by many abusers: the child wanted it, or the child needed it for its own good. If such arguments seem outrageous, it should be remembered that these same arguments are used by pornographers to defend themselves against the charges of victimizing women. The women in pornography, say the pornographers, choose to be in it, the women make money, perhaps more money than they could in "straight" jobs.

To answer such arguments and to understand what constitutes abuse, we must, I believe, understand how people learn abusive behavior. I will examine this process in detail shortly. What I will argue is that abusive behavior is *not natural.* That is, it does not appear spontaneously without contact or instruction from others.

This means, of course, that the person involved with abuse could have been taught other behavior, that there are options which have been denied to that person. And because of the narrowness and one-dimensional quality of the world of abuse, I will argue that abuse represents a loss of knowledge about oneself and the world, and, therefore, a loss of freedom.

3

A boy is sitting on the steps with his uncle. It is August, fireflies sparking in and out of the dark, a few mosquitoes. The night films their bodies with sweat, they are not talking. The boy is eight. Slowly the uncle takes the boy's hand, rubs it against his groin. Soon the boy has grabbed the uncle's penis, is kneading and stroking it through the khaki pants. The uncle says they should go inside.

What does this boy feel? He scarcely knows himself. Perhaps he should not talk about what they are doing. Surely he feels fear: at the size of his uncle's penis, at their mutual silence, at the sense, vague yet strong, that what they are doing is wrong. The boy does not protest. He fears his uncle's anger. The boy fears that the uncle will blame him for what they are doing, will say that the boy made the uncle do this. The boy fears the uncle will tell his parents, fears the excitement the act incites in him, his sexual feelings. Since no one has talked to him about such feelings, he does not know what they are. And yet he is drawn to them, to the dream-like quality of doing something he has never done before, yet knowing, somehow, how to do it. The boy wants to know what is happening, but fears asking questions. He knows questions are not what his uncle wants. The boy fears the attraction this act has for him, how it brings his uncle's attention, how it brings caressing, how it makes him feel that his uncle must love him. The boy feels important. He fears being caught, going home afterwards, facing his mother and father, his brother.

Most of all the boy learns this: to love his fears.

 *accepting as normal* **4**

But there are other lessons in this one act, lessons even more difficult for the boy to articulate. These lessons have to do with power and what to do with feelings. The uncle has used his power over the boy. This power consists partly in the uncle's size, his physical superiority over the boy. In turn, the boy knows the uncle is stronger, could take what he wants by physical force; even if that threat is never exercised, both the boy and the uncle know it is there. But more than physical superiority, what gives the uncle power is knowledge. An adult might repel the uncle's advances, would know he or she has the right to say stop. The boy does not know he has this right. He does not know whether others would believe him if he told them about this act. He does not know what they would do, or whose fault they would say it is. All the boy senses is that he knows less than the uncle, and he looks to the uncle, the adult, to guide him. In turn, the uncle knows the boy will accept his authority on what is right and wrong. The uncle knows the boy will believe his warnings against telling anyone, his threat that the boy will be punished. The uncle exploits the boy's ignorance, the boy's un-awareness of choice. The uncle exerts power, control.

There is, in the boy, something that resists this power, this control. This resistance is, in part, the boy's semi-conscious knowledge that what he and the uncle are doing is wrong. Part of this knowledge comes from society, but part, I would posit, does not. We might say there is something in each of us that cries out against an injustice, and we might call the source of this cry the soul or spirit, but we cannot prove the existence of this source. We can only witness or, at times, dig for, its cry. What the boy's cry says is that he is being used as an object, a source of energy for the uncle. As such the boy is not valued for anything but his sexuality and his weakness, which allows that sexuality to be exploited. The uncle does not wish to apprehend, to know who the boy is. He does not wish to know how the boy feels, his fears, his rage and sadness at not knowing what is happening, his vague sense that what is happening is wrong. The uncle does not care what effects his actions will have on the boy in the future, nor does he want to acknowledge that the boy is a child, though some part of the uncle, which he represses, knows this. In short the uncle does not truly love the boy. Perhaps later, if confronted, the uncle may maintain he did love the boy, but at the moment the uncle commits the act of abuse, this love is banished, destroyed. The cry of the boy says, "I want to be loved, to be known and cared for, to have my whole being acknowledged. In committing this act you are telling me I am nothing, a tool, that I am not allowed to express my feelings, that I have no feelings."

Once the cry is suppressed, and given the circumstances, it must be, the boy may then take this act for love. Whether verbally or silently, this is what his uncle has told him.

5

In taking the act of abuse for love, for the standard of sexuality, the boy carries this message: sex is the exertion of power by the stronger over the weaker, sex is the denial of feelings, sex is fear and secrecy, sex is shame (shame keeps us from speaking what we know, tells us we are unworthy), sex uses the other as an object, sex is not a means of knowing the other, sex is a devaluing of the self, sex is the maintenance of distance, of control over one's feelings, sex is how I can make others pay attention to me.

How deeply these messages are imprinted depends, in part, on whether or not they are congruent with the boy's family system. A boy from a healthy family will be able to recover from such abuse, but a boy whose parents have given him the same messages as the uncle will have no other choice. The latter boy lives in a system where the ideology of abuse is the only available way of knowing the world. He grows up thinking power, secrecy, shame, fear, distrust, lack of feelings, and distance are the bases of human relationships.

Is it any wonder, then, that such a boy comes to crave pornography?

6

Although the boy I have described above is a victim of sexual abuse, it should be mentioned that physical and emotional abuse both have similar effects on a child. Also, therapists have argued that there may be "covert" forms of incest. In covert incest, while no sexual act occurs between the child and adult, the relationship between the two carries with it strong sexual overtones. For instance, many addicts of pornography grew up in families where they served as a surrogate husband for their mother and took care of her emotional needs. Such men grow up with an enormous amount of rage at how they became a target of their mother's misdirected rage and sadness, her lack of fulfillment. Pornography functions as an outlet for rage the boy could never express.

7

Of course the development of the child's addiction, its etiology, is never made clear to the child. Most of this remains buried beneath consciousness. Confronted with abuse, the child is confronted with his own powerlessness to stop it. Such powerlessness is terrifying, too terrifying for the child to contemplate. So the child invents an alternative reason for the presence of abuse in his world: he, the child, wanted it. In this way the child attempts to gain control, to stop his terror. After years of living with this alternative reasoning, the child can scarcely remember ever not wanting to experience abuse. All he knows is that he wants it; he cannot explain why. It is simply part of his nature. And his nature is bad.

8

What is the family system like where the seed of abuse grows into addiction? It is one where the abuse is denied. The child knows that if he or she tells about the abuse, no one will believe it. Or the parents will tell the child not to tell anyone else, to forget it ever happened. The feelings the child has concerning the abuse will not be acknowledged. The child will be told, verbally or non-verbally, that feelings are to be repressed.

The rules of such a system do not have to be stated out loud. Facial expressions or body posture can tell the child what not to express. Or the child discerns tabooed areas of speech by observing what the family fails to talk about and how the family acts as if what is not talked about does not exist. This silence is a common occurrence in alcoholic families. Since no one admits the existence of alcoholism, no one can express his or her feelings over the damage done by the alcoholic.

9

Because the parents can enforce the zones of silence without verbalization, they can feign surprise when the child confronts them years later in therapy. "We never told you you couldn't express your feelings," say the parents. They refuse to see that by not providing their children with the tools to express those feelings, they were dooming their children to silence almost as effectively as if they had ordered them to be silent. In essence, what they have done is denied their children a right to recognize a part of the self. Their children, like them, live in alienation.

Of course the parents were taught by their parents and were raised in a similar system. And because of the silence, no new knowledge may enter.

10

In abused children, one often finds a troubling self-assurance, an adult-like manner that seems to deny any suffering or turmoil. This act of self-assurance protects the child from what would happen if the child were to feel the terror, rage, sadness and shame of abuse. It is a tool of survival.

As the child grows to adulthood, so much of what has happened, so much of what the child felt while being abused, is banished from consciousness. If the adult talks at all about acts of abuse, the acts are recounted without feeling, with a numbness that leaves each detail dull and grey, devoid of resonance or color. Or perhaps a story is substituted which focuses only on those elements which can portray a picture of happiness, postcards from a childhood the adult wishes had occurred. In such stories, the defeated child identifies with the parents and their official version of the past. (History, as Walter Benjamin has remarked, is the tale of the victors.) There is simply no record of any crime. The victim has disappeared in a conspiracy of silence.

We must admit the possibility of alternative histories.

11

So much of Kafka's world seems uncanny, as if we've dreamed it all before. In this world, the terror is that one will be punished, one does not know when or why. One is punished, and the reasons given do not make sense, or else no reasons at all are given. Afterwards, one knows punishment will come again, yet between the first and second punishment, one has been unable to learn anything to prevent the second punishment. Oftentimes, reading a work such as *The Trial* or *In the Penal Colony* as a political allegory, we probably repress the true horror of what Kafka presents. Sufferings like those K. undergoes are not limited to adults. In fact, for some, much of childhood is exactly like the world of Kafka. To undergo such experiences without the psychic defenses and skills of an adult, that truly is too horrible to contemplate. We know this world intimately and that is its uncanniness. We cannot bear our knowledge.

III EVIL & IGNORANCE/KNOWLEDGE & INTIMACY

1

When a child repeats a self-destructive action he or she has learned, we generally do not accept the child's explanation that he or she genuinely desires to commit such an action. But when adults repeat such actions, we often listen to their reasons and may even become convinced that the self-destructive action is something the adult freely chooses. There are, of course, sound reasons for this difference. Children depend upon adults for the requirements of life, and do not have the option of leaving an abusive family system. But what if the only choice the adult knows is self-abuse and addictive behavior?

To adults, abuse seems natural, the only way to live. They lack sufficient knowledge of another way of acting, and this lack of knowledge denies them a choice. Viewed in this way, abuse is the very opposite of freedom. To speak of its victims as free to choose their victimization is a lie.

2

In imposing abuse, the abuser attempts to keep the victim from any knowledge of how to resist the abuse. In this way, abuse represents a closed system; any information which implies the abuse is wrong or which even implies the existence of a world beyond the system must be repressed.

This repression explains why children are so easy to abuse. They learn of the world mainly through adults, and what adults keep from them is nearly impossible for children to know, much less act upon. Moreover, once the system is in place within the child, he or she will automatically filter out or disregard any evidence which contradicts the system. This filtering out includes the child's own feelings.

3

Why does a child feel pain, sadness, rage and anger, rather than joy, at being abused? One explanation is that since abuse seeks to cut off knowledge, to impose a closed system, it is only sensible that our being would revolt against it. More, rather than less, knowledge would increase the chances of our survival as individuals as well as a species.

4

Feelings are a way of knowing the world: they tell us how the world moves beyond our control, beyond whatever boundaries or categories are set up by our intellect. In a sense, then, feelings are prior to language, closer to our animal being. Though they are expressed in language, they are much less erasable than other forms of knowledge and much less dependent upon learning. Abuse may be a learned behavior, but a child's emotional reactions to abuse are not.

This is true despite the fact that the child may quickly learn to suppress or circumvent the expression of these emotions. How then are we able to recognize them? To start with, the denial which the abuser forces on the child takes place through language, and the net of language is never without its loopholes, the spaces between the netting. It is through these spaces that alternative messages flow. As post-structuralists like Jacques Lacan have pointed out, the very structure of language is multivalent; each word in a sentence can be read as an endless chord whose composition constantly changes as the speaker or writer continues. Poets have known this for years, and the resonance of poems relies on and implies the inability of language to contain just one meaning, to communicate only the "official" message. In contrast, the parent who wishes to hear from the abused child a message of pure acceptance or obedience, a message with no other meaning, denies this quality of language. Such a parent strives for a control or power which does not exist.

Thus, with a child or the child grown into an adult, a therapist listens to the pain behind the words, behind the official or accepted version of the past, the white-wash of a happy or "normal" childhood. In this listening or reading, the therapist also acknowledges the language of the body, which communicates neither ideas nor facts, but the feeling self.

5

To link sexuality and intimacy is to link sexuality with knowledge, with an opening up of possibility rather than a closing down. In the choice between addictive sexuality and intimate sexuality, one trades a finite set of possibilities against an infinite set of possibilities. Addictive sexuality wishes to deny itself knowledge of the lover, of the lover's emotions, history, human fallible self and the possibilities of that self. Such sexuality views the other only in one dimension, for that is all it believes sexuality can contain. In contrast, intimate sexuality believes that sexuality can contain not only the other, but also one's own emotions, history, fallibilities and possibilities. Such an acknowledgement, though, is extremely frightening. It is an affirmation of all we do not control, a letting go of our defenses. It admits the knowledge of the pain we bear.

Men, Feminism and Pornography: An Attempt at Reconciliation

by Alex Rode Redmountain

In the simplistic, adversarial spirit of the times, a strange alliance of fundamentalists and feminists has declared war on all pornography as a manifestion of evil. I believe the feminists have cast their lot—with their declared enemies—in grievous error. There is nothing inherently "evil" in pornography, although I know that it, like almost anything else, can be utilized for evil ends. There is also nothing inherently anti-feminist about pornography, though it might superficially appear that way. All I ask of you in this essay is an opportunity to present a different point of view.

I write this as a heterosexual male, 55 years old, who has enjoyed erotica and pornography since puberty. Like many of my friends, I still enjoy it. It turns me on and reminds me that I'm a sexual creature. It satisfies my curiosity about all the women I'll never be with. It has, I believe, made me a better lover, and it has certainly helped make me a more tolerant human being.

I know that I've been addicted to pornography at times and like any other addiction it is a burden to the spirit. I've "wasted" many hours of my life on it, but I don't know that I wouldn't have wasted the same time on sitcoms and mysteries. For better or worse, I must admit that I've almost never been bored by it; this is just as curious to me as it might be to some of you.

Some confounding additional facts: I've been a feminist for as long as I can remember, even in grade school and in the high school locker room, long before most of my *female* friends had any idea what I was talking about; I have a wonderful, intensely satisfying, monogamous sex life with my wife, ranging from just plain old "down and dirty" to highly intimate to spiritual; I've been a full-time father (and a pretty good one, I think) to three children; and I've been a best friend and true partner to each of my two successive wives. That doesn't mean that I think I'm any kind of repository of virtue, or that I haven't screwed up in lots of ways—I have—but my flaws are not the "traditional" ones, anyway.

I also happen to be a psychotherapist, and as such find it hard to deal with people or ideas from a right/wrong perspective. This *doesn't* mean that I don't have strong social and political beliefs; I've acted on these as far back as I can remember, too. But a topic like pornography, in my opinion, does not lend itself to polarization.

It's not that I'm unaware of the arguments raised by women about exploitation and degradation. I've heard all the anecdotes about snuff films, sado-masochism, sexual violence, and "kiddie porn." I have even seen some examples of these, and have found them truly repulsive. But the truth is that all of these extremes add up to a tiny fraction of all pornography. And I invite anyone who doubts that, to get on a "sexually explicit" mailing list and check the offers that start pouring in.

An attack on the glorification of murder, rape, violence, and the sexual exploitation of children is different in kind from an attack on all pornography. Apart from the fact that banning such material raises serious First Amendment issues (e.g., Nabokov's *Lolita*), I am not interested in defending its right to exist nor its moral stature. What I wish to emphasize is that, almost without exception, pornography both straight and gay is not degrading to anyone.

Many feminists will of course disagree. They might argue that the porn industry is predominantly in the hands of men, that the vast majority of directors is male, and that the actresses are exploited while their bodies are young and supple, and then discarded. They would point to the parallels with prostitution, to the pimp-hooker/director-actress parallel, and to the obvious fact that pornography and prostitution intersect in many places.

All of this is *partially* true, and I'll come back to it. First, I want to take a detour, a less politicized one, to write about pornography and me—and by extension, I hope, to say something about other men as well.

Throughout my life, the major purpose of pornography has been to get me excited prior to and during masturbation. Although I like to play with myself even when I'm flaccid, it's a lot more exciting when I have an erection. Now even masturbation, or jerking off, is a pretty complicated topic when you start thinking about it. Some of it is just plain self-comfort and reassurance of a very primitive kind: it's still there, I'm still here, everything is okay with the world. Often it has an addictive quality: I'll do it and then all my anxiety goes away and I'll get a tension release and a temporary high (just like drinking or shooting up or binging and purging). Once in a while, it's even sexual.

I feel horny, or what I interpret as horny, and want to have an orgasm right there and then. Many women don't seem to understand why any male would masturbate if he has a willing and available partner. Again, the answer is both simple and complex. Sometimes, he is in fact rejecting her, just as she fears, because he's turned off to her, or mad at her, or infatuated with someone else. More often than not, masturbation is less difficult and less threatening (can I get it up, will I satisfy her, will it bring us closer or drive us apart?). It's also less threatening because sexual contact can make us more vulnerable (yes, even us males!), and everyone knows that we are emotional cowards by and large.

More typically, I'm distracted by work and kids and a hundred other things, and I want to make love with my wife that evening or the next morning; the pornography helps focus my attention. Sure, if it's the only way to make it work between us, and it goes on for a while, I have a problem and I have to deal with it. But the occasional use of pornography, like the occasional use of anything else, is subject to all kinds of moralistic condemnation rather than reason.

Most pornography, admittedly, is pretty basic and uncompli-cated. People fuck and suck and don't have much contact with one another. What does this have to do with love and intimacy? Nothing, really. What it has to do with is something that prudes, romantics, idealists, and some feminists are loath to accept: the male principle (animus) in sexuality, by no means restricted to the male gender, is aggressive and goal-oriented and, at times, pugnacious. It is inter-ested in excitement rather than closeness. Its manifestation seems to be more rare in women, either because of biology or culture or both, but it is by no means absent in an uninhibited, sexually-aroused woman. Since some 98 percent of regular pornography con-sumers are men, it is not surprising that it is fashioned to appeal particularly to them. The comic Lenny Bruce used to say that "Guys'll make it with anything—mud, sticks, trees. If they're hot enough, they don't care where they stick it, as long as it doesn't have teeth!" This was certainly true for most of us males in the pre-AIDS world. And it was just as clearly *not* true for most females, even in the "liberated" sixties.

As I stated earlier, the issue of degradation still needs to be addressed. It seems to me that feminists err seriously when they automatically label all heterosexual prostitutes, and, by extension, pornographic models and actresses, as victims of exploitation. Many prostitutes and porn actresses, including members of *Coyote* (a prostitutes' "union"), have said repeatedly that they do not feel exploited, that in many cases they have more control over their destinies than women in traditional occupations, that they enjoy their work and feel in control. In pornographic films, for example, women are paid at least three times the going rate that men are. There are several highly intelligent porn actresses who have become directors, producers, and magazine editors.

Having said all this, I'm aware of course that there's another side to the story. Drugs, criminal elements, and various sleazy people are mixed up with pornography. Recently a well known porn actress admitted that she had only been sixteen years old when many of her films were made; I'm sure this isn't a one-time event. Many women *are*, in fact, exploited by pornographers—as are some men. In various storefronts and on magazine racks, and in Dad's dresser drawer, our children are sometimes prematurely exposed to material they can't put in context. For some people, pornography may reinforce violence toward women, other perversions, and perpetuate addiction.

Even so, I believe that these evils do not justify a "war against pornography." Legalization, zoning controls, protection of minors— as with prostitution—will do far more to address these evils than will prohibition. The exploitation of women is a worldwide disease, of long duration, which must soon be healed. It is not a function of pornography, but of economics, tradition, and patriarchies. I can envision a world in which pornography and humane, non-sexist values co-exist peacefully. It is hard to envision one in which banning, censorship, and the inevitable thought police would not brutally clash with such values.

Thoughts of a Putative Pornographer

John R. Nierenberg

A Personal Revelation

A few months ago, I was reading a mystery story that took place in a fictional Supreme Court. Although the subject was not central to the plot, accepted legal opinions on pornography were mentioned frequently in the book. Suddenly, I realized that there are people in this world—including the *real* Supreme Court judges—who would consider me a pornographer.

About every six months for the last seven or eight years, I have had works published in several nationally- and internationally-distributed gay "men's magazines." While all of my writings have not been sexually oriented, the magazines themselves definitely are.

Generally, I have been very pleased with the editing and presentation of my work, enough so to brag a little about them to my friends and carefully chosen acquaintances. (And, yes, my mother knows that I write for "those" kinds of magazines. In fact, she keeps asking me to send her copies, but somehow I never get around to it.)

It doesn't bother me that people who know me know I write "dirty stories." What bothers me is that the people who see my name in magazines like *Torso, Mandate, Honcho* and other "skin mags" probably don't know that I have published anything else, like my essay on straight and gay misogyny in a small press anthology or my computer user's manuals. Strangers don't know that my Men's Movement novel languishes for a publisher; that I've written poetry and plays; that I have stacks of treatments, plot outlines, and opening chapters, all of which I consider my *real* work.

I sometimes feel uncomfortable being two different writers: the popular pornographer/eroticist and the obscure "serious" author. And I wonder how many other creative people suffer this sort of existential angst.

But regardless of this larger metaphysical question, I am not now—nor have I ever been—ashamed of my homoerotic writings. On the contrary, a couple of these stories and comic essays are among the best work I've done so far. I also derive a great deal of satisfaction knowing that quite a few gay men around the country and even around the world are reading—and presumably enjoying—stories *I* have written. I even fantasize now and then that those "wonderful people out there in the dark" anxiously await my next appearance in print.

More to the point of this discussion, though, is that when the subject comes up, I always think of my stories as being erotic rather than pornographic. It was not until recently, however, that I began to wonder how my work fits into the ideas our culture has about the function and validity of sexually-oriented works. Like so many other writers and artists, I wonder if the differences between erotica and pornography are political, esthetic, psychodynamic—or all of the above. I also find myself asking (especially in this time of flagrant political paranoia and conservatism): who has the right to decide what creative work is pornographic and what is erotic?

Searching for Distinctions

After much thought, I decided that for me, at least, erotic writing differs from pornography because it shows respect for the wide range of emotions that can occur—even in the most casual and seemingly impersonal sexual experience. (I like to think that many writers of erotica—from Sappho to Lytton Strachey to Phil Andros—would be comfortable with this distinction.)

Once I came to this conclusion, however, I fell prey to my earlier training as an academic: nagging doubts about the value of my own opinion began to impinge. I felt compelled to have my opinion confirmed by other, more "established" writers and thinkers. Consequently, I started to research the matter and verified something I suspected all along: the main public library of a major American city contains virtually no works at all dealing specifically with homosexual erotica or pornography. I turned to the available works: those that exclusively discuss heterosexually-explicit writings.

Thanks to the efficiently straight, white, and male supremacist Dewey Decimal System—which sandwiches the subject between sexual perversion and organized crime—I found several helpful volumes. I had heard of an essay by Gloria Steinem and found it in *Take Back the Night: Women on Pornography*. The essay, "Erotica and Pornography: A Clear and Present Difference," supported my ideas.

Steinem's essay begins with a lucid discussion of the complex nature of human sexual expression (especially non-procreative sex) and the social problems it creates. Sexual behavior, Steinem contends, becomes a means of communication as well as a physical act. And "(s)ex as communication can send messages as different as life and death; even the origins of 'erotica' and 'pornography' reflect that fact."

She reminds us that etymologically the word "erotica" is "rooted in 'eros' or passionate love, and thus in the idea of positive choice, free will, the yearning for a particular person." On the other hand, Steinem points out, "pornography" is derived from the Greek word *pornos* and means the "writings of prostitutes or captive women." She indicates that such writings involve domination and violence which are inimical to the love among equals described in erotica.

I must, in all fairness, point out that the symbolic and linguistic distinctions Steinem makes are not necessarily so clear-cut. First, prostitution was a well-established, respected and lucrative vocation in ancient Greece; "pornography," therefore, may also be the carefully calculated products of socially-accepted female creators. In a similar way, the commercially successful storytelling skills of traditional geishas and the current popularity of "telephone sex" suggest that traditional pornography can, in fact, be used by the prostitute to control, manipulate and even dominate the client instead of the other way around.

Second, with regard to the positive, egalitarian nature of "eroticism," we must remember that Eros is the son of the god of War, as well as the goddess of Love. And the method he traditionally uses to inspire love is to shoot arrows into the heart or eyes of his "victims." (Some mythology scholars show that the Greeks and Romans perceived Eros as representing blind and blinding lust, while his enemy-brother Anteros stood for open-hearted and mutual love.) In any case, the basic psycho-linguistic link between love and violence cannot easily be denied.

Nevertheless, I find Steinem's differentiation between two types of sexual depictions to be essentially valid:

> The first is erotic: a mutually pleasurable, sexual expression between people who have enough power to be there by positive choice. It may or may not strike a sense-memory in the viewer, or be creative enough to make the unknown seem real; but it doesn't require us to identify with a conqueror or a victim. It is truly sensuous, and may give us a contagion of pleasure.
> The second is pornographic: its message is violence, dominance and conquest. It is sex being used to reinforce some inequality, or

to create one, or to tell us that pain and humiliation (ours or someone else's) are really the same as pleasure. If we are to feel anything, we must identify with conqueror or victim. It means that we can only experience pleasure through the adoption of some degree of sadism or masochism. It also means that we may feel diminished by the role of conqueror, or enraged, humiliated, and vengeful by sharing identity with the victim.

Perhaps one should simply say that erotica is about sexuality, but pornography is about power and sex-as-weapon—in the same way we have come to understand that rape is about violence, and not really about sexuality at all.

The Politics of Pornography: Straight vs. Gay

The main reason I had never thought of myself as being a pornographer is because my "dirty stories" are part of the gay male subculture and have been virtually excluded from most serious discussions of pornography. None of the sociologists, moralists and humanists whose writings appeared on the library shelves seemed to care about the causes and effects of male homosexual eroticism. Only pornography created by and for heterosexual men has been dissected, debated, defamed and defended.

To the dominant, heterosexual culture, any male homoeroticism is either doubly condemned as pornographic because of its "deviant" as well as "prurient" nature, or it is dismissed as politically insignificant since it is considered different from "real," i.e. heterosexual, male eroticism. As outsiders to the mainstream culture, what difference does gay men's pornography and eroticism make to mainstream politicians and polemicists? Gays are not *real* men, after all: only queers.

Therefore, the erotic world of gay men and its social implications has been virtually ignored by the dominant culture. The fantasies that gay men create and how they affect our feelings and actions have generally remained unexamined.

Unfortunately, the gay community has not been able to speak out effectively on the meanings and messages of homoeroticism, either for lesbians or gay males. The intellectual gay press is still so geographically isolated and poorly distributed that even when these matters are discussed, there is little public knowledge or awareness of the opinions expressed.

I did become aware, well after the fact, of a forum on "Gay Male Pornography" held in Philadelphia. Reading transcripts of two of the major speeches offered me at least some solace. It is always heartening to discover, once again, that I am truly not alone in searching for some clarification of the issues.

John Stoltenberg presented the more conservative view by condemning gay male pornography as being equally dangerous and opposed to "good sex" and positive humanist principles as is heterosexual male pornography.

Scott Tucker, on the other hand, raised several points that challenged the largely accepted feminist link between domination in fantasy and violence in action.

In this transcription of his speech at the Philadelphia forum, Tucker brings up the very important issue of the difference between fantasy and reality in sexually-explicit writing. He refutes the so-called radical feminist notion that violence in art or fiction leads to violence in life:

> In the course of insisting that rapists practice what pornographers preach, radical feminists have often confused fantasy with reality, and have done so with great conviction and consistency. And since any form or degree of sexual objectification *may* lead down the slippery slope to rape and murder, the same feminists have found it useful to take the sex out of erotica, and to equate sexually stimulating material with sexually violent material.

Despite the existence of such forums and the occasional article in the various regional gay presses, it was still a shock to me to think I would be considered a pornographer. Under the influence of heterosexual hegemony, I hadn't taken my own work seriously enough to think it might need defending. Since it appears in gay men's magazines, I accepted the trivialization and invisibility of my work that comes from being considered outcast. I accepted the idea that my works "didn't count" because they involved only gay men.

Pornography as Patriarchal Phenomenon

On the contrary, I have become utterly convinced that gay and straight male pornography are essentially the same. Both *Hustler* and *Drummer* use culturally-induced male images of sexuality that inevitably involve power, dominance and violence more than the affection, caring and mutuality considered the basis of any true "erotic" work.

A straight woman friend expresses an interesting perception of the difference between gay and straight pornography:

> . . . (I)n gay porn what takes place happens between two equals. Whatever differences the participants have as individuals, they are both (or all) still members of the same club: males. And they are

> equal culturally in a way that women cannot yet be. Men can play
> S/M [sadism/masochism]-D/S [dominance/submission] games
> starting from an equal place. If a woman is the dominant one in a
> straight relationship, she's "reversed" her "normal" role. It gives a
> different flavor, allows all kinds of hidden resentments to surface,
> twists the meanings and makes the games impure. On the other
> hand, what's the fun of being submissive to a member of the
> species born to dominance in this culture—economic, social and
> political power. How can you give the power to someone who had
> it anyway, by virtue of his gender?
> Certainly D/S is not the only kind of gay or straight porn, but it
> enters into each relationship in some way, skewing the results. In
> a gay relationship, it's more like starting with clean slates on both
> sides.

While I feel that much of what she wrote is true, I think the issues
are necessarily more complex than society's stereotypical idea of
male dominance over females. If that were the case, if male dominance were so implicit in every male/female relationship, the need
for pornography and rape would probably be lessened rather than
increased—albeit for the worst possible reasons.

It is precisely because men feel uncertain with their putative role
as master that they must constantly re-create situations that
reinforce the mythology of their "natural" dominance. (Or accept the
opposite role as some proof of their "sickness.")

More to the point, as my friend so wisely points out, dominance
and submission appears to be part of any sexual encounter, regardless of the genders, ages, races or social statuses of the persons
involved. The need that some men—straight or gay—have to be
dominated seems very strongly ingrained in our culture. The images
of the cruel heterosexual dominatrix are virtually indistinguishable
from those of the heartless gay leather master.

Even in less severely-drawn situations, I think it is crucial to keep
in mind that the so-called dominant male culture is highly seg-
mented and there is a very subtle, but inescapable hierarchy among
males. Race, age, beauty, strength, and especially material wealth,
create a pecking order in our patriarchal culture, whether the men
are straight or gay. And men in the lower ranks, tend (like their
heterosexual female counterparts) either to use sexual situations to
reinforce their feelings of inferiority or to deny them by adopting the
dominant, even potentially dangerously violent role.

Thus, gay male pornography involves the dominance, humiliation and often physical abuse of one partner as a means to
perpetuate the ambivalence that the vast majority of gay men feel
about themselves. In a dominantly heterosexual culture, gay men

are seen as anomalies at best, but more often as deviants from their "natural" role, i.e. to control women, first sexually and then in every other aspect of their lives.

While gay men are not usually involved with women sexually, the gay male subculture still expects its members to have and express their "natural" male need to dominate. Often this need to be hypermasculine leads gay men to behave even more "macho" than their straight counterparts. This compulsion also leads many gay men to enjoy written and pictorial fantasies of raping straight men or "forcing" them to recognize and accept their own homosexual desires.

As mentioned earlier, since many gay men are also, on another level, alienated from their "maleness," they may feel obliged to adopt the "female" role in sexual encounters and find it both psychologically and physically satisfying.

In this very complex world of unspoken, often subconscious feelings, the sadist or dominant male appears to be asserting his so-called masculinity precisely to deny society's accusations that he is not a "real" man because he is homosexual. His partner, the masochist or submissive, is, in many cases, accepting that same judgment. But instead of refuting the claim of his non-maleness, he seems to willingly adopt the role of the sexual inferior, "playing the woman." Some elements of self-hatred and desire for self-abasement or punishment also enter into this pornographic dynamic.

Again, it seems to me that the line between pornography and erotica is thinly-drawn, but no less important for its delicacy. In the classic pornographic situation, one partner is literally and figuratively stripped of will and integrity. The victim is presented as being unworthy of respect or affection. Such feelings are reserved for love among equals, where the roles of dominance and submission, "top" and "bottom," usually shift. In these "erotic" relationships, the possibility of changing roles is apparently understood by both parties.

But what if both partners consciously prefer fixed, and perhaps even violent, roles? Does that mean their relationship is automatically "pornographic" rather than "erotic"?

The Leatherworld Twist

Nowhere is the fragility of the distinction between erotica and pornography clearer than in the literature and photography of the sadomasochistic or leather subgroups. Most of the relationships (ranging from bondage to extreme forms of physical torture) have a curiously ritualistic, even intellectually detached, quality. The awareness of the "gamesplaying" involved blurs the true psychological distinctions between top and bottom. In fact, it is the first axiom in some of the SM culture that "the bottom rules," meaning that it is the seemingly submissive partner who establishes the rules and limits of the sexual encounter.

The question then is ultimately arbitrary and even moralistic: if a person seeks out and "enjoys" verbal humiliation, restraint or even physical pain, is the person who accommodates his desires performing violent, abusive and therefore pornographic acts?

If a man enjoys being tied to a post and then teased and tickled until he achieves orgasms, does society have a right to declare him "sick"? And what if the pleasure another seeks includes scarring and bloodletting, or the use of urine and feces during sexual encounters? Who draws the line? When does deviance slip into madness? And who has the right to say when consenting "adults" have gone "too far"?

None of these are easy questions to face, let alone answer, particularly when issues of safety also involve the control or spread of life-threatening diseases like AIDS. But these questions do shed light on the phenomenon of the current culture's idea of male sexuality. For the extremism of some of the members of the Leather Community (which includes ever-increasing numbers of lesbians and heterosexuals of both genders) is just that: an exaggeration of the roles and games implied even in the most "innocent" of sexual relationships.

Is the "missionary" position, generally considered acceptable by the most conservative communities, any less sexist and degrading to women? After all, they are still on the bottom, expected to be almost completely receptive, passive and submissive.

Some Final Thoughts

Ultimately, there are no definitive, unarguable answers to any of these questions. Instead, we are left with the same distinctions with which we began: a truly erotic situation involves mutual respect, understanding of needs, a certain level of affection and the desire to see to it that each partner is satisfied when the encounter ends. I have always tried to create characters and situations in my stories that are exciting as well as excited, as lustful as they are caring, both passionate and compassionate.

And if the Supreme Court feels my work is pornographic, then I will have to defend it as have so many others before me. Sex, in all its strange and various guises, is not evil or dangerous in and of itself. Like so many great ideas—like Christianity and Democracy—it can be twisted and perverted into a vicious and dangerous parody of itself. But that need not happen: we are all, regardless of gender or preference, capable of preventing that violence to the nature of humanity when we choose to be loving, caring and considerate—both in and out of bed.

Men and AIDS[†]

Michael S. Kimmel and Martin P. Levine

Over 93 percent of all adult Americans with AIDS are men (as of December, 1987). 73 percent of all adult AIDS cases occur among gay men (and all cases among homosexuals are male). Eight out of every ten cases linked to intravenous drug use are men (AIDS Surveillance Report, Center for Disease Control, December, 1987). In New York City, AIDS is the leading cause of death among men aged 30 to 44.[1] Most instances of the other AIDS-related diseases are also among men. These conditions mark earlier stages of infection with the virus causing AIDS, the Human Immune Deficiency Virus (HIV). They include AIDS-related complex (ARC) and AIDS virus antibody positivity (HIV seropositivity). Although the prevalence of these conditions is presently unknown, they appear to be concentrated among male intravenous drug-users and homosexual men (Institute of Medicine, 1986).

And yet no one talks about AIDS as a men's disease. No one talks about why men are so overwhelmingly at greater risk for AIDS, ARC, and HIV seropositivity. No one talks about the relationship between AIDS and masculinity. In fact, the rhetoric is more often about AIDS as a moral disease. Christian Voice leader Bob Grant says that people with AIDS are simply "reaping the results" of their "unsafe and immoral behavior" (Kropp, 1987). Evangelist Jerry Falwell calls AIDS "the wrath of God among homosexuals" (cited in Altman, 1986: 67).[2] These pronouncements enjoy some popular acceptance. Almost one-third of the respondents in one survey believed that "AIDS is a punishment that God has given homosexuals for the way they live." (This understanding, echoing Falwell's, seems to be unaware that lesbians who are not IV drug users are virtually risk free.) And one-fourth of those same

[†] This essay is dedicated to the memory of José A. Vigo, 1950–1988.

respondents believed that AIDS victims are "getting what they deserve" (*Los Angeles Times*, 12 December 1985). "The poor homosexuals," explained Patrick Buchanan, a conservative columnist and aid to President Reagan, sarcastically, "they have declared war upon Nature, and now Nature is exacting an awful retribution" (*The New York Post*, 24 May 1983). And almost two-fifths of the respondents (37 percent) to another survey said that AIDS had made them less favorably disposed towards homosexuals than they had been before (*The New York Times*, 15 December 1985).

Such beliefs confuse the cause of the disease with transmission. Sin does not cause AIDS, a virus does. Homosexual intercourse and sharing intravenous needles are but two of the ways in which this virus is transmitted. Other forms include heterosexual relations, blood transfusions, and the exchange of blood during pregnancy. In fact, in Africa, most people infected are heterosexual non-intravenous drug users (Quinn, Mann, Curran and Prot, 1986).

But in the United States, AIDS is a men's disease. The seriousness of the disease demands that we pose the question: what is it about masculinity that puts men at greater risk for AIDS-related illness? To answer that question, we will explore the links between manliness and practices associated with risks for HIV infection; that is we will examine the relationship between masculinity and risk-taking. To do this, we will first outline the norms of masculinity, the defining features of what it means to be a "real" man in our society. Then we will look at how these norms predispose men to engage in behaviors that place them at greater risk for AIDS. And finally we will discuss how this perspective may shed new light on strategies of AIDS prevention.

I. Masculinity as Social Construction

What does it mean to be a man in contemporary American society? Most experts believe that the answer to this question lies in the prevailing cultural construction of masculinity.[3] This perspective maintains that our understanding of masculinity and femininity derive less from biological imperatives or psychological predispositions that from the social definitions of what is appropriate behavior for each gender. Men acquire the scripts that define gender-appropriate behavior through socialization; the family, educational and religious institutions, and the media all contribute to this cultural definition. Such a perspective insists that the cultural definitions of masculinity and femininity are not universal, but culturally and historically specific; what it means to be a man or a woman varies from culture to culture, within any one culture over time, and over the course of one's life.[4]

What, then, are the expectations of gender behavior that men in the United States learn? What are the norms of manliness? Social scientists Deborah David and Robert Brannon group these rules into four basic themes: (1) *No Sissy Stuff*: anything that even remotely hints of femininity is prohibited. A real man must avoid any behavior or characteristic associated with women; (2) *Be a Big Wheel*: masculinity is measured by success, power, and the admiration of others. One must possess wealth, fame, and status to be considered manly; (3) *Be a Sturdy Oak*: manliness requires rationality, toughness and self-reliance. A man must remain calm in any situation, show no emotion and admit no weakness; (4) *Give 'em Hell*: men must exude an aura of daring and aggression, and must be willing to take risks, to "go for it" even when reason and fear suggest otherwise.

This cultural construction of masculinity indicates that men organize their conceptions of themselves as masculine by the willingness to take risks, their ability to experience pain or discomfort and not submit to it, by their drive to accumulate constantly (money, power, sex partners, experiences) and their resolute avoidance of any behavior that might be construed as feminine. The pressures accompanying these efforts cause higher rates of stress-related illnesses (heart disease, ulcers) and venereal diseases among men. The norms encouraging risk-taking behaviors lead men to smoke, drink too much, and drive recklessly, resulting in disproportionate incidences of respiratory illness, alcoholism, and vehicular accidents and fatalities. And the rules urging aggressiveness induce higher rates of violence-related injury and death among men. Over a century ago, Dr. Peter Bryce, director of a mental institution in Alabama, underscored the relationship between masculinity and mental health. "The causes of general paresis," Dr. Bryce wrote (cited in Hughes, 1988:15):

> are found to prevail most among men, and at the most active time of life, from 35 to 40, in the majority of cases. Habitual intemperance, sexual excesses, overstrain in business, in fact, all those habits which tend to keep up too rapid cerebral action, are supposed to induce this form of disease. It is especially a disease of *fast life*, and fast business in large cities.
>
> "Warning," writes one modern psychologist, "the male sex role may be dangerous to your health!" (Harrison, 1978).

II. Masculinity and Male Sexuality

These norms also shape male sexuality, organizing the sexual scripts that men follow in their sexual behaviors. Men are taught to be rational, successful, daring in sex: Real men divorce emotions from sexual expression, have sex without love and are concerned solely with gratification. Real men "score" by having lots of sex with many partners, and they are adventurous and take risks.

The norms defining masculinity also significantly increase men's vulnerability to AIDS. The virus causing AIDS is spread through bodily fluids such as blood, semen, and vaginal secretions. To become infected with this virus, men (and women) must engage in practices that allow these fluids to enter the bloodstream. Such practices are known as "risk behaviors" (see Frumkin and Leonard, 1987: Ch. 4).

The most common risk behaviors among adults are unprotected sexual intercourse, oral sex, and sharing needles. Heterosexual or homosexual intercourse can cause tiny breaks in the surface linings of these organs, through which infected bodily fluids can enter the bloodstream directly. In oral sex, the fluids enter through breaks in the lining of the mouth.[5] Sharing needles allows these infected fluids to enter the bloodstream directly on needles containing contaminated blood.

Fortunately, there are ways one can avoid contact with the AIDS virus. Authorities recommend avoiding risk behaviors. This can be accomplished in several ways: (1) abstinence: the avoidance of sexual contacts and use of intravenous drugs; (2) safer sex: the avoidance of all sexual behaviors in which semen or blood are passed between partners (this is usually accomplished by the use of condoms); (3) safer drug use: avoidance of all unsterilized needles. Safer drug use means that one must not share needles if possible; if one must share needles, they must be cleaned (with bleach or rubbing alcohol) before each use.

Unfortunately, these types of risk-reduction behavior are in direct contradiction with the norms of masculinity. The norms of masculinity propel men to take risks, score, and focus sexual pleasure on the penis. Real men ignore precautions for AIDS risk reduction, seek many sexual partners, and reject de-pleasuring the penis. Abstinence, safer sex, and safer drug use compromise manhood. The behaviors required for the confirmation of masculinity and those required to reduce risk are antithetical.

III. Strategies of AIDS Prevention

Given this perspective, how might we evaluate the various strategies that have been developed to combat the AIDS epidemic? To what extent do they reproduce or encourage precisely the behaviors that they are designed to discourage? The procedures developed to combat the AIDS epidemic ignore the links between masculinity and risk behaviors. The battle against AIDS relies heavily upon the public health strategies of testing and education (Gostin, in Dalton and Burris, 1987). But each of these are limited by the traditional norms of masculinity, as well as other factors.

Testing

Testing involves the use of the HIV antibody test to screen the blood for antibodies to the AIDS virus, and post-test counseling. People who test positive for HIV antibodies are regarded as infected, that is, as carrying the virus and capable of transmitting it to others. These individuals are counseled to avoid risk behaviors.

AIDS antibody testing, however, even when coupled with counseling, is not a sufficient method to deal with the AIDS epidemic. The rationale for testing has been that it will encourage safer-sex behavior among those already infected but not yet ill, and thus curtail the epidemic. While this procedure may have been successful in the past with other infectious diseases, Dr. William Curran of the Harvard School of Public Health argues that it does not apply to AIDS. One study found that a positive result on the AIDS antibody test does not necessarily promote safe-sex behaviors. "It is not the test that promotes safe sex," the author writes, "but education and social support for safe sex" (Beeson, et. al., 1986:14).

AIDS antibody testing also has negative side effects such as psychological distress, the possibility of social sanctions such as losing one's job, loss of medical care or life insurance, or the possibility of forced quarantine, if specific public policy recommendations are adopted by voters. Thus, antibody testing is opposed by nearly all medical and epidemiological experts. The Institute of Medicine of the National Academy of Sciences recently summarized their findings, concluding that testing was:

> impossible to justify now either on ethical or practical grounds . . . [raising] serious problems of ethics and feasibility. People whose private behavior is illegal are not likely to comply with a mandatory screening program, even one backed by assurances of confidentiality. Mandatory screening based on

sexual orientation would appear to discriminate against or to
coerce entire groups without justification (Institute of Medicine,
1986: 14).

From our perspective, as well, we must examine the ways in which the norms of masculinity impede the effectiveness of AIDS antibody testing. These rules compel men to shun stereotypical "feminine" concerns about health. "Real" men don't worry about the dangers associated with smoking, drinking, and stress—why should they worry about the risks associated with intravenous drug use and sex? Manly nonchalance will keep men from getting tested. Early reports from New York City indicate that more women than men are being tested for AIDS (Sullivan, 1987).

These norms of masculinity also impede the effectiveness of counseling. During counseling, men are warned against spreading the virus. Such warnings, however, contradict the dictates of manliness. "Real" men score, and their sexuality is organized phallocentrically, so counseling, which would encourage men to de-emphasize the penis and emphasize sexual responsibility, may fall on deaf ears. To demonstrate manliness, seropositive men may actually give the virus to someone else.

Public Health Education
Public health authorities have also utilized education as an AIDS prevention strategy. The Institute of Medicine of the National Academy of Sciences recommends "a major educational campaign to reduce the spread of HIV" and that "substantially increased educational and public awareness activities be supported not only by the government, but also by the information media, and by other private sector organizations that can effectively campaign for health." For IV drug users, the Institute recommends "trials to provide easier access to sterile, disposable needles and syringes" (Institute of Medicine, 1986: 10, 12, 13).

Educational efforts have been developed by both public sector agencies, such as federal, state, and local health departments, and private organizations, such as local AIDS groups, and groups of mental health practitioners. These public and private efforts are each faced with a different set of problems, and each confronts different components of the norms of masculinity.

Public health education campaigns, funded by taxpayer dollars, have utilized mass transit advertisements, billboards, brochures and hotlines to explain the medical facts about AIDS, its causes, how it affects the body, how it's transmitted, and who is at risk. Such campaigns de-emphasize information about safe sex behaviors, because such information might be seen as condoning or even encouraging behaviors that are morally or legally proscribed. As Dr. James Mason, undersecretary for health in the Department of Health and Human Services said, "[w]e don't think that citizens care to be funding material that encourages gay lifestyles" (cited in Anderson, 1985). Editor and writer Norman Podhoretz criticized any efforts to stop AIDS because to do so would encourage homosexuality so that "in the name of compassion they are giving social sanction to what can only be described as brutish degradation" (cited in New York Times, 18 March 1986). And North Carolina Senator Jesse Helms, one of the nation's most vocal critics of education programs, sponsored an amendment that stipulated that no federal funds be used to promote or encourage homosexual activity, and emphasized that AIDS education emphasize abstinence outside a sexually monogamous marriage as the only preventive behaviors that the government would fund. The choice that Helms offers, he claims, is "Reject sodomy and practice morality. If they are unwilling to do that, they should understand the consequences" (Helms, 1987).

The content of these educational campaigns reflects the political ideology embedded within them. The pamphlet issued by the U.S. Public Health Service's Center for Disease Control, "What You Should Know About AIDS" counsels that the "safest way to avoid being infected by the AIDS virus is to avoid promiscuous sex and illegal drugs." Teenagers, especially, "should be encouraged to say 'no' to sex and illegal drugs" (Center for Disease Control, 1987).

The effectiveness of such strategies is extremely limited by the myopic moralizing that is embedded within them. "It is too late to be prudish in discussing the crisis with youngsters," warns an editorial in The Washington Post, urging explicit safe-sex education in the schools ("AIDS Education," 1987). But more than this, they are limited because they violate the traditional norms of masculinity. Just saying "no" contradicts the norms that inform men that "real" men score in sex, by having many sexual partners and by taking risks, or, more accurately, by ignoring potential risks in their pursuit of sex. Because of the norms of masculinity, which are especially salient for teenagers and younger men, the burden of just saying "no" will undoubtedly fall upon the shoulders of women. Efforts to halt the spread of a sexually transmitted disease by encouraging men to abstain have never been successful in American history, although such strategies have been attempted before, during the syphilis epidemic following World War I (see Brandt, 1986).

Private-Agency Educational Campaigns
Educational campaigns sponsored by privately-funded agencies have developed various mechanisms that are far less negative about sexuality, and may, therefore, have far greater chances of reaching male populations. These campaigns vary in tone and effect. Some organizations that have emerged from within the gay community in major cities across the nation have given explicit information about safer sex practices. "Plain Talk about Safe Sex and AIDS" (published by Baltimore Health Education Resource Organization and also distributed in Boston) uses scare tactics:

> You must be aware that AIDS will almost certainly kill you if you get it. No fooling. It's that deadly. And at this moment it's incurable. This is no wishy washy Public Health 'warning' from the Surgeon General, determining that cigarette smoking is dangerous to your health. The medical breakthrough hasn't happened yet. In other words, if you contract AIDS, the chances are that you'll be dead within a year, probably. Got it? Let's put it in plain language. If you develop AIDS, kiss your ass goodbye.

The San Francisco AIDS Foundation condemns past practices among gay men, such as anonymous sex, bathhouses, backrooms, bookstores and parks, while giving this advice:

> We do know that the long standing health problems caused by sexually transmitted diseases in the gay community could be reduced if everyone were to heed the suggestions outlined here. If, as many believe, repeated infections also weakens the immune system, these suggestions can help you lead a healthier and safer life. If our comments sound rather judgemental or directive, understand that we, too, have and are experiencing these diseases and are trying to follow our own recommendations. . . . [W]e believe that intimacy, both sexual and emotional, is necessary as we move toward a more healthy regard for our own bodies and those we love.

Other educational efforts attempt to remain sex-positive, such as Houston's "AIDS Play Safe" campaign, whose slogan is "Adapt, Enjoy, Survive." Their pamphlet states:

> You don't have to give up good times, being social, having fun, going out, or even having sex, but you can change to safe sex, accept the experience and enjoy it. The results are lower risk of AIDS, less fear and anxiety, your health, and possibly your life. Come on, let's party. Don't be left behind, don't sit at home fretting. You can still have a good time, you can still enjoy your sexuality, you can still enjoy your lifestyle, you can still party, dance, play, have sex, and get the most out of life. You don't have

> to deny it to yourself. Adapt, enjoy and survive. And we'll see you
> around next year.

This position is echoed in the "Healthy Sex is Great Sex" pamphlet published by the Gay Men's Health Crisis in New York City. Other efforts to educate gay men about safe sex practices include safe sex videos, house parties where information and free condoms are distributed on a model of Tupperware parties, and workshops run by professionals on eroticizing safe sex encounters.

In general, these campaigns developed by local gay organizations have had remarkable success. By a variety of measures—impressionistic, comparative, and surveys—unsafe sex practices have declined sharply among those groups who have access to explicit information about safe sex behaviors. Impressionistic journalistic reports indicate that gay baths and bars are less crowded and monogamous coupling is on the rise. The rates of other venereal disease, a certain marker of promiscuity and unsafe safe practices, have plummeted among gay men across the country.

The results of survey data reveal a significant decrease in unsafe sex practices among gay men. The San Francisco AIDS Foundation found in 1984 that almost all respondents were aware that certain erotic behavior could result in AIDS, and two-thirds had stopped engaging in high risk behavior (*Advocate*, 428, 3 Sept. 1985). Another San Francisco survey found widespread awareness about safe sex guidelines, and a continued decline in high risk behaviors among subjects between 1984 and 1985.

Some Lingering Problems
But we are concerned not with the significant numbers of men who have altered their behavior in the face of serious health risk, but with the residual numbers who have not changed. How can we explain that one-third of those men surveyed in 1984 and one-fifth of the men surveyed in 1985 continued to engage in unsafe sex? How do we explain the conclusion of the 1985 study, which reported that the "men in these groups were uniformly well informed for AIDS risk reduction. Despite their knowledge of health directives, the men in this sample displayed discrepancies between what they believed about AIDS and their sexual behavior" (McKusik, Hortsman, and Coates, 1985). It appears that a significant number of men continue to engage in high risk behavior, even though they know better.

Such continued high risk behavior cannot be attributed to homophobia, since the information provided is by local gay groups. And it is unattributable to sex-negativism, since much of the material is also sexually explicit about safe sex practices and gay-affirmative in tone. We believe that the cultural norms of masculinity compose one of the hidden impediments to safe sex education. That men's sexuality is organized around scoring, associates danger with sexual excitement, and is phallocentric, limits the effectiveness of safer-sex educational campaigns. In one study, 35 percent of the gay men who agreed that reducing the number of sexual partners would reduce risks had sex with more than five different men during the previous month. Over four-fifths of the men who agreed with the statement "I use hot anonymous sex to relieve tension" had three or more sexual partners the previous month. And almost 70 percent of the men having three or more sexual partners the previous month agreed with the statement "It's hard to change my sexual behavior because being gay means doing what I want sexually."

IV: Challenging Traditional Masculinity as Risk Reduction

Here we see the equation in its boldest form: gay male sex is, above all, male sex, and male sex, above all, is risky business. Here, we believe, the social scientist can inform public health campaigns and epidemiological research. We need to recapitulate our understanding of how masculinity informs sexual behavior, and how masculinity might serve as an impediment to safer sex behaviors among men. Since there is no anticipatory socialization for homosexuality, boys in our culture all learn norms for heterosexual masculinity. This means that, gay or straight, men in our culture are cognitively oriented to think and behave sexually through the prism of gender. Gay male sexuality and straight male sexuality are both enactments of scripts appropriate to gender; both have, in their cognitive orientations, "male" sex.

What this means concretely includes the meanings that become attached to our sexual scripts in early adolescence. Through masturbation and early sexual experiences, boys learn that sex is privatized; that emotions and sexuality are detached; that the penis is the center of the sexual universe; that fantasy allows heightened sexual experience; and that pleasure and guilt are intimately linked, that what brings sexual pleasure is also something that needs to be hidden from one's family. Masculinity is enacted in sexual scripts by the emphasis on scoring, by its recreational dimension (the ability to have sex without love), and by the pursuit of sexual gratification for its own sake, and by the association of danger and excitement (enacted through the link of pleasure and guilt). The male sexual script makes it normative to take risks, engage in anonymous sex, have difficulty sustaining emotional intimacy, and validates promiscuous sexual behavior.

In such a script, "safe sex" is an oxymoron. How can sex be safe? How can safety be sexy? Sex is about danger, excitement, risk; safety is about comfort, security, softness. And if safe sex isn't sexy, many men, enacting gender scripts about masculinity, will continue to practice unsafe sex. Or they may decide not to engage in sex at all. "I find so-called safe sex comparable to putting my nose up against a window in a candy store when I'm on a diet. I'd rather not go near the window at all, because seeing the candy makes me want to eat at least three or four pieces," said one man explaining his two-year voluntary celibacy as a response to AIDS (*The Advocate*, July, 1986). To educate men about safe sex, then, means to confront the issues of masculinity.

Despite the efforts of some policy makers, whose misplaced moralism is likely to cost thousands of lives, we know that "health education is the only tool that can stem this epidemic," as the executive director of the Gay Men's Health Crisis put it. "AIDS education should have started the moment it was realized that this disease is sexually transmitted," wrote one medical correspondent (cited in Watney, 1987: 135). It would appear that a public health policy that was truly interested in reducing the spread of AIDS (instead of punishing those who are already stigmatized and at risk) would need to add two more considerations to the impressive educational efforts already underway. First, we will need to make safer sex sexy. Second, we will need to enlarge the male sexual script to include a wider variety of behaviors, to allow men a wide range of sexual and sensual pleasures.

Safer sex can be sexy sex. Many organizations are developing a safer sex pornography. GMHC in New York City offers safe sex videos as a form of "pornographic healing." In his important new book, *Policing Desire: Pornography, AIDS and the Media*, English author Simon Watney argues the gay men "need to organize huge regular Safe Sex parties in our clubs and gay centers . . . with workshops and expert counseling available. We need to produce hot, sexy visual materials to take home, telephone sex-talk facilities, and safe sex porno cinemas" (Watney, 1987:133).

And while we make safer sex into sexy sex, we also need to transform the meaning of masculinity, to enlarge our definition of what it means to be a man, so that sexuality will embrace a wider range of behaviors and experiences. As Watney argues, we "need to develop a culture which will support the transition to safer sex by establishing the model of an erotics of protection, succour and support within the framework of our pre-AIDS lives" (Watney, 1987:132).

Conclusion

The process of transforming masculinity is long and difficult, and AIDS can spread so easily and rapidly. Sometimes it feels as if there isn't enough time. And there isn't. While we are eroticizing safer sex practices and enlarging the range of erotic behaviors available to men, we must also, as a concerned public, increase our compassion and support for AIDS patients. We must stand with them because they are our brothers. We are linked to them not through sexual orientation (although we may be) or by drug-related behavior (although we may be), but by gender, by our masculinity. They are not "perverts" or "deviants" who have strayed from the norms of masculinity, and therefore brought this terrible retribution upon themselves. They are, if anything, over-conformists to destructive norms of male behavior. They are men who, like all real men, have taken risks. And risk taking has always implied danger. Men have always known this and have always chosen to take risks. Until daring has been eliminated from the rhetoric of masculinity, men will die as a result of their risk taking. In war. In sex. In driving fast and drunk. In shooting drugs and sharing needles. Men with AIDS are real men, and when one dies, a bit of all men dies as well. Until we change what it means to be a real man, every man will die a little bit every day.

NOTES

1. New York City Department of Health, personal communication, January 11, 1988.

2. For an overview of moralistic interpretations of AIDS, see Fitzpatrick, 1988.

3. Our work here draws upon the "social constructionist" model of gender and sexuality. The pioneering work of John Gagnon and William Simon, *Sexual Conduct* (Chicago: Aldine, 1973), has been followed up by our recent work. See, for example, Michael Kimmel and Jeffrey Fracher, "Hard Issues and Soft Spots: Counseling Men About Sexuality," and John Gagnon and Michael Kimmel, *Gender and Desire* (Basic Books, forthcoming), and Martin P. Levine, *Gay Macho: The Ethnography of the Homosexual Clone.* PhD dissertation, Department of Sociology, New York University, 1986.

4. Gender norms also vary within any culture by class, race, ethnicity and region. Although there are many masculinities or femininities in the contemporary United States, we will elaborate the standard for white middle class in men in major metropolitan areas because this is the model that is the hegemonic form that is defined as generalizable and normative. It is essential to understand its universality as a power-relation and not as a moral ideal. (See Connell, 1987).

5. The evidence for oral sex as a mode of transmission is only speculative. To date, there are no reported instances of transmission in this way (Green, 1987).

13-12

Ich hab mich schon wieder auf eine Person fixiert. versuche möglichst alles davon zu kriegen, ohne auf die Konsequenzen zu schauen. Erreiche Löffar was von auf den Teppich zu kommen und bin dort selbst nur am laufen!

Race, Masculinity and Sexuality: An Insider's Perspective

Robert Staples

It is difficult to think of a more controversial role in American society than that of the black male. He is a visible figure on the American scene, yet the least understood and studied of all sex-race groups in the United States. His cultural image is typically one of several types: the sexual superstud, the athlete, and the rapacious criminal. That is how he is perceived in the public consciousness, interpreted in the media and ultimately how he comes to see and internalize his own role. Rarely are we exposed to his more prosaic role as worker, husband, father and American citizen.

The following essay focuses on the stereotypical roles of black male heterosexuality, not to reinforce them, but to penetrate the superficial images of black men as macho, hypersexual, violent and exploitative. Obviously, there must be some explanation for the dominance of black men in the nation's negative statistics on rape, out-of-wedlock births, and premarital sexual activity. This is an effort to explore the reality behind the image.

Black Manhood

As a starting point, I see the black male as being in conflict with the normative definition of masculinity. This is a status which few, if any, black males have been able to achieve. Masculinity, as defined in this culture, has always implied a certain autonomy and mastery of one's environment. It can be said that not many white American males have attained this ideal either. Yet, white males did achieve a dominance in the nuclear family. Even that semblance of control was largely to be denied black men. During slavery he could receive the respect and esteem of his wife, children and kinsmen, but he had no formal legal authority over his wife or filial rights from his children. There are numerous and documented instances of the slave-owning class's attempts to undermine his respect and esteem in the eyes of his family.[1]

Beginning with the fact that slave men and women were equally subjugated to the capricious authority of the slaveholder, the African male saw his masculinity challenged by the rape of his woman, sale of his children, the rations issued in the name of the woman and children bearing her name. While those practices may have presaged the beginning of a healthier sexual egalitarianism than was possible for whites, they also provoked contradictions and dilemmas for black men in American society. It led to the black male's self-devaluation as a man and set the stage for internecine conflict within the black community.

A person's sex role identity is crucial to their values, life-style and personality. The black man has always had to confront the contradiction between the normative expectations attached to being male in this society and the proscriptions on his behavior and achievement of goals. He is subjected to societal opprobrium for failing to live up to the standards of manhood on the one hand and for being super macho on the other. It is a classic case of "damned if you do and damned if you don't." In the past there was the assertion that black men were effeminate because they were raised in households with only a female parent or one with a weak father figure. Presently, they are being attacked in literature, in plays, and at conferences as having succumbed to the male chauvinist ideal.

Although the sexual stereotypes apply equally to black men and women, it is the black male who has suffered the worst because of white notions of his hypersexuality. Between 1884 and 1900 more than 2,500 black men were lynched, the majority of whom were accused of sexual interest in white women. Black men, it was said, had a larger penis, a greater sexual capacity and an insatiable sexual appetite. These stereotypes depicted black men as primitive sexual beasts, without the white male's love for home and family.[2] These stereotypes persist in the American consciousness.

It is in the area of black sexual behavior, and black male sexuality in particular, that folk beliefs are abundant but empirical facts few. Yet public policy, sex education and therapeutic programs to deal with the sex-related problems of black people cannot be developed to fit their peculiar needs until we know the nature and dynamics of black sexual behavior. Thus, it is incumbent upon researchers to throw some light on an area enmeshed in undocumented myths and stereotypes.

Sexuality of the Male Adolescent

The Kinsey data, cited by Bell,[3] reveals that black males acquire their knowledge about condoms at a later age than white males. The white male learns about sexual intercourse at a later age than black males. Because of poorer nutrition, the black male reaches puberty at a later age than his white male counterpart. A critical distinction between black and white males was the tendency of the more sexually repressed white male to substitute masturbation, fellatio and fantasy for direct sexual intercourse. Masturbation, for instance, was more likely to be the occasion of the first ejaculation for the white male while intercourse was for the black male. A larger percentage of white males reported being sexually aroused by being bitten during sexual activity, seeing a member of the opposite sex in a social situation, seeing themselves nude in the mirror or looking at another man's erect penis, hearing dirty jokes, reading sado-masochistic literature and viewing sexy pictures. Conversely, black males tended to engage in premarital intercourse at earlier ages, to have intercourse and to reach orgasm more frequently. As Bell notes in his analysis of these data, the black male's overabundance of sexuality is a myth. The sexuality of black and white men just tends to take different forms and neither group has any more self-control or moral heroism than the other.

Among young black American males, sexual activity begins at an earlier age, is more frequent and involves more partners. Apparently white males are more likely to confine their associations in the adolescent years to other men. Larson and his associates found that black male adolescents were twice as likely to be romantically involved with women than white males.[4] The kind of rigid gender segregation found in white culture is largely absent from black society. For example, blacks are less likely to be associated with all male clubs, organizations or colleges.

The sexual code of young black males is a permissive one. They do not, for example, divide black women into "good" (suitable for marriage) and "bad" (ineligible for marriage) categories. In the lower income groups, sexual activity is often a measure of masculinity. Thus, there is a greater orientation toward premarital sexual experimentation. In a study of premarital sexual standards among blacks and whites in the 1960s, Ira Reiss found that the sexual permissiveness of white males could be affected by a number of social forces (e.g., religion), but the black male was influenced by none of them.[5] Leanor Johnson and this author found that few black male adolescents were aware of the increased risk of teenage pregnancy, but there was an almost unanimous wish not to impregnate their sexual partner. Another survey of black male high school students reported their group believed that a male respects his partner when he uses a condom.[6]

Poverty and the Black Father

The period of adolescence, with its social, psychological and physical changes (particularly sex-role identity and sexuality), deems it the most problematic of the life cycle stages. The prolongation of adolescence in complex technological society and the earlier onset of puberty have served to compound the problem. While adolescents receive various messages to abandon childlike behavior, they are systematically excluded from adult activity such as family planning. This exclusion is justified not only by their incomplete social and emotional maturity, but by their lack of marketable skills which are necessary to command meaningful status-granting jobs. Unskilled adolescents are further disadvantaged if they are members of a minority racial group in a racially stratified society.

Parenthood at this stage of the life cycle is most undesirable. Yet, recent upsurges in teenage pregnancy and parenthood have occurred, specifically among females younger than fourteen. Approximately 52 percent of all children born to black women in 1982 were conceived out-of-wedlock. Among black women under age twenty, about 75 percent of all births were out-of-wedlock compared with only 25 percent of births to young white women.[7] Although the rate of white out-of-wedlock pregnancy is increasing and that of non-whites decreasing, black unwed parenthood remains higher than that of whites.

Because life and family support systems of black males are severely handicapped by the effects of poverty and discrimination, the consequences of becoming a father in adolescence are more serious for the minority parent. Many family planning agencies offer counseling to the unwed mother, while the father is usually involved only superficially or punitively—as when efforts are made to establish legal paternity as a means for assessing financial responsibility. This omission, however, is not unique to black males. It is, perhaps, the single fact of inadequate economic provision which has resulted in the social agencies' premature conclusion that unwed fathers are unwilling to contribute to the future of their child and the support of the mother. Furthermore, sociological theory purports that slavery broke the black man's sense of family responsibility. Thus, it is assumed that black women do not expect nor demand that black men support them in raising their children.

Family Planning

Recent evidence, however, suggests that the matrifocality of present theory and social services is myopic. Studies have demonstrated that most unwed fathers are willing to face their feelings and responsibilities.[8] The findings suggest that unmarried black males do not consider family planning a domain of the female, but rather a joint responsibility to be shared by both partners.[9]

Throughout the world one of the most important variables affecting birth rates is the male attitude toward family planning and the genesis of this attitude. Too often we are accustomed to thinking of reproduction as primarily a female responsibility. Since women are the main bearers and main rearers of children in our society, we tend to believe that they should be primarily concerned with planning the size of a family and developing those techniques of contraception consistent with family's earning power, their own health and happiness and the psychological well-being of their children.

However, in a male-dominated world it is women who are given all the burden of having and raising children, while it is often men who determine what the magnitude of that burden should be. Unfortunately, the male's wishes in regard to the size of his family are not contingent on the effect of childbearing on the female partner, but are often shaped by his own psychological and status concerns.

Within many societies there is an inseparable link between men's self-image and their ability to have sexual relations with women and the subsequent birth of children from those sexual acts. For example, in Spanish-speaking cultures this masculine norm is embedded in the concept of "machismo." "Machismo," derived from the Latin word "masculus," literally means the ability to produce sperm and thus sire—abilities which define the status of a man in society. In male-dominated society other issues involved in reproduction are subordinated to the male's desire to affirm his virility, which in turn confirms his fulfillment of the masculine role. The research literature tells us that the male virility cult is strongest in countries and among groups where the need for family planning is greatest.

Thus, we find that in underdeveloped countries—and among low-income ethnic groups in industrialized societies, including much of the black population in the U.S.—men are resistant to anything but natural controls on the number of children they have. Studies show that males who strongly believe that their masculine status is associated with their virility do not communicate very well with their wives on the subject of family planning. As a result the wives are less effective in limiting their families to the number of children they desire.

Sexual Aggression

Sexual attacks against women are pervasive and sharply increasing in this country. The typical rapist is a black male and his victim is most often a black female. However, the most severe penalties for rape are reserved for black males accused of raping white women. Although 50 percent of those convicted for rape in the South were white males, over 90 percent of those executed for this crime in that region were black. Most of their alleged victims were white. No white male has even been executed for raping a black woman. [10]

As is probably true of white females, the incidence of rape of black women is underreported. Ladner reported that an eight-year-old girl has a good chance of being exposed to rape and violence if she is a member of the black underclass. [11] While widespread incidents of this kind are rooted in the sexist socialization of all men in society, it is pronounced among black men who have other symbols of traditional masculinity blocked to them. Various explanations have been put forth to explain why black men seem to adopt the attitudes of the majority group toward black women. Poussaint believes that because white men have historically raped black women with impunity, many black males believe they can do the same. [12]

Sexual violence is also rooted in the dynamics of the black dating game. The majority of black rape victims know their attacker—a friend, relative, or neighbor. Many of the rapes occur after a date and are what Amir describes as misfired attempts at seduction. [13] A typical pattern is for the black male to seek sexual compliance from his date, encounter resistance which he thinks is feigned, and proceed to forcibly obtain his sexual gratification from her. Large numbers of black men believe sexual relations to be their "right" after a certain amount of dating.

Rape, however, is not regarded as the act of a sexually starved male but rather as an aggressive act toward females. Students of the subject suggest that it is a long-delayed reaction against authority and powerlessness. In the case of black men, it is asserted that they grow up feeling emasculated and powerless before reaching manhood. They often encounter women as authority figures and teachers or as the head of their household. These men consequently act out their feelings of powerlessness against black women in the form of sexual aggression. Hence, rape by black men should be viewed as both an aggressive and political act because it occurs in the context of racial discrimination which denies most black men a satisfying manhood.

Manhood in American society is closely tied to the acquisition of wealth. Men of wealth are rarely required to rape women because they can gain sexual access through other means. A female employee who submits to the sexual demands of a male employer in order to advance in her job is as much an unwilling partner in this situation as is the rape victim. The rewards for her sexual compliance are normatively sanctioned, whereas the rapist does not often have the resources to induce such sexual compliance. Moreover, the concept of women as sexual property is at the root of rape. This concept is peculiar to capitalistic, western societies rather than African nations (where the incidence of rape is much lower). For black men, rape is often an act of aggression against women because the kinds of status men can acquire through success in a job are not available to them.

Recommendations

To address the salient issues in black male sexuality, I offer the following recommendations:

1) An educational program for black men must be designed to sensitize them to the need for their responsibility for, and participation in, family planning. This program will best be conducted by other men who can convey the fact that virility is not in and of itself the measure of masculinity. Also, it should be emphasized that the use of contraception—or obtaining a vasectomy—does not diminish a male's virility.

2) An over-all sex education program for both sexes should begin as early as kindergarten, before the male peer group can begin to reinforce attitudes of male dominance. Sex education courses should stress more than the physiological aspects in its course content. Males should be taught about the responsibility of men in sex relations and procreation. Forms of male contraception should be taught along with female measures of birth control.

3) The lack of alternative forms of role fulfillment available to many men, especially in industrialized societies, must be addressed. In cases of unemployment and underemployment, the male often resorts to the virility cult because it is the only outlet he has for a positive self-image and prestige within his peer group. Thus, we

must provide those conditions whereby men can find meaningful employment.

4) Lines of communication must be opened between men and women. A supplement to the educational program for men should be seminars and workshops involving both men and women. Hopefully, this will lead to the kind of dialog between men and women that will sensitize each of them to the feelings of the other.

NOTES

1) Robert Staples, *The Black Family: Essays and Studies*. (Belmont, CA: Wadsworth, 1978.)

2) Robert Staples, *Black Masculinity*. (San Francisco: The Black Scholar Press, 1982.)

3) Alan P. Bell, "Black Sexuality: Fact and Fancy" in R. Staples, ed., *The Black Family: Essays and Studies*, pp. 77–80.

4) David Larson, et al., "Social Factors in the Frequency of Romantic Involvement Among Adolescents." *Adolescence* II: 7–12, 1976.

5) Ira Reiss, *The Social Context of Premarital Sexual Permissiveness*. (New York: Holt, Rinehart and Winston, 1968.)

6) Leanor Johnson and Robert Staples, "Minority Youth and Family Planning: A Pilot Project." *The Family Coordinator* 28: 534–543, 1978.

7) U.S. Bureau of the Census, *Fertility of American Women*. (Washington, D.C.: U.S. Government Printing Office, 1984.)

8) Lisa Connolly, "Boy Fathers." *Human Behavior* 45: 40–43, 1978.

9) B.D. Misra, ""Correlates of Males' Attitudes Toward Family Planning" in D. Gogue, ed., *Sociological Contributions to Family Planning Research*. (Chicago: Univ. of Chicago Press, 1967), pp. 161–167.

10) William J. Bowers, *Execution in America*. (Lexington Books, 1974).

11) Joyce Ladner, *Tomorrow's Tomorrow: The Black Woman*. (Garden City, New York: Doubleday, 1971.)

12) Alvin Poussaint, *Why Blacks Kill Blacks*. (New York: Emerson-Hall, 1972.)

13) Menachim Amir, ""Sociocultural Factors in Forcible Rape" in L. Gross, ed., *Sexual Behavior*. (New York: Spectrum Publications, 1974), pp. 1–12.

Male Privilege and Male Violence: Patriarchy's Root and Branch

Dick Bathrick and Gus Kaufman, Jr.

Male violence and male abuse of power are undeniable facts of our lives. Their effects are felt by women, children, other men with less power, and the earth. We will be examining in particular male violence against women, situating it within the context of male privilege.

To look at male violence against women it may be instructive to start with rape. Male rape of women is male violence against women in one of its most devastating forms. It involves the total violation of a woman's body, mind and spirit. And when we listen to and take victims seriously, we know that its effects are debilitating long after the act itself.

What is almost as horrifying as rape itself is how normative it is in our culture: one in 2.5 women is a victim of a sexual assault in her lifetime. One in three females is sexually abused before age eighteen. In a 1988 survey of 1,700 Rhode Island junior high school students, a quarter of the boys and a sixth of the girls said that a man has a right to have sex with a woman without asking if he has spent money on her. A majority of the boys and a near majority of the girls said it's permissible for a man to force sex on a woman if the couple has dated for six months. Historically, the cultural response to rape has been to ask questions like, "What was she wearing?" "Where was she walking?" "What did she do to stop it?" Now battered and raped women are requiring us to label victim-blaming for what it is and to see how victim-blaming relieves us from asking more disturbing questions like, "Who is doing this to women? And why?"

One reason it's difficult for men to answer these questions is because it threatens to lessen the distance between us and "those other guys" who brutalize women. When we first began working with men who batter women, we kept waiting for the monster to come through the door. Seven years later we're still waiting. Most of the men we've seen, whether self-referred or mandated by the courts or the military, seem normal to most of the people who know them. They just happen to be committing criminal offenses at home. FBI crime statistics tell us that close to 40 percent of all men living intimately with women have battered their partners during the course of the relationship. By "battering" we mean the use of and repeated threat of physical force to dominate and control a woman. From this definition and these statistics we might conclude that battering is "normal" behavior in this culture. Seventy-five to ninety percent of rapes are committed by male acquaintances: family members, co-workers, classmates, dates, boyfriends, husbands. Battering and rape aren't, as many of us would prefer it, being committed by pathological freaks. Women are most often victimized by men whom they once trusted and loved. Why?

The answers that generally mean most to the men going through our program include the following: Men batter women because, in the short term, it works; i.e., the violence temporarily stops a woman from doing what threatens or challenges our authority. Men batter women because they can get away with it. Until recently men could batter women without experiencing consequences such as her leaving or their arrest, prosecution, conviction, and sentencing. Most men know that no matter who starts the fight, they can generally physically overpower a woman. And finally, men have been socialized to believe we have the right and the privilege to dominate and control women. Physical force (battering and rape) are the extremes to which we resort if necessary to maintain that control.

When we say men batter because we can get away with it and it "works," we are describing some of the workings of patriarchy, a system of male control over women, a system of male privilege.

To talk about male privilege we have to talk about ourselves from the perspective of the other. From within male reality the term "male privilege" doesn't signify; it has no meaning—it's invisible; it's just the way things are. How does a fish talk about water? This famous conundrum applies to white men talking to other men about our position in the world. The name feminists have given to our position—male privilege—doesn't exist in "common parlance," which is the language of the dominant group, the culture definers. Rich Vodde notes that

"It is doubtful that the term (male privilege) existed or had any meaning until women began to expose their oppression and name their oppressors. It is a phrase whose meaning was articulated by the experience of women who were its victims . . . It is a new phrase, born of broken silence . . . As it left the mouths of those women who

did not need a definition to know what it meant and entered the
realm of general discourse, its meaning became contested . . . " [1]

Notice we again have circled back to the problem of the difficulty of expressing certain thoughts in general discourse or common parlance. The above quote includes two more terms from women's reality: "oppressors" and "oppression." In the battle for the power to define reality, most men reject those terms as applying to us. We label them and those who use them as "strident," "hysterical," "man-hating," because it is in our interest to discredit them. Men of color in a white-dominated, i.e. racist, society also experience oppression, but they share some of the "perks" of sexism in terms of power over women, especially in relation to women of color. Gay men experience the benefits of male privilege *and* the oppression of homophobia.

When we began to work with men who batter, we ran into this problem of conflicting definitions, conflicting realities. We entered the work with an assumption you the reader probably share—that we were good guys (non-batterers). The guys we worked with were bad guys (batterers). This assumption was immediately confronted from two directions: first, many of the guys referred seemed quite like us. And second, the women who hired and supervised us began confronting us on *our* behavior.

At first they insisted we audiotape the group. We resisted, claiming some men wouldn't tolerate that and might even drop out. At the time that thought came to our minds more readily than the implications for the women's safety. Once we began recording, our supervisors critiqued our conduct of the group as revealed by the tapes. They pointed out the ways we accepted at face value statements from the men that they knew from the men's partners were lies and distortions. They challenged the ways we didn't confront assumptions of dominance and privilege. A man who was a "star" in group (he was verbal and concerned for other men) turned out to be requiring his partner to stay home and to answer the telephone for his business. She had no car and wasn't allowed to leave at any time. He drove a Cadillac.

The supervision sessions were difficult for all of us. Gus would get sinus headaches and have to go sit in the bathroom. Our supervisors had to face fears—that we would feel they didn't have the authority to criticize us, that we would quit or at least go away mad if they were too critical (i.e., honest), that they would betray themselves and other women to avoid hurting our feelings.

Gradually through being confronted, from listening and reading, we came to acknowledge that the experience of oppressed peoples, those not in power, is different from ours in the dominant class. Our group so controls the definition of what is, that we need not even know there is any other view. We came to see that we shared the dominant world view, that there wasn't as much difference between us and batterers as there was between men and women. So there wasn't much of a we/they split (in our groups). We were all participants/beneficiaries in the "continuum of male controls over women."[2]

Most of us can see how we benefit from sexism in terms of having easier access to higher-paying jobs. But we balk at the idea that we benefit from women being raped or battered. To understand how all men "benefit" from battering is to see something of the complicity we all share in the act. While many of us don't rape or batter women, those of us in relationships with women find that our partners frequently make decisions based on how to avoid subjecting themselves to male violence: Decisions like where and when to walk, whom to talk with, and what to wear. These decisions are often powerfully influenced by whether or not a man (spouse, lover, friend) is available to accompany a woman on that walk. They have an unspoken agreement that she depends on a man to protect her from being raped or threatened by violent men. So men end up determining if women get to go out and where they go. And we don't mind having that control. More than once, batterers in our program have noted the irony in their partners' relying on them for protection from "those violent men out there." This form of control never gets named. It's classic male privilege, in all its invisibility, with all its power.

This information came to us by listening to women's reality. Listening, we began to get a better sense of who we are and how we operate. We came to see that a cardinal principle of male-dominated reality, of male privilege, is the assumption that *others are there for me*. By "others" we mean whoever we can put in one-down (service) positions. Thus this principle might be called the principle of hierarchy. Each of us according to his own position in a hierarchy has access to the services of those below him.

In our Western version of patriarchy, traditionally this meant a white, male god at the top, the Pope, secular leaders like the President and corporate executives next, followed by middle management, professionals and religious leaders, then workers (who might still be heads of households), then white families (women, children and maiden aunts) and, at the bottom, people of color.

As you can see, male privilege also includes the assumption that *reality is what I (and my kind) say it is*. Adrienne Rich has said, "Objectivity is just male subjectivity made (sacrosanct)." A man is defining a woman's reality and claiming the truth when he says:

1) "She was being provocative; she had on a see-through (too short) dress."
2) "I didn't want to hit her. She provoked me. She kept nagging."
3) "Women lie."
4) "I don't notice the mess. You're just being compulsive. If it bothers you, you pick it up."

Note how we describe reality in ways that justify our position. Implicit in this is another male operating principle: *the rules apply to others; not to me.* Think of how we handle jealousy, anger, name-calling, expectations of service. In all we apply the notorious double-standard.

What can a man do once he becomes aware of all this, of how things are? We propose that listening to women, systematically instituted, is an alternative to using power and control tactics to silence them. Listening is thus a path toward justice. In "Men Stopping Violence" we have instituted principles and practices to further this goal. We invite the reader to try these out.

1) *Listen without interrupting.* This doesn't mean "white knuckle" listening, where you're actually planning your rebuttal as she speaks. It doesn't mean listen until you've had enough and then interrupt. It means give her your full attention and seriously consider her point of view.

2) B*elieve her and take her seriously.* This means accepting her feelings, her version, her vision. It means fully recognizing her right to her opinion and acknowledging that her opinion is as valid as your own.

3) *Change what is wrong.* This is about giving up pornography since pornography reinforces our assumption that others are there for us. It's about recognizing the amount of rage she feels from being constantly endangered, from being expected to serve us, and then labeled "bitch" or "nag" if she complains about it. It's about pay equity, abortion rights and doing our share of the housework without being reminded.

Listening to women is hard for us. If we listen, we'll hear things said that are hard to hear. Our lies, our injustices, our faults will be exposed. We'd like to think we can act to correct these without having to go through the ordeal of hearing about them. We can't. If we listen, and don't start acting angry ourselves to divert her, we may begin to have feelings. Somehow we must learn to feel without acting, rather than act without feeling. To do or say nothing in the face of her rage is to step into the unknown. We're likely to feel confused and scared if we don't emotionally withdraw, go numb or get angry. Our confusion and fear can be palpable. At this point we feel like we're not being a man. And in fact we aren't being the kind of man we grew up trying hard to be.

We're relinquishing control over a space so that there is room for her to live. In the process we're vulnerable, we're passive, and we're opening ourselves to all sorts of feelings we've not allowed ourselves in a long, long time. For after the guilt and shame we've warded off are not only terror and confusion, but tears, tenderness, sorrow, and love. When we allow ourselves these feelings, the women and children in our lives may be able to feel a commonality and closeness with us, rather than feeling driven by us.

Some of our best moments come when we're not in control. Remember the flow between us and others when we're laughing uncontrollably, crying deeply, feeling deep love. Remember orgasms. Or even a sunset, the oceans, a gorgeous day . . . We don't make these things happen.

Becoming comfortable not being in control, being patient, listening, offering care, being of service—if power and dominance are essential to who we are these will always be alien. But if we want love and connectedness, rich relationships with women, children, men, other living creatures—ourselves—let us open ourselves to these.

NOTES

1. Rich Vodde, M.S.W., "Male Privilege," unpublished manuscript (Men Stopping Violence, Inc.).

2. David Adams, "The Continuum of Male Controls Over Women," (EMERGE, Cambridge, MA).

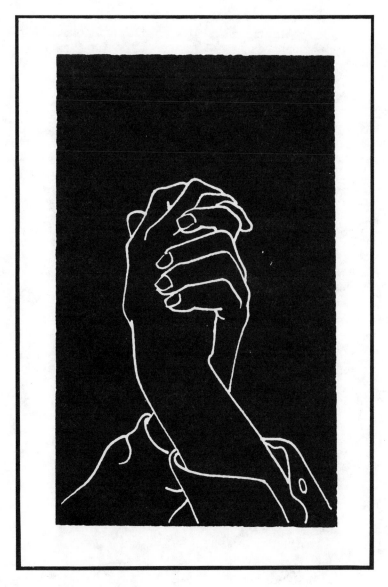

Part II: *Understanding Intimacy*

Lost

Christopher Wiley

I'm
losing
myself
through you,
going
gently
underneath an
inescapable
skin
holding
your body's
universe
of soft
movements.
Be still
while I
climb
down
your body
like a
ladder
until
even
moles on
your back
that once
charted
stars
to my
touches,

can't
bring me
back
again,
not fully,
because
your
skin's
edge
begins
something
all too
deep
and just
too wide
to escape.
I'm
losing
myself
in you
like a
diver
submerged
in a
translucent
sea
with
only
one
breath.

Some Enchanted Evening

Sy Safransky

My friend Ron is in California now, making movies or waiting tables; we never write and I don't know when I'll see him again. But I'll always remember something he once said, which was one of the most honest things I've ever heard a man say. "The only time I'm happy, really happy," Ron said, "is when I'm in a woman's arms."

I know, I know. . . . There are men about whom this isn't true at all, or so it seems, men who are happy only when they're making money, men for whom happiness is found only in another man's arms, men who are devoid of passion for anything or anyone, because their heartache is too great or because their hearts were never broken—yes, men to whom women are no more important than poetry to a rock. Or so it seems. But I wonder whether this kind of indifference isn't always a lie, whether it doesn't mask the greatest need. There's a howling in all of us. Some admit it; others say it's the wind, and shut the window, and go to sleep. But in their dreams everything they touch screams.

What have I ever craved more than a woman's arms? To be up half the night, talking, laughing, making love—have I ever been closer to heaven? The bed becomes your church; you pass the collection plate back and forth until you've given too much, then your poverty becomes your gift: your tears, her tears—I mean, when it's right, who can tell laughing from crying? And though, in days or months or years to come, you'll swear you were fooling yourself, you weren't, it really happened: in the midst of all that fluttering, between the spilled wine and the giggling and the breathless kiss, your hearts billowed out like great white sails, and above you for a moment hovered the dove.

For a long time, I disparaged romantic love, even as I yearned for it; better, I said to myself, to long for true love, total selflessness without thought of return, saintliness. Better to crave God's embrace than a woman's embrace. What is romance, after all, but a golden chain that winds first around the heart, then around the neck? What sweeter lie do we whisper to ourselves than that another person can save us? The truth is they do, for a while—days or weeks or months, even years. But eventually we find out that no one can save us from ourselves. The realization is stunning, like seeing a photograph of the earth taken from space. How mysteriously alone we are! How tempting to imagine that if we're loved our loneliness will be dispelled.

Yet here I am, celebrating with champagne and flowers my second anniversary, with my third wife. My conceit, lustrous as her skin in the flickering candlelight, is that I've finally learned something about love. She's been married before, too: in the lines around her eyes, I trace the scars, but when she smiles, the pain is transfigured; I trust her pain, and what she's learned from it, and the light in her eyes—how can I not trust that? It's a beacon to me, a refuge; more than four walls can ever be, it's home. Am I a man in love, which is to say, as big a fool as God has made? A friend, asked if she trusts eye contact, says, "I trust it foolishly."

If I've learned anything, hasn't it been how little I've learned? Norma and I sip our champagne; a breeze from the window slaps the candle, and my memory, like a breeze, calls up other nights, other eyes, other women I've lived with and loved—how with each, I built a temple of hope, and placed upon the altar the unclaimed future, with the sunny side up; how our hands and tongues and lives wound around each other as effortlessly as morning light filling a room; you could no more separate us than take the blue from the sky. Yet here we are, in the long night of disbelief we were sure would never follow: we're together no more. With each, in turn, the tears became a rain, the rain became a river, and we are rushed down the waters of life with about as much control as a barrel.

In the movie, *Last Tango in Paris*, there is a heart-rending scene which evokes, for me, the impenetrable mystery of loving someone: why two souls, different as sky and sea, are called from opposite ends of the universe to make together a home, a life.

The estranged wife of Paul (Marlon Brando) has killed herself. Alone with her, in the funeral parlor, Paul contemplates her lifeless body upon its bed of flowers, her face set in a smile that is nearly beatific—a death mask which betrays his memories of her as in life she betrayed him, as they betrayed each other, with bad decisions, indiscretions, broken vows. He curses her, vilely and furiously—it is shocking; we expect, foolishly, something different for the dead—and then, suddenly, he begins to cry, his hatred dissolving into remorse and longing and grief, as time itself dissolves, and she is again his darling, his tender love, the one he reached for across the aeons, and who reached for him, and then let go, and now has let go for good. "A man can live for two hundred years," he weeps, "and never understand his wife."

Is it the women I haven't understood, or myself? The need to love and be loved—how much of it really had to do with them, their individual temperaments, charms, braininess, magic, their faces so ordinary and so adored? What have I looked for in their eyes but a truer reflection of myself? How passionate I've been, in pursuit of life through these other lives. What a devotee of desire! But not merely of the honey breasts and milky thighs, not merely of tastes tasted, the stuttering tongue appeased—but desirous, most of all, for desire itself. I've been hungry for hunger. I've come before my women like a starving man to a banquet table, laden with everything delicious and suddenly within reach, and sat there scowling, insisting that someone feed me, feed me with a smile, with her hair brushed back just so, with nothing else on her mind, with undying devotion to my hunger, my awful hunger. No one could do it right, at least not for long. And so we hurt each other, terribly—I, convinced I was starving; they, convinced my appetite was grotesque, for sex, for sorrow, for sympathy, but mostly for the party not to end. My need, finally, was to keep alive the possibility of deliverance, no matter that I knew, deep down, that no one would deliver me this way. To give up the yearning for a woman to save me was terrifying, because it meant facing an ancient anguish my heart just couldn't bear. To give up the promise of love— the dizzying romance that someone else could meet my needs, fill my emptiness, still the howling—would mean acknowledging just how profound my pain was. To be lost, like a child, in my memories of childhood, to be drawn deeper and deeper into that maelstrom of grief—no, anything but that. Better the bruised look, the turned back, the slammed door. Better the quixotic search for the next shapely savior. But, of course, it would happen again. We seek our completion in the strangest ways, but seek it we must. We reenact the old hurts, we summon forth the ghosts of Mom and Dad and resurrect for them a new body, a new face, a voice with just a hint of the old, and we bid them to sit down beside us, here at the banquet table, and beg them once again to feed us, please, and please, this time, with a little love.

The truth is, there are no love substitutes. There's love, and there's everything which masquerades as love, all those diamonds that turn out to be glass: the world's prizes, and the prizes of the flesh, and the prizes of the spirit, too, so that God became the one I turned to when the fairy tale sputtered and the night came on: God as Mom, God as Dad, a God as distant and unattainable as the painful memories I used God to mask. But did it really matter whom I knelt before? What I worshipped was my own longing, what I loved was what I was able to get.

My children sometimes play a game called "Opposites," in which everything you say is the opposite of what you mean; they are learning, as they grow older, that most of us speak that way all the time. Every time I've said, "I love you," hasn't it been a lie? What I loved was *the way I felt* when a woman talked to me, when I thought of her, when her sunlight slid across the big dark barn of my heart after a night of rain. I loved the end of storm and loneliness, the clouds opening.

But this is like loving the postman because he brings you a letter you wrote to yourself a long time ago, in a time before time when you were whole, and love was as natural as breathing, and you hadn't yet bought the lie that you needed someone else's approval to be complete, that enchantment resided in another's eyes not yours, that security needed to be sought, that you could find yourself in someone else! Deep within us that knowledge still throbs, in our heart of hearts, the heart that can't be broken, where the words God and love and truth are not distant signposts but closer than two bodies can ever be—closer than her hair, dark and storm-tossed the way I like it, splayed across my face; closer than her breath, smelling of me, and mine, of her, mingling above us; closer than her secret wish, whispered in my ear, for a finger here, and mine, for a tongue there, blazing like fire and going up like smoke; yes, closer than memory and regret; closer than that. Closer than my mother a thousand miles above me, bending down to pick me up; closer than my father at the door. Closer than close—where the tyranny we call "love" is seen for what it is: our human prison, to which we've fashioned the lock, and the key, and forever go on confusing the one with the other, and always in the name of love.

Have I learned a thing or two? Knowing what something isn't, isn't the same as knowing what it is, but it's a start. Some humility about love is a start. I start with what is dead in me, what hungers for the kiss of life, what wants to live in astonishment—not *through* but *with* a woman—and I acknowledge how difficult this is: did I say difficult, or impossible?

For example, I learn to leave my wife alone. For someone as unsure as I of his self-worth—longing for the kind word, the hand-out, the pressing of flesh on flesh—this is no small accomplishment, and often I fail, but then I get the chance not to blame her for my pain. Of course, it's always more complicated than that, for there's her pain, too. Does she rub my wounds with the balm of a little lie? If I realize what she's doing, do I merely get angry, or do I have to consider why? Do I, like a blind man, give her my hand, to run across her hidden face, so I might know her darker features, her fear? Do I lose myself in sympathy, or judgment—or reach through to real compassion? Do I stay the distance, or jump the wall—love her, or write a poem about love gone astray?

I have a desk drawer full of poems, for my ex-wives; for the other women I've lived with; for the women I've known briefly, and slept with once, or known no less intimately for never having touched them; for friends who, had we cared less for each other, might have been lovers, and lovers who cared enough to become friends. Knowing that my love is nine-tenths lie, I say I love them still, that they're here with me on this anniversary night as the men Norma has loved are with us, too, that if togetherness is mostly illusion, so is separateness, and that everyone we've loved, however imperfectly, has left their mark on us, and we on them.

I fasted for a week before our wedding day, to "purify" myself, but by the time the ceremony started I was more dizzy than pure. I promised Norma the sweet air of me, but knew I'd deliver the meat. No angel touched me as I nervously recited the vows—which, two years later, seem both practical and preposterous: either you need volumes to get you through the hard times, or nothing so much as silence.

We lift our glasses and gaze at each other romantically, before one or the other of us breaks the spell with a wink. We both know what an absurd yet touching drama this is: this marriage rooted in human frailty and conceit but rooted, too, in God's will. Yes, we know—until the next awful moment when we forget, and have to struggle against the amnesia drawn before us like the darkest of curtains. The grief becomes our bond. Grief, joy—one turns to the other quicker than you can say, "How was your day?"

And who's to say which is more love's measure? I didn't know I'd fallen in love with Norma until the first time I saw her cry. Through my tears and hers, which no lover's hand can stay, I'm falling still: through our shared loneliness, gathered into our hearts like a wild bouquet, then hurled away; through the sounds our bodies make, rolling together like chords; through echoes of pleasure. . . .

One moment we're "in," the next moment we're "out" of love; we agree, over the flickering candlelight, that we can scarcely say which serves us better. The pain of love always leads us down to a deeper, more compassionate love—but who can remember this? Who can bear the pain of love for what it is: the heart's unbearable treasure?

Eros and the Male Spirit

Thomas Moore

> "I am in the hands of the unknown God,
> he is breaking me down to his own oblivion
> to send me forth on a new morning, a new man."
> —D.H. Lawrence

Gender is one of the grand metaphors for the human condition and for the nature of the cosmos, used by visionaries and poets in all places and in all times. Like all metaphors, this one participates in the concrete reality that gives rise to the image: differences between men and women. However, it takes a poetic sensibility to appreciate the metaphor, and the metaphor is primary. Without a taste for image, the mind slips quickly into literalism. Not catching the poetry in gender, we tend to place all our gender talk onto actual men and women; so that no matter how hard we try to resolve the war of the sexes, antagonism and polarization remain.

The Latin people of the time of Cicero, for example, understood that the male spirit is not the same as a male person. They called the male spirit "animus,'" a word that suggests a male element in the breath. This spirit was present in a family, in a place, in a marriage, and in an individual. Shrines were set up to honor the male spirit or genius of the family. This spirit, they believed, was conveyed from generation to generation when a young person kissed the dying father and received the family spirit from his breath. They believed that adultery dishonored the spirit of the marriage bed, not the marriage partner. Masculinity was not identified with men.

Jung picked up on this Latin idea and wove the notion of animus into his psychology; however, he tied it more concretely to actual gender. For Jung an animus or male spirit is felt in thinking, judging, acting, and valuing. But even in Jung's thought, where gender is treated less metaphorically than it could be, the male spirit has a life of its own. Because women adjust themselves to a split-gendered society, they, Jung said, have to work extra hard to accommodate this male spirit, just as men have trouble aligning themselves with the feminine anima.

Jung thought that one of the most pressing psychological needs of every person is to reconcile these two figures of the psyche: anima and animus, or soul and spirit. That is to say, so as not to be at war within oneself, one has to find a way to befriend the female and male figures within oneself and out in the world. This implies that male is not simply a man's way of being. Man is the source of the metaphor, but the male spirit is something needed by men and women, by both societies and individuals.

We don't realize how deep existential secularism runs in our approach to everyday life. We tend to take everything onto ourselves. There is no room for spirit and soul. Peoples of other times and places have taken for granted that all of life cannot be squeezed into conscious, controlling, intentional subjectivity. In moods, enthusiasms, fantasies, obsessions, depressions, and addictions spirits flow through and captivate us. Only a secular attitude tries to deal with these encounters literalistically with medications and exercises of will. A sensibility attuned to the sacred can respect larger-than-human factors without denying them in a spirit of modernism and without reifying them in an attitude of religious fundamentalism.

I am saying, therefore, that we will not deal with gender in depth until we recover a sense of the sacred. I am not talking about a sectarian or even New Age belief, but simply an awareness of a spiritual dimension. With D.H. Lawrence I would define renewed manhood by saying: "I am in the hands of an unknown God, he is breaking me down to his own oblivion." I find my manhood and masculinity not by identifying with some faddish notion of what a male is, but by letting this male spirit course through my being. I am male through my participation in *him.*

Cicero said that it is the animus that gives a sense of identity and character. We tend to think that identity is persona, self-image. Therefore, much gender talk gets its feet stuck in the surface linoleum of image and role. An alternative would be to understand that what gives character and identity is the spirit that drives and motivates a person. In Renaissance times this spirit was called the daimon, the more than rational source of fate and special destiny. I am what I am because of the powerful forces that well up within me and which place me in history.

The secular life that denies the world its animism places the full cosmic weight of gender upon the shoulders of the mere human being. Men are expected to embody masculinity, women femininity. Naturally, we all fail. It is too much to expect of us. In Renaissance times a writer having trouble getting the words out didn't talk about *his* writer's block, he worried that the spirit of Mercury, the daimonic source of a writer's inspiration, might not pass by. This is more than simple rhetoric. It is a way of being in the world, a way of imagining experience that allows for the non-human elements in the face of which human life defines itself.

Therefore, one of the symptoms of loss of masculinity or the male spirit is the frustration of trying to *be* it instead of being its priest. But the symptomatic manifestations only begin there. They become quite outrageous.

Symptomatic Masculinity

For example, because the animus grants power, creativity, authority, and drive, its symptomatic forms exaggerate all of these. With no real animus, power turns into tyranny, creativity into productivity, authority into authoritarianism, and drive into manic impulsiveness. Women struggling for equality with these exaggerated substitutes for masculinity run the risk of establishing their own gender neuroses. They also, of course, have to dare the blind reactions of bogus authorities who, ultimately void of power, have no limits on the extent of their tyranny. True power enjoys its own inherent inhibitions, but inauthentic power is capable of atrocity.

Symptoms of any kind tend toward literalism, exaggeration, and destructiveness.Where ordinarily a quality should be quite subtle and interior, symptomatically it takes absurd external forms. Power becomes the display of instruments that suggest power. Armies march in stiff profile, bayonets and barrels raised in caricature of the phallus. Nations hoard stockpiles of weapons. If an individual were to do this, he would be arrested and hauled off to the local mental hospital. It is obvious to most that the more weapons a person carries or hoards, the less secure and stable that person is.

The male spirit is creative, but producing great numbers of things with no regard for quality and no sense of inhibition in the proliferation indicates symptomatic creativity. The creative drive can go wild in spasms of production in which there is no genuine creation. It is not the male spirit that values only growth: economic, psychological, territorial, financial. It is not the male spirit that measures a man's success by his W-2 form. And it is not the male spirit that conquers and collects women.

We know from religions that the male and female factors in all of life—yin and yang, lingam and yoni, creator and wisdom, Zeus and Hera, Jesus and Mary—live a certain tension and yet complement each other and nourish each other. Keeping them together is not always an easy task. We see these tensions lived out among men and women. Zeus and Hera do not symbolize the man and woman in matrimony. The man and woman in their struggles toward marriage represent and provide an instance of the cosmic couple. Every coming together of a man and woman is the *hieros gamos*, the sacred mingling.

Sex has nothing to do with biology. The love or lust between a man and a woman only set up the altar on which the Gods and Goddesses mate. Physiology is the sacred technology of the Gods. That is both a limitation on human personal love—it's not all about me and the other person; and it is a wondrous exaltation of human love and a great gift from one person to the other. Renaissance psychologists recognized this aspect of love when they applied their Neoplatonic world-view to the love between people. Marsilio Ficini, intellectual advisor to the Medicis, writes of human love: "It descends first from God, and passes through the Angel and the Soul as if they were made of glass; and from the Soul it easily emanates into the body prepared to receive it." Then this love returns to its divine source. Bodily love is a point on the circuit of the soul, and from that transpersonal circulation it takes its nobility and its sacredness.

The male spirit, so full of vision and creative promise, longs for a female soul to impregnate. The world needs the audacity and daring of the male spirit. But it also needs the receptive, reflective feminine alchemy of the soul to give spirit its context, its material, and its vessel. Naturally, the two seek each other out.

But what hapens in a time like ours in which the male spirit is elusive, supplanted by its surrogate, hyperactive male? Then there is no movement toward inner marriage. Human marriage cannot hold together. The whole society becomes captivated by the daring of the titanic male and undervalues the female. It is not women, precisely, who are oppressed in this culture; it is the feminine. Women suffer this oppression to the extent they are identified with the feminine, but the oppression is aimed at the feminine. Simple proof of this is male acceptance of the woman who honors the plastic phallus of commercial success and power. The masculine, too, is oppressed in a secular, ego and will-centered culture. It is axiomatic that as long as one gender is debilitated and undervalued, the other will also suffer complementary wounds.

Jung described the animus as "spermatic." It impregnates. Women look for this engendering spirit because the feminine soul requires it. Women look to men, but often they find the fetish of male potency, unqualified growth, instead of true fertility. They look for drive and strength and instead find muscles and machines. The male spirit, if it were the real thing, would fertilize the imaginations and lives of women. It would offer security, not brutality. A man doesn't lord it over a woman or treat her violently if he has the male spirit pumping through him. He turns to violence in a desperate search for the lost spirit. These are not strong men who have to possess and bind women. They are the weakest, the least masculine, those most lacking in masculine spirit.

Confusion about this distinction between flaunting men and the male spirit keeps the breach wide between men and women. As a result, women often fall too much into the feminine. Neither men nor women thrive when the gender in them is lopsided. Men have the opportunity, being male, to radiate ritually the male spirit needed by both men and women. Women need the male stuff from the man. Men also need it from each other.

Women abused by men become attached to the abuse because they crave that spirit, finding it only in its twisted, emaciated manifestation. They are attached, too, because they are only-feminine. We always become destructively attached to that which we give over fully to another or to the world. On their part, men require the woman's opening, the eternal wound, the flow of blood, the moon-friendship, the vegetative strength that comes from vulnerability to the rhythms of the stars and seasons. But those very things ardently desired by the male are also a threat to his spirit. The male spirit, animus, can survive the encounter. But the symptomatic male, non-animus gender, has nothing to fall back on, nothing behind the facade of masculinity to stand up to the feminine mystery. He can only puff up and thrash that feminine being he needs, loves, and cannot abide.

The marriage sought after in every affair, every dalliance, every flirtation, every spat, and every matrimony is the union of these spirits. We know this in part from the dreams of those contemplating such actual unions. In these dreams partners may vary, circumstances chance, moods fade, outcomes vary. Gender and its marriage are in no way literal. All gender is dream gender, except when it falls disastrously into literalism.

The male spirit that hovers in the heart longs for the feminine, not to be completed—it is as complete as it ever will be, but to find fulfillment in its reaching out to lattice itself in that other different, responding, echoing, resonant partner. The man's radiance of femininity in the subtle airs of his soul plays the overtones of the woman's fundamental womanhood, and the woman sings the upper partials of the man's familiar male spirit. Marriage is a consonance, a vertical harmony. Men, of course, in their loves with each other sound rich overtones of the harmony as well.

A woman is not always befriended by a female nymph. She may be as remote from the feminine spirit as a man who feels the longing for female stuff. Women sometimes resent and reject the feminine sphere. Often their dreams are filled with women's mystery rites. An anorexic woman dreams of many old women washing her and presenting her with long tables of food. The dream offers her the healing services of archaic womanhood. A man may not know the male spirit that is his brother, yet in his dreams an unknown male companion walks by his side sharing in his adventures. The soul has its own homoerotic desires that may or may not find themselves breaking into life.

Eros and Aggression

For the Greeks Eros is one of the male spirits. Masculinity is erotic by nature. It is male to be erotic, erotic to be male. The rush of desire for another soul is the male spirit doing his job, taking us along, making connections. He mingles and unites. He makes friendships. He hammers out unions. He keeps us within certain orbits. In art Eros is adolescent, brash, active, uncontrollable. He has wings. He shoots arrows. This is the natural aggression of the male: to bring things together, to join what is joinable.

To be masculine, therefore, is to tolerate the rush of eros, to live by desire.One gets masculine strength from the strength of the desire. It is eros who has power, and the individual becomes powerful in a deep way through participation in that erotic power. William Blake says that desire that can be suppressed is not true desire. Centuries before Christ Hesiod sang that Eros breaks the strength in the arms and legs of Gods and humans. By all accounts, Eros is a source of immense power.

There is a fundamental difference, however, between the power that eros brings and the manipulative opportunity created by the abuse of eros. A man can enslave another person who is in love (in eros) with him. But he does that only as a defense against the true power of eros that stirs in himself. All false, inhumane loves betray the abuse of eros: addictions, obsessions, fetishes. We are in love with the nuclear bomb because explosive, powerful eros has been blocked. The bomb is our fetish.

But Eros is not only powerful, he is also beautiful, full of life and grace. He is brilliant. He shines. His erection is not an emblem of blunt power, it is his showing. The pornographic imagination, repressed wherever Eros is abused, wants to see the display of Eros.

The name "Zeus," the high God, means "shining." He is known in his brilliant displays of lightning. According to Jung, phallos among other things means "light." To be phallic, the great emblem of the male spirit, is to shine. When we don't shine, we swing our fists and butt our chests. People become violent when their male spirit cannot shine forth. When we can't shine, we expect our metallic missiles and our military shoes to shine, as fetishes. Shining is the ultimate aggressive act; anything else is symptomatic and therefore deeply unsatisfying. Isn't the satisfaction of boxing in the shining and not the bruising? In the bravura, the exaggeration, the show? Doesn't the ice hockey free-for-all manifest the latent male force that wants to shine?

I don't shine; the male spirit shines through me. My passions burn and glow in my maleness. When the male spirit is vibrant, my character, my daimon, my archon, my angel shines its halo of spirit in my slightest gesture. There is no need for violence when the spirit radiates. The glint of the steel gun barrel replaces the glow of the angel who is the guardian of light—Lucifer, Light-Bearer.

Lucifer is a dark angel. Sometimes the male spirit shines with an Underworld aesthetic, with the beauty of dark mystery. Only a sentimental misunderstanding of religion believes an angel to be superhumanly good. The male spirit has to shine sometimes in his mischief, like the great God Hermes, archetypal thief and liar.

Light and desire are almost indistinguishable, like the penis of sex and the phallos of shining. Desire, the aura of eros, is warm and phosphorescent. It shines. To let desire shine is to heal that man who beats the woman who he thinks has smothered his desire. When desires are not allowed to glow, they turn into addictions and odd loves. There is love within all those things to which we are madly attached: alcohol, sex, money, home, wandering, oneself. These odd loves are the egos of the male spirit. The Greek Orphics said that eros arises from a great egg. We might look for eros in the eggshells that render life brittle and concealed as phobias, depressions, and dysfunctions. We need not get rid of these eggshell complaints. We have only to look closely into their interior spaces.

We carry our desires around like eggs, going from romance to romance, orgy to orgy. But eros appears only when the egg is incubated, when it opens and reveals its inside. The heaviness of eros we feel in love and desires is its own maturing nature, its burden, its pregnancy, which is not revealed from the beginning. The true objects of eros sometimes appear only after a long period of engagement with its decoys. Our crazy loves and attachments may be destructive, but they are important as unique embryos of authentic love.

The egg from which Eros appears is often a long-standing obsessive love. It is a truism that in loving another we are in love with love. Love is the object of our love, and the other gives us love that he or she has been holding for us as in a shell. Aphrodite, the great Goddess, the awesome and profound mystery of love and sex, was recognized for centuries in the scallop shell.

Part of the mystery of Aphrodite, for a man, is the ironic truth that his sexual fantasy, drive, and emotion are feminine. It is she, the shell, Venus the sea, Aphrodite whose name means "foam-Goddess" or perhaps, the scholars say, "the Goddess who shines," who grants the wet and sea-surging tides of sex to a man. Sex itself is a union, then, of male Eros and female Venus. In some ancient stories, she is his mother. But Apuleius, the second-century writer of the *Golden Ass*, shows her giving her son a passionate kiss. The world of Eros is never contained in the rectangular boundaries our morals and customs and expectations built to fence him in. Eros, the Orphics said, is a maker of worlds. We know that he makes relationships, friendships, families, communities, even nations. He also inspires poetry, letters, stories, memories, shrines. In short, erotic sex makes individual and social culture. Or, it makes soul. As James Hillman has said, where Eros stirs, soul is to be found. Soul is sign that eros is truly present. If there is no sign of soul, then the sex is symptomatic, on the path toward eros, but not yet out of its shell.

The mystery of male sexuality, therefore, is not to be found and lived in literal gender or literal sex. The other can only be loved and pleasured when one has discovered the cosmic couple, inside oneself and in the world at large. Only when the male and female have coupled in our buildings and economies and schools and politics will the God and Goddess take their long night together with us, like Zeus and Hera on their three-hundred year honeymoon, radiating the truth of sex into all our lives. Then the act of sex would be what it is meant to be: a ritual act epitomizing and celebrating the marriage of heaven and earth. Only when the genders of culture enhance their love can two human beings find the fullness of sexuality.

Of course, it works the other direction, too. Culture is us. Our rediscovery of eros in our own microcosmic lives is the beginning of the cosmic union. When we realize what the Orphics understood, that desire is the fundamental motive force of life and soul, that its power is true aggression, its action authentic creativity, then sex can be released from its captivity in literalism. At the moment our world is frightened by desire, knowing that its limits are not the limits of heroic will and Promethean secularism. But perhaps we can risk the pleasures of desire and glimpse the new worlds it engenders. Then we may discover sex for the first time.

Bisexual Husbands: Integrating Two Worlds

David R. Matteson

I am a married man with two children. I like to wear a wedding ring as a symbol of my commitment to my family. My wife has been wonderfully supportive throughout our 27 years together, and she is an imporant part of my life.

I am also a gay man. To take off my ring when I am in a setting where I meet gay men would feel hypocritical to me. I hide neither the importance of my gay life from my wife, nor the importance of my wife from my gay friends. Yet much of the time being this bisexual person—both heterosexual and gay—feels a bit like being a "man without a country."

Picture in your mind a married couple with whom you've been friends for years and assume that you've just learned that the husband is involved in a gay relationship. Regardless of whether you are gay or straight yourself, you probably have emotional reactions as you try to digest this new information.

If you are part of the mainstream heterosexual community, this information confronts you with two taboo issues at once: homosexual behavior, and extramarital sex. Many heterosexuals have a more difficult time accepting homosexual behavior in persons whom they identify as like themselves than in those clearly different from themselves. When a heterosexual man meets another man who is married, has children, and seems to live a lifestyle much like his own, the discovery that this man is bisexual threatens the safe division of the world into the neat categories of gay and straight.

The categorizing of lifestyles into "them" and "us" is not unique to heterosexuals, of course. If you are gay the struggle to affirm your own orientation may have required that you reject the idea of "fitting in" to the heterosexual model of the "normal" family. Gradually you may develop or locate a community or network of your own, but it is a community hidden from, or rejected by, the mainstream. The division of the world into these two communities becomes a real, but unfortunate, part of gay life-experience. Because of this, some may view my "bisexuality" as self-deception or a waystation on the voyage to exclusively gay orientation.

Bisexual lifestyles, and especially mixed orientation marriages, are often misunderstood by both gays and straights. This may be because much published information about these marriages is based on clinical studies, and thus perpetuates myths about the neurotic character of such marriages. In this chapter, I will rely primarily on studies of bisexual husbands and wives which used either non-clinical (more representative) samples, or were conducted in gay-affirmative settings. For reasons to be discussed below, it appears that mixed-orientation marriages in which the husband is bisexual, the wife straight, are far more prevalent than those in which the wife is bisexual and the husband straight. For this reason I will refer to the bisexual spouse as "he," and the straight partner as "she" in this chapter.

How Mixed-Orientation Marriages Develop

In my research on mixed-orientation marriages, less than one-third of the husbands thought of themselves as bisexual or gay before they met their wives-to-be and committed themselves to marriage. The vast majority of these husbands were predominately heterosexual in behavior at the time they married. The majority of men in such marriages presumed themselves to be heterosexual or believed that their bisexuality would make monogamous marriage possible. Eighty-three percent of us expected to remain monogamous when we were married, and most of us did so for a number of years.

Most of us bisexual husbands have had some adult homosexual experience before we married, but we also have found ourselves sexually attracted to women, or at least to the particular woman we fell in love with and chose to marry. Our reasons for marrying were similar to those of most men who marry: we wanted a wife and family, and, we loved this particular woman. Most of us were not aware of "the male couple" as a viable alternative lifestyle. Only 20 percent of the bisexual husbands in my study implied that negative attitudes toward being gay were part of their motivation for marrying.

Disclosure or Discovery

In mixed-orientation marriages which became stable, the first five or more years of the marriage is a period of developing the primacy of the marital relationship. It seems crucial that a high level of intimacy and trust be developed before extramarital relationships can be tolerated. However, in almost all cases, some years into the marriage the husbands' same-sexed desires become compelling, and are acted upon. Usually a year or two of sporadic homosexual activity occurs before these bisexual husbands experience a crisis in sexual identity, leading to questions about their marriages.

Some of us shared our re-experienced homosexual desires with our wives early in the process. Our decisions to disclose early seem to have been related to more open communication in our marriages, a higher comfort level with our own homosexual feelings, and a perception that our wives were strong and independent enough to tolerate the disclosure.

Other men made decisions to keep their homosexual behaviors separate and secret from their wives and families. Perhaps they dropped hints, and got responses they interpreted to mean that their wives were too dependent, or too rigid, to handle more complete disclosure. There is some evidence that the men who did not tell their wives were more homophobic to begin with; perhaps they chose wives who were also less comfortable with sexuality and sexual differences. In any case, these men delayed disclosure, and were left with guilt both for being "queer" and for "cheating." Frequently, the conspiracy of silence results in a spiral of mistrust and distance which often destroys the emotional intimacy of the marriage, though the outward appearance of a conventional marriage may be maintained. (There are notable exceptions: some secretive couples appear to share a high degree of sensitivity and respect for each other.)

At the point of disclosure or discovery of the husband's same-sex involvements, the wife must deal with three emotionally-charged issues at once: the husband's sexual orientation, the marital infidelity, and the fact that information affecting her life was not available to her until now. The degree of deceit that has occurred is an important fact in whether trust and renegotiation can occur (though sometimes the "deceit" appears to be better described as a conspiracy of silence involving both partners).

Renegotiating the Marriage Contract

The period immediately following the disclosure or discovery is usually a tumultuous one. At first we husbands are so intensely involved in issues relating to our emerging or re-emerging gay or bisexual identity that we may be insensitive, or at best only reactive, to our wives' needs. In some cases the wives quickly make the decision to reject the "negative" characteristics they have now discovered in their husbands, and act to end the marriage. Less frequently the husbands move to that decision, often on the assumption that if they are indeed gay (rather than bisexual) then the marriage can't be continued. However, most often both partners experience a difficult period of ambivalence. Typically, we husbands are hoping things can work out, but unwilling to surrender our newly affirmed gay life; our wives are deeply hurting and longing for support. At this stage there is a tendency for all the previous and present problems in the marriage to be blamed on this particular issue. Marriage counseling (with counselors who are not heterosexist and are familiar with open marriages) or peer support groups are particularly useful at this phase.

After a year or so, if the wives are able to acknowledge and accept the husbands' bisexuality, our marriages typically move into a re-negotiation stage. Either the couple renegotiates the marriage as an acknowledged mixed-orientation marriage (often with extra-marital sexual experimentation on the wives' side) or they move toward an amicable divorce and friendship. If the couple survives two years of this renegotiation phase and the partners are still together, chances are they will remain together. It appears to take four or more years before mutually acceptable guidelines are developed and adhered, stabilitizing the marriage and securing intimacy.

What is learned during this process? The wives learn that they cannot control their husbands' activities, but that they can state their own needs clearly and firmly, set their limits of tolerance, and find ways to care for themselves when we are not available to them. We husbands gradually move through our identity crises and begin to take initiative to nurture our marriages. In my study, husbands in the couples that stayed together took more initiative in spending time and doing things with their wives, rather than relying on their wives to initiate or demand time. These husbands were also more empathic toward their wives, and had an appreciation of the pain their wives had experienced during the tumultuous years. While the wives learned to stop trying to control their husbands' gay relationships, the husbands learned to stop defending and to listen to the wives' feelings and needs, and to act in the interests of the marriage.

In a mixed-orientation marriage where open communication prevails, the couple may learn a responsive pattern of negotiation, compromise, and, most importantly, a deep appreciation of differences. The marriages gradually restabilize with each spouse understanding and respecting the other more fully, desiring to remain intimate and committed to the other, and developing secure areas of individual identity apart from the other.

The Closeted Husband

Not all of the couples who stay together move through open disclosure to a renegotiated relationship. A large portion seem to stabilize their marriages in an ongoing "mutual conspiracy of silence." Since it would not be ethical for me to contact the wives in such marriages, we have only their husbands' impressions of how these wives know about their husbands' double lives. It is clear that these husbands typically experience much greater conflict about their secretive gay activities, and do not develop as positive a gay/bisexual identity as do the husbands in the more open or acknowledged mixed-orientation marriages. Both husbands and wives in the latter marriages appear to achieve more optimal levels of mental health, communicativeness, and intimacy than do those in the secretive marriages, although some of these differences probably were present in the individuals even before the marriages, and are reinforced and amplified by the style of the marriage.

Stable Marriages, Positive Identities

Three further findings about mixed-orientation marriages are noteworthy. First, it is clear that marriages in which the husbands are actively bisexual can become stable marriages. Most of the subjects in the "acknowledged" marriages in my longitudinal study were still in the early years of renegotiation at the time of the first interviews. When contacted two years later, two-thirds of the acknowledged mixed-orientation marriages *and* two-thirds of the secretive marriages were still intact. Six years after the initial interviews, we did not find a single couple that were together at the two-year followup who had separated since. Interestingly, a number of couples previously in the "secretive" group had now become more open. Clearly, once the couples have survived the crisis it is possible for these marriages to stabilize and endure.

Second, although earlier research disputed this, it is now established that we bisexual men in open marriages can develop congruent sexual identities which affirm the gay component. A positive sexual identity is far more difficult to achieve in a traditional marriage in which the husband's bisexuality is not acknowledged by the wife.

Third, a comparison of couples married before the emergence of gay liberation and those married after showed increasingly positive attitudes towards gays for both husbands and wives in the latter group. More of these husbands accepted and disclosed their sexual orientations to their wives before marrying. For these couples it appears that the most serious crisis in the development of the marital relationship is not in the disclosure, but in the establishment of the primacy of the marital relationship, since they may not undergo a period in which the marriage relationship is sexually exclusive.

The Bisexual Wife

Large-scale studies of homosexuality suggest that a larger proportion of lesbians than gay men have been in heterosexual marriages. However there appear to be fewer bisexual wives than husbands actually living in mixed-orientation marriages. There are at least two reasons for this: first, the overall incidence of homosexuality is considerably lower in women than in men; second, lesbian/bisexual mixed-orientation marriages are less likely to survive than gay/bisexual mixed-orientation marriages.

Only one study exists describing heterosexual marriages in which the wife is lesbian or bisexual. Several differences emerged in that study, as compared to the above description of gay/bisexual men in heterosexual marriages. Not only did the women not think of themselves as lesbian or bisexual at the time of their marriage, the great majority of them had not had *any* homosexual experience prior to marriage (or, in most cases, until years into the marriage). This may be explained by the fact that women are socialized to do less sexual exploration than men (especially during the late 1960s when most of these women entered their marriages), and the fact that these women were three years younger than their male counterparts when they entered their marriages. For the majority of these women their first awareness and exploration of lesbian sexuality occurred when they already had marriage and family commitments. Thus, for the majority of bisexual wives, as for the minority of bisexual husbands who first explored gay sex *after* marriage, a higher incident of dissolution of the marriage occurred.

Further, women seem to have more difficulty tolerating multiple relationships than do men. Perhaps partly because of internal conflicts about extramarital sex, 76 percent of those wives who had extra-marital lesbian experiences kept these a secret from their husbands. Most of the wives who did tell their husbands were unable to negotiate with their husbands for open marriages. It appears that the lesbian/bisexual marriages seldom moved to or through the negotiation stage that is so important to the survival of the mixed-orientation marriages.

Another difference in male and female socialization that perhaps affects the survival of mixed-orientation lesbian/bisexual marriages concerns the development of intimacy skills. Men tend to develop their deepest emotionally intimate relationships with women. Women tend to develop theirs with other women, as well as with their husbands. Lesbians/bisexuals in marriages report more *emotional* attachments with their homosexual friends than do their male counterparts. The gay male scene typically accepts recreational sex, while women's socialization stresses relationship-oriented sex. The married gay is not likely to see his gay buddies as a replacement for the intimacy he has with his wife. By contrast, when a married woman enters a lesbian relationship she is likely to have already had a deeply intimate friendship with the woman, which then developed into a sexual relationship. The wives' belief in monogamy, and their dissatisfaction with men's weaker training in intimacy skills, lead them to think of their lesbian relationships as replacements for marriage.

A final speculation concerning the earlier and more frequent dissolution of lesbian/bisexual marriages has to do with the fact that when couples divorce, the women are usually assured of having custody of the children. One of the reasons bisexual men give for staying in their marriages is that they don't want to lose their home life and children. Women are less likely to lose the children and home life (especially if they have keep secret their bisexual identity so that it can't be used against them in the divorce proceedings). The fear of losing the children may, of course, be a factor in the lower disclosure rates of lesbians to their husbands.

It seems clear from the above discussion that bisexual wives are more likely than bisexual husbands to terminate their marriages because of conflicts arising from their bisexuality. However, it must be remembered that very little is known about lesbians in heterosexual marriages, partly because it is so difficult to find a sample of these couples when they are still together. It is possible, then, that there may be a hidden population of such marriages which may or may not fit the above description.

The Meaning of Intimacy

By now it should be clear that there is no single pattern for the relationships of persons in mixed-orientation marriages. Bisexuals in heterosexual marriages live a wide variety of lifestyles varying on at least four dimensions:

—the degree of self-affirmation about being bisexual.
—the degree of secrecy or openness about their gay/lesbian

activities, with spouse, family, friends, and the community.

—the degree of comfort (vs. guilt) about deviation from monogamous heterosexual marriage as the model for intimate relationships.

—the awareness of and sensitivity to gender roles.

It is crucial to recognize that the conflicts experienced by persons in these marriages are not simply conflicts regarding sexual orientation. Rather, bisexuals in these marriages struggle with redefining intimacy for themselves, expanding its meaning beyond the narrow confines that our society has sanctioned in heterosexual love. Homophobia and the sex role stereoptypes that inhibit deep friendships between men, or between women, are problems for heterosexuals as well, though gay, lesbian, and bisexual persons may be more sensitized to these issues. The issues with which these couples struggle are merely intensified reflections of the more general crisis about intimacy in our culture.

Resources: Some Organizations That May Provide Support to Persons in Mixed-Orientation Marriages

One of the most helpful resources for partners in mixed-orientation marriages who feel alone and overwhelmed is a peer support group that includes others struggling with the same issues. Most large cities now have support groups for gay married men. The quickest way to locate them is to call the local Gay Hotline or Gay Switchboard. Many of the organizations also have a rap group for the wives also. To the best of my knowledge, at present there are no groups solely for lesbian wives.

Since bisexuals often feel their marital situation is not understood in either the gay or straight community, groups which consciously attempt to foster dialog between gays and straights are often supportive. For women, consciousness raising groups of chapters of NOW may be helpful. For men, local affiliates of NOCM are usually supportive. To obtain local addresses contact:

National Organization for Women
1401 New York Ave., N.W.
Washington, D.C. 20005 (202) 347-2279

National Organization for Changing Men
794 Pennsylvania Avenue
Pittsburgh, PA 15221 (412) 371-8007

142 David R. Matteson

I want to thank the men in two Chicago support groups for married bisexuals (Gay & Married Men, and Review) and the men and women in two workshops at the 10th National Conference on Men and Masculinity (St. Louis, June 1985) for their suggestions and personal anecdotes. My thanks also to my wife for her help in editing and for her continuing support and love.

Joining

Jim Long

"Which one of them d'you suppose plays the woman?" I'd heard that phrase many time over the years, but maybe I never listened to the words before. Or, maybe the words rang strongly in my head because I wanted a real relationship, and the fear lurked in my brain that it would be said about me at some future time. Don's saying the words was nothing new. He wore his homophobia the same way he wore his clothes, poorly and with too many gaps.

Don was a dumpling, one of those spirits that seemed to me to have jumped into the simmering stew of life head first, without much purpose in living. He ate constantly, and thus, came to physically look like the analogy that I saw in him. He made life miserable for his family, as well as for those of us who worked under him. He was a self-centered, thoughtless but often good-natured dumpling. My crews on the job were usually made up intentionally by me of both gay and straight men and women. In groups, even in twos, Don was cordial, gregarious, good-natured. But if he would catch one of the crew whom he thought to be gay alone, he would call them "cocksucker," "queer," "faggot," those words we all knew too well, but not words you liked to hear while doing your job, (and never within hearing of witnesses, so he could deny saying it).

So when Don said out loud to me "Which one d'you suppose plays the woman?", I was even more startled to have *heard* his words. These were ugly words from a man I didn't even like, much less respect. But I heard them, and for the first time in my life really thought that I understood what the words meant. In this bigoted straight man's eyes the people he was referring to didn't fit into any cubbyhole of his experience, and that was threatening.

The recent object of ridicule had been two elderly queen-types, too much jewelry, too much cologne, blazing grass-green suits with rhinestone buttons. I didn't automatically feel comfortable in their presence, either, but for quite different reasons. However, they had lots of money, something that Don did respect. So, he was genuinely confused. Money, success, status, all belonged to this pair of human parrots, this couple of people who chose to live together. In Don's eyes there had to be standard roles to play, and these men didn't fit well into those roles. One must be the husband, and the other the wife. One dominant, the other recessive. We are taught that from childhood on, and not only do the Don's of the world buy into that philosophy and cultivate it, so do we as gay people, very often.

I had a ten year marriage, and had friends whom I had been in love with, and none of those had given me the kind of real relationship I longed for. But those experiences helped me know a lot about what I *didn't* want in a relationship. By knowing what I didn't want, I could better judge what I wanted. I wanted equality and communication, right up there on the list next to love and loyalty. I didn't want role-playing in a relationship; I'm too stubborn to be dominated and too conscientious to dominate. I was not choosing to be a husband *or* a wife, any more than Don's objects of ridicule were, but rather a life-partner with someone. But our society, even though it is changing, doesn't have accepted categories for such relationships yet.

There isn't a time in my memory when I wasn't gay. Even as a small child, I knew. When Jimmy Stricklin walked past my house the summer when I was five, wearing tight jeans, no shirt and his fishing boots open, I *knew* how attractive he was. He would pass by my house each morning about 10:00 o'clock, when he had returned from running his fishing lines in the river, walk up town to the store and buy soda pop and a Snickers. I was very aware of his schedule, and anticipated his daily trips. He was just the best-looking thirteen year old that I knew, and he made me feel different inside. Now I recognize the feelings as sexual, but then, at five and six, it seemed like a strange sense of anticipation inside, a yearning that needed to be filled; something strikingly different went on in my insides when I saw him walk by and I tingled inside.

Jimmy Stricklin had a cousin his age who came to visit every summer. They would fish and hunt together, and had an enviable friendship. By the time I was seven, I had noticed the same feelings for his cousin Foxy as I felt for Jimmy. Both were muscled and tanned, and I just liked being around them and watching them work or play.

There had to be strong attractions to those boys, because I put up with a lot to be around them. They never invited me, I always showed up where they were, and they didn't want some little kid hanging around. Usually I brought along Betty, Jimmy's little sister, too, which meant two suspected spies to watch out for. Usually the big boys would tolerate us for awhile, then find a way to run us off. To make conditions worse, Foxy had a real thing for being mean to little kids. Looking back from the standpoint of an adult, I recognized him as a battered and abused child with very little self-esteem. Back then however, he was just a bully in a very attractive body. To feel better about himself, he would hit, knock down or humiliate someone smaller.

Foxy and Jimmy were the attractions and I'd go for the show. I enjoyed seeing them wrestle, play ball, sweat. But when the crowd got rowdy, I'd go home. Sometimes I'd just go far enough away that I wasn't a temptation to be picked on, but could still watch. However, one time I misjudged the show and Foxy caught me.

The yard was full of kids, cousins of the pair of my attraction. I was there, ready to play any game to be around the big boys, maybe gain their tempered attention. We were in a good game of tag, and everyone was in fine spirits. We all played hard, and the big boys were beautiful with no shirts and lots of sweat and laughter. Suddenly a basket appeared from somewhere, brought out by Jimmy or Foxy. Eggs. Old, rotten eggs from a nest that a hen had forgotten months ago. The boys knew quite well the eggs were rotten. The rest of us kids just knew that they were eggs.

War broke out. It was the big kids with the eggs against the little kids with no eggs. It was still fun, and we knew enough to stay out of range, even though both of the boys were capable of pretty mean pitches with rocks and dirt clods. Soon, Foxy combined tag with the egg war. He would chase then throw. Or, in the instance with me, chase, catch the victim by the arm and smash a rotten egg on the side of his head. My head.

I was so humiliated. I ran all the way home crying, hearing Foxy's laughter dying away in the distance behind me. How could someone who looked so good, who I admired so, physically, do that to me? My attraction for him wilted in seconds, replaced by my hurt, not understanding the heat of the moment, the passion of the chase, nor Foxy's need to feel superior to something or someone in his life. All I knew was that I didn't want to be around him again. I didn't go back again, either, but I continued to admire that beautiful body and those piercing eyes from a distance over the years.

Within, I knew that I was attracted to men, all of those early years, and my experiences taught me indirectly. I didn't have ways of telling others. I didn't express my desires and attractions, but wanted very much to be able to do so with someone in my life. I wanted a life-mate, and through years of coming to know myself, I learned to be trusting of others. I learned too, that pretty things don't always come in pretty packages.

When I met my own true love, I first saw the pretty package, and then became attracted to the person within. We have different anniversaries that we celebrate. I met *him* on Halloween at a party. "What a neat guy, why can't I meet someone like him?", I said to myself, But he has no memory of me that evening at all. I was invisible. *His* anniversary of our meeting is Thanksgiving. We were both guests of the same host for dinner, and his curiosity and interest were stirred. We exchanged addresses, that old custom of gentlemen everywhere.

I started dropping by to visit Josh. We actually dated. We'd go to community plays, or out for vegetarian food. Lots of times we'd cook at his place. He had been seeing someone before me, and I was actually horning in. I'd been dumped painfully by a would-be love affair that had never left the ground. But we saw each other for six months with regularity and passion, spending nights reading books out loud together, walking in the woods, visiting friends. We're from very different backgrounds, but share the same values and aspirations. We found a spiritual bond that seems like it has always been there, like we have known each other for all of eternity. Maybe we have.

Neither of us wanted to be a wife or a husband. There aren't terms or words for our roles. We knew we wanted to be joined together, to be bonded in a way that we could look back on and celebrate together in years ahead. We wanted an official *beginning* to our relationship, and we wanted to express verbally what we were willing to promise to the other. Our months of dating had helped us be sure of what we felt and what we wanted. We chose May first for our day of joining.

Josh went back home to visit for two weeks. Home is often a place you left years ago, but where a lot of who you are is hanging around in the dark corners of your old closets and rooms. Home can give perspective at important times in your life. So he went away for that time, leaving me for my own perspective-gathering. It was the longest we've been apart, and it took effort for both of us, even though we knew the advantages of gaining perspective.

During the two weeks, I worked on the spring garden, and built a new little pergola in the middle of the garden in preparation for our joining day. He came back, and we made our other preparations. We cleared the day of chores, unplugged the phones and put away our daily routines. We invited a witness for our special day, someone who was a dear friend, to hear and witness our commitments to each other.

When the day arrived, it was full of silliness and excitement. We were both self-conscious about contriving this ceremony, and yet very dedicated to the purpose of it. The appointed hour came and our witness arrived, bringing a delightful cake he had baked, all decorated with spring flowers for after the joining. We put on robes, not because they were robes, but because we wanted something plain, something that made us as equal as possible. We each wore a garland of leaves on our heads, and we walked to the pergola and sat down.

Invitations were given to the farm spirits and to the Spirit within us, to join us. We verbally exchanged what we were promising to each other . . . to possess the other's love, to be loved, to be honest, to give freely, to care and grow together as persons and as spirits. Our witness tied our hands together in one knot, to signify our bond. We kissed. He kissed us both, took our pictures, and we retired to have his wonderful cake.

Our day of joining is very special to us, even after all of these years. We always acknowledge our day to each other, celebrate it in some way. It signifies our beginning, our commencing life together. We neither one play the wife nor husband. We're not married, in the sense that society recognizes, nor do our close friends even recognize our special day. But we were joined together as partners, as lovers, many years ago. We choose to nurture and cultivate that relationship in the same way that any other relationship must be cultivated. We love, and after all, what else is there?

Pictures From a Memory Book

Charlie R. Braxton

I was around ten years old when I first began to pay any real attention to the fact that, aside from the pony tails and dresses, girls really were/are quite different from the fellas. My best friend and road buddy Carey, whom we all called Spat—don't ask me why—stole a couple of girlie magazines from his older brother simply because we were curious as to what was all of the fuss the older guys were making over girls. We couldn't understand it all. We knew that the older girls like Sue and Jolene and Paula were built different from the girls our age. They looked more like our Moms only younger and to some extent a lot prettier (even though we wouldn't admit it to ourselves). None of the girls who were our age were built like them. So what was so different about them, we wondered. We thought that maybe books like *Playboy* could tell us . . . or at least I did at the time . . . boy was I ever wrong!

We all met around the back of Spat's house just under the huge wooden stairway with open panels that allowed the sun to seep through to the grass and us. We called this place our secret hideout—it was the only place our moms never thought to look for us and we loved it. After making sure that the coast was clear we sat down and began to carefully examine the nude women with the air brushed breasts and waxed pubic hair. I remember now how sorely disappointed I was upon looking at the buxom blonde playmates all sprawled across the pages of the magazine. "Where were the Black women?", I asked, "How come they don't have any Black women in here?" Spat looked at me utterly annoyed and said, "I don't know and don't really care." The rest of the fellas howled at Spat's snappy remarks (he was known in the neighborhood for his wisecracks) while I just sat there and looked confused. I kept thinking to myself as I thumbed through the pages looking at various pictures of nude white women, is this it? Is this what all women are supposed to look like naked; will my wife look like this when and if I get married? None of these girls look real! They all reminded me of those Barbie dolls that little girls used to play with, all white and waxen with that stupid come hither look on their face. This can't be where it's at, if so, it sho' nuff ain't for the kid (meaning me). Where were the girls who looked like Sue and Jolene and Paula and Sheila . . . where are the girls whose hips spread peacock proud and breasts come in all shapes and sizes . . . where are the women who I saw do the Bugaloo and Belly-rub on the porch every Saturday evening at Miss Annie's Cafe? These were the women that I held close to my heart because something about them keeps me in tune with myself . . . affirms my reality . . . and makes me whole again.

It is extremely dangerous to be charmed by an image for it's images that really run the world and most if not all images are controlled by ruthless men who rape the minds of the poor and ignorant via the mass media for sole sake of power and profits. At the time Spat, the fellas and myself were looking at the so-called men's magazines none of us could realize the dual exploitation that was taking place. But it didn't stop there for me. In my future there was to be more . . . much more, only this time it didn't involve magazines.

At fourteen my hormones kicked in full force and I was feeling the results hard and fast. Spat and I were still the best of friends only the rest of our crew had changed slightly. We had dropped Dave, Daryl and Joe White, in turn we added Shorty, Tob and a guy by the name of Danny Smith whom we called Smut because he was, as my folks used to say, the color of Jesus himself. Dark, dark black. Most of the guys in my crowd had girlfriends with the exception of Smut and myself. We were loners. Most of the talk we had revolved around girls and ultimately . . . sex. I would sit and listen as the guys would swap various myths about sex and sexual conquests. As each guy told his who, when, where and how I kept thinking, "Hotdog, I can't wait 'til it's my turn!" One day I made the stupid mistake of telling the fellas this and much to my surprise Shorty started laughing and saying "Nigger please! You know damn well you can't fuck!" (Shorty was also known for his very short vocabulary.) Without thinking I retorted, "Oh yeah, well bring yo' bald headed sista over here and we'll see." The rest of fellas howled in delight as Spat slipped me five and Shorty burned in embarrassment singed in anger. I walked away looking triumphant on the outside but bruised and battered on the inside. And the really bad thing about it was, I couldn't understand why.

In junior high school I was known among the fellas, even though I didn't have a girlfriend, for having the coolest raps in the county. I got this reputation because I used to write love letters and poems for some of the fellas who were too "macho" to say what they didn't think they could feel. Sometimes, I would even pretend to be one of my buddies and talk on the phone for some of them who were meeting a girl over the phone for the first time. But as far as me actually talking to a girl on my own behalf—face to face—I couldn't. I was just too shy to do it. I suppose the real reason why I felt this way toward asking girls for a date was the fact that almost every girl that I had ever asked to "be my lady" (goodness what a sexist thing to say—I repent) I was turned down cold. They would always say things like "I'm sorry Charlie (shades of Starkist tuna, Batman!!!!!), you're real sweet dude n' all but you're just not my type." At first I thought that there was something seriously wrong with me . . . you know like . . . bad breath, body odor, severe dandruff . . . stuff like that. So after a hundred showers straight in a row, several bars of soap, a bottle or two of Head and Shoulders and tons of cologne I tried again. Still no dice. So I thought, maybe it's my personality, perhaps I need to change. So I began to read books on how to improve your personality, how to improve your image and how to make friends—self-improvement sort of stuff. I learned a whole lot from some of those books but apparently not enough to impress any girl into dating me.

Eventually, I got around to asking some of my close female friends what is it that girls look for in a man. Like any subjective questionnaire, I got all kinds of personal answers. Some of the more common answers were: girls prefer men with long hair (Afros were in big at the time), nice bodies, good personalities (I already had that covered) and handsome. After gathering this "valuable" info I grew an Afro, lifted weights, read more of those "I'm Okay, You're Okay" type books and used as much Clearasil as I could buy (I had bad skin back then—too much chocolate candy). Little did I know at the time, I was on the verge of being a serious victim. Not so much because I was growing an Afro or lifting weights or clearing my skin or reading those silly "how to get what you want" books . . . none of this was bad in and of itself. Self-improvement is a normal and healthy thing for any and everybody as long as he or she is doing it for their own satisfaction, not just to please someone else, which was exactly what I was trying to do. I was trying to fit an image, someone else's conception of what a man is supposed to be . . . and it just wasn't working.

By the fall of '77 I entered high school a totally new person . . . or so I thought. Where I was once a short haired, skinny, shy dude whose face looked like the flip side of a Nestle's Crunch bar, I was now a muscular, clear complexioned kid with an outgoing personality and a huge Afro to boot. As for my personality improvements, I learned one thing that I believe to this day has made me a much better person, and that was I learned to listen to and talk to women openly and honestly. No bullshit lines and half baked confessions of love. Any kind of real relationship with a man or woman is based on love (real love), trust and mutual respect. With women, men must learn to demonstrate these three things by learning to open up and be vulnerable to them emotionally or else our relationship with them will fall like a house of cards.

So there I was, the "new" Charlie Braxton with a whole lot of love to share with some lucky girl. This time I just knew I would find somebody to go with (our term for going steady). But much to my dismay I still couldn't find a girlfriend even though this time most of the girls I asked did tell me that I was cute. Again I tried to tell myself that there must be something I am not doing right . . . maybe if I just keep trying a little harder . . . do the right things . . . talk the right talk . . . wear the right clothes (my parents were very poor and couldn't afford all of the expensive styles and name brands that most of the "hip dudes" were wearing at the time) . . . maybe if I did all of these things maybe it would change. It didn't.

By the time the school year had rolled around it became absolutely crystal clear why I couldn't get girls to date me. My disability. I'll never forget the day I first realized this. It was on a Saturday in late May, I was madly infatuated with a new girl named Gina who had moved into our neighborhood, and I wanted to talk to her real bad—my Mom said that I was in "Puppy Love" with her. Maybe that was true but at the time I didn't think so. As far as I was concerned this was it . . . love at first sight. But I had a slight problem, I was absolutely scared to ask her out on a date. The word was, through the home-boy grapevine, that Gina had already turned down John and Obie, two of the most popular dudes in school. And most of the guys in my crowd who tried to approach her got turned down so fast it would make a fish's head swim . . .

Somehow Gina and I befriended one another. At this point I don't remember which one of us initiated the friendship. (I think that it started over a class project that we were assigned to work on together.) We would call each other on the phone and talk to each other for hours about our problems, our dreams (Gina wanted to be an artist and I a writer) and fears. We were close but she never suspected that I was in love with her. And I never told her . . . I couldn't find the nerve. I remember one time when I did her a much needed favor for school and she gave me a quick kiss on the lips. I remember how good her soft full liips (Gina had lips like Sade or Chaka Khan) felt pressing against mine and, for a brief second, I almost melted like ice in an oven . . .

I couldn't take the heat. I smiled at Gina, said you're welcome and walked away. Later that night I fantasized about Gina and I having long intimate talks, walking hand in hand and making beautiful love together with me in the missionary position (you know the position; God, what a sexist way to make love!). Then suddenly it occurred to me that I can't walk hand in hand with her, I need my hands to hold on to my crutches while I walk. And as for assuming the missionary position, forget it, I have a hard enough time getting my legs to move so I can walk (I have Cerebral Palsy, a disease that affects the brain's ability to coordinate muscle functions properly.). Suddenly the realization of Shorty's words hit me like a ton of bricks. I thought to myself Shorty's right, there's no way that I could stack up to all those other guys sexually . . . there's just no way. No wonder I couldn't find a girl to go steady with, they all thought that I couldn't make love to them (most of the girls that I knew in high school were sexually active and made no bones about it).

There is something strange about the way a lot of women view the sexuality of handicapped males. For my part, most of the women that I've talked to about it sort of naturally assume that because I am unable to walk that must mean that I am unable to use my so-called third leg. Even today, in the so-called age of enlightenment, I still get those same stupid assumptions only now they ask my wife . . . at first these kinds of things used to tickle me to death but now that I am a little older and a little wiser I usually just feel real sorry for them. I pity them because they are pitiful. Their minds having been so roped, robbed and raped by this vicious racist/sexist Capitalist system, they fail to see the humanity within myself and my compatriots almost in the same way that a racist fails to see the humanity within the Black/Brown/Red/Yellow/Jewish flesh that he or she has come to hate so.

For me, a disabled non-sexist male, the struggle is not to overcome some poor sister or brother who, due to no fault of their own, refuses to recognize my humanity. Nor is it a struggle to get every female in America and beyond to sample the virtues of sex with the disabled. To me the struggle is about changing the images that say to the world that a real man (i.e. a sexually desirable man) is "free, white and 21" with two good eyes, ears, arms and legs; has a huge penis, lots of money and power galore. This can only come about once we have totally transformed this Capitalist system and replaced it with a more just and humane one. Until then love and sex, the image and the act will always be at odds with one another.

A Date?

Arthur Levine

Gay men do not know how to date. I say this, of course, meaning "*I don't know how to date,*" but for a few pages I'll take the liberty of projecting. See, I had this date last night. But actually, I wasn't sure it was a date until it was over. I wasn't even sure that I wanted it to be a date. And, in fact, maybe it wasn't technically a date at all.

Oy. I've been going on like this for a week now. Changing the sheets because, well, they were due to be changed anyway. Then making sure I had plans for the morning after with other friends . . . just in case. Since I actually called this guy up and made date-like plans, I've been doing more flip-flopping than Greg Louganis! Until then my "date" had just been someone I'd met at a few parties—a tall man with neatly kept dreds, round intellectual glasses, snug black turtleneck sweaters, and interesting opinions on Spike Lee and Springsteen's early records. Until I made that phone call, I knew that I liked him. I also knew that he had forearms of death. Now I felt as if I didn't know anything. Did I want him to become a buddy—someone to fill the void left by the diaspora of my college friends? Or did I want him to be the torrid love-god of my dreams? Or both? Why the confusion?

I think part of the answer can be had by examining a question posed by the movie *When Harry Met Sally*, a film that asks "Can men and women be friends?" Harry says no. Sally says yes. By the end of the film, Harry has come around to Sally's point of view, but by that time they've fallen in love, gotten involved, and left the meat of the question unanswered.

Now I have to say right off that for me the specific question, "Can men and women be friends?" has never been too puzzling. Starting in kindergarten, my best friend was a girl with a long, thick braid named Amy. We were lumped together as the "smart kids" and though she took to chasing me around the tiny desks demanding kisses, our bond was purely platonic from the start. We did art projects together using yarn and popsicle sticks and sometimes we "checked" our homework against each other. It was a simple friendship born of two over-achieving, brainy personalities and agnostic, culturally jewish backgrounds.

Of course, the other kids in our elementary school would have none of it. In later grades, when we sat next to each other on the bus to district band practice (I was first clarinet, she was second) the other kids would sing "Amy and Arthur sitting in a tree, k-i-s-s-i-n-g." Like a gestapo of the social order these kids instinctually tried to humiliate us out of our friendship using sexual imagery in their taunts that none of us could have understood. With remarkable idiot-savant prescience they anticipated the "Harry and Sally" question and acted to keep the lines of friendship in order. There were to be no alliances across gender lines—lines that would supposedly be left clear for heterosexual romantic involvement. But Amy and I held on and took our gleeful revenge by privately making fun of our tormentors in ways that we thought were impossibly clever and precocious. We proved that we could be friends and laugh in the face (albeit one chubby with baby fat, in need of braces) of cultural norms.

But my experience with Amy did not teach me anything about dealing with boys. In straight culture boys are *supposed* to be friends; from the normative perspective it's anything else that would be questioned. The real issue brought up for me by *When Harry Met Sally* would more accurately (though less euphoniously) be phrased, "Can one be friends with a person who is the gender of one's sexual preference?"

This was one of the things on my mind as my "date" and I sat down to see a sad British film about a romance that ends tragically. An educated, upper class "gentleman" visits a farm and falls in love with a "peasant" girl, but in the end he is unable to take her back to the city and marry her. She dies. He lives a life of emptiness and moral bankruptcy.

Fortunately my "date" and I are both the sort of mushy-hearted intellectuals who love to talk that kind of movie to death. We vilified the spineless British fellow for his inability to take risks. My "date" agreed with my analogy that love is like an exceptionally difficult gymnastics routine—you can't achieve the highest levels of beauty without constantly putting your neck on the line. Our knees brushed under the small wooden table as the check came. It was too early to go home and too early to face the decision of who would go to which home, when. So we went for a walk in the thick August humidity, talking and bumping shoulders as we went. It was so tense, and so overtly innocent, I kept thinking of the first time I fell in love.

It happened my senior year of high school with a straight boy named David. David was six-foot-two, with soccer player's thighs, a slow, shy smile and a habit of straightening his fine blond hair by running two fingers back from his forehead. Being near him made me feel so close to paralysis that I went into social overdrive in defense; I cracked jokes, I danced, I did imitations . . . I was never still unless he picked me up and put me on his lap (another disconcerting habit he had). And then I'd be still as the earth, terrified that anyone would see how this struck to my core. I became fluent in the foreign language of straight-boy affection. I'd ask, "New contact lenses, David? That color blue is not found in nature!" He would respond with tickling, wrestling or the patented "smile"—all equally, satisfyingly wonderful.

So with him enigmatically silent and physical; me energetically verbal and kinetic, we struck a solid balance. We would go to movies on Friday nights and drive back to his house full of banter, laughing. Then we'd go up to his room and put on jazz and a black light and just sit quietly for hours, holding hands. The intensity of our thumbs circling one another—my hand quietly engulfed by his—was enormous. But with these circles we defined our limits, our rules. No speaking. No questions. No words. Only the saxophone and our hands connecting us. No kissing. No admission that this was at all unusual. And when I inevitably left at 2:00 or 3:00 in the morning my throat would hurt, unused. But I would still drive home convinced I was unbelievably lucky and blessed to be able to feel that deeply for someone and to have it returned.

Which is not to say that I saw this as a perfect situation. Yes, I sometimes wished that we were boyfriends; I wished we could have confirmed our unspoken connection with words, whispered vows, public declarations. I wished we could have had sex. But my fear of mis-step and my determination to preserve the unique and powerful bond we did have drove me to accept the terms of our friendship: perfect integrity within strict limitations. Hell, I didn't care as long as I got to hold his hand. I simply became practiced at maintaining a gap between sexual attractions and sexual action. It was an inevitable side effect of growing up in the closet.

My "date" and I reached the Hudson River and turned up a side street so we could sit on some steps. I talked about my group of close friends—all women—and how it was frustrating to me that I seemed to be able to reach my ideal of closeness and intimacy there, but not in love and rarely with men at all. (Was I testing him? What response was I fishing for?) He said he didn't consider himself to "do friendship" well, especially with men. Especially with sexual tension involved. Gay men, he said, were rarely clear with each other about their "agenda," rarely open enough about their feelings to see clear to an honest friendship without the residue of lingering sexual tension covertly undermining things.

We sat in silence for a short while that seemed long. The traffic hurtled by on West Street. Laughter came up from the crowds by the piers. A couple entered the building across the street.

"I'd like to be your friend." I said finally. "Although I have to say . . . your forearms kill me."

He didn't say anything, but he wrapped the aforementioned forearms around my waist.

"So where do we go from here?" I mumbled.

"To the subway, I think." he said. I laughed. We hugged and let the feeling of vulnerability slide away into relief and end-of-the-evening tiredness.

"I'm not sure how this will turn out either," he said finally. "But I'd like to be your friend too. Anything else would be gravy." Then we walked hand and hand to the subway where we each rode home—alone.

And at home the good feelings burn a question mark on my bedroom ceiling. Is it true that gay men don't have gay male friends, only unrealized lovers? Or do we have the potential to use the skills we've won the hard way with the help of our Amys and our Davids? Can we answer the "Harry and Sally" question in our own gay way, making conscious choices about where to take our relationships? Or do we have to learn to grope around blindly like everyone else?

I come up with no answer, only my "date's" smile hanging in place of the question mark, like the grin of the Cheshire Cat. I hope we have the time to figure it out for ourselves—slowly and cautiously if we have to. I hope we have the courage of gymnasts, to throw ourselves into space with only our inner vision to guide us. And I hope we see another movie soon—one with a happy ending.

Choiceful Sex, Intimacy and Relationships for Gay and Bisexual Men

Jeff Beane

Gay and bisexual men are becoming increasingly aware of the difficulties we have in being intimate with each other and in establishing committed relationships. We are also beginning to examine the tyrannical role sex has played in our lives and relationships over the past twenty years. Through the men's movement, psychotherapy and other self-help methods, we are discovering that many of the roots of these dilemmas stem from our early gender and sex role socialization as males. Some of us want more choice than traditional socialization gives us in how we define ourselves and how we feel about ourselves as men. We want more options about how we relate to other gay and bisexual men, including the ability to form lasting relationships that are loving, intimate and sexually fulfilling. Having more choice necessitates becoming aware of how we were taught by our families and culture to be male and the avenues of change which are available.

This article is an overview of these concepts and does not address their comprehensive nature. My information and perspective come from being a gay man, a gestalt psychotherapist, and a participant and leader in the feminist men's movement for fifteen years. The feminist men's movement has studied the impact of male gender and sex role conditioning on gay, bisexual, and heterosexual men. It has been an invaluable source of information, encouragement, support, and healing for men who are in the process of change. Gestalt psychotherapy with its emphasis on awareness, contact, phenomonology and an I-Thou relationship between client and therapist has been an invaluable tool for me personally as well as professionally. Perhaps the richest vein of knowledge has been that of my own journey from being a Pennsylvania Dutch country boy in the '50s to a healer, social activist, and writer from West Hollywood in the 1990s.

To illustrate that gay and bi men have a difficult time getting close to each other and establishing relationships, I'd like you to meet Joe, a hypothetical client. Joe came to psychotherapy twelve months ago with the following complaints: at thirty-four he had been out of the closet for twelve years, but had never had a long term relationship, his intimate relationships with gay men lasted one to three months, were romantic and highly sexualized. His relationships were intense and intellectual, with little emotional closeness, or direct, open, communication and problem solving. He was concerned about his frequent use of 976 numbers for sex and as a method of meeting gay men. He was a successful professional, but was confused about whether he really enjoyed his work. A written exercise early in therapy revealed lots of "shoulds," constant references to what was right or wrong, and particular attention to what others thought of him or his actions. In the sessions he seemed stiff, physically and emotionally controlled, very analytic, tough, and at times a little abrasive.

How It Began—Boys Will Be Boys

Boys will be boys because that's what we were taught. We had little choice in that matter. The forties, fifties, and early sixties were post WWII, McCarthyism, conformity, starched shirts on Sunday school days, and serious bar mitzvahs. Families were nuclear then—dad was the center, home his kingdom, mom and the kids his serfs.

Around age six, hugs with dad turned to distant handshakes, lest too much closeness develop between these two males. Too much time in the house with mom created the "sissy" scare, so outside to play (usually sports) with the boys (girls not allowed). If he got hit with the ball, god forbid he cry about it, he had to be tough and take it like a man even though he was a boy. Being scared of the dark or being alone at night, got responses like "Hey, you're eight now, got to learn how to be on your own." "Scaredy cat, you're acting like a girl, boys aren't afraid." "Stop that crying, or I'll give you something to cry about." Additional training in how not to express feelings. After all you're ten. "It was only a hamster, we'll get you another one." "Don't you think you should be playing outside with the other boys at recess, instead of doing art inside with the girls?"

So from our early training we learned that it was not okay for two males to be close to each other, in any form. To acknowledge pain or to cry was to betray our gender. It was more important to act like a man than be one's self. There were rules to be followed in order to be a man. It was more masculine to be distant and detached, than close and caring.

As we grew into adolescence we were faced with the terrors of junior high school. Age twelve brought rules for how to walk and carry books. Athletics loomed larger. Got to want to kill the other team. By now girls were completely off limits as friends, yet clandestine forays to the girls' locker room were a sign of real budding masculinity. The sensitive men who taught English, French, and humanities were clearly not as manly as the coaches who taught math, history and chemistry. Natural curiosity about what was happening to other boys' bodies led to downturned eyes in the shower lest our wonderings be discovered.

The rules were confusing. Our roles as males began to focus more and more on impressing and getting girls. We were taught not to respect girls, yet our masculinity was directly tied to how we were succeeding with them. There was no one to talk to.

Senior High Pressures

In high school impressing others with athletic letters, class presidencies, or grades became the signs of true masculinity. Sex education was a parental question about how babies were made. Lots of jokes and teasing about how far she let you get on the first date were signs of masculine development. Tales about dates imagined or real were as regular as pop quizzes in algebra. Emphasis was always the score: how many, how far, and whether she had big bazookas or not. To be different at all was not to fit in, was to withdraw into fantasy, books or work.

Very little of our early training addressed self-esteem or identity based on being ourselves or our intrinsic worth as male human beings. Most early male gender role training in fact absolutely discouraged being in touch with one's physical or emotional experience. Closeness or tenderness towards another male was "queer." We were taught that other males were the enemy, not to be trusted, and whenever possible we were supposed to beat them in whatever the activity was.

The messages about sexual turn-on were primarily about her looks, body part specifications and packaging, and had nothing to do with closeness, caring or affection. Our early teachings about sexuality included doing it with easy girls, as long as you weren't thinking about marrying one of them. The further one got with as many girls as possible added notches to one's masculinity rating. Clearly they were objects, not persons. We were taught to focus only on our sexual experience, not our partners', and that the entire purpose was physical gratification which had little to do with emotional closeness.

An Extra Burden

Most of us who knew we preferred the attention, closeness and affection of other males, knew it only in conjunction with anxiety, discomfort, and fear. If we dared to fantasize about or look desirously at the bodies of other males (this early sex role learning generalized), depression and self-hate were not far behind. A major task for many of us who recognized our attraction to other males was convincing ourselves and others that it wasn't so. There were no positive role models for us. Information was overwhelmingly negative and stereotypic. Effeminate, hairdressing, child-molesting, lonely old men were the negative images we tried to shut out. Again, there was no one to talk to.

The Role of Gay Liberation

Gay liberation was the beginning of many wonderful changes for millions of lesbians and gay men around the world. The personal liberation and sexual freedom of the seventies were essential ingredients to a broad base of positive self identification for gay and bisexual men. But there were inevitable pitfalls for us because of our male socialization.

Prior to gay liberation, most gay and bisexual men were confused about their identities, often had low esteem and negative self-images, were full of hurt, anger, fear and sadness, and had few skills for getting support from or being close to other men. This lack of positive gay identity, the restrictiveness of the male role, and the lack of intimacy between men set the stage for rocky relationships between gay men and for sexuality to be glorified and over emphasized.

Sex has always been an antidote for pain, loneliness, depression, isolation and low self esteem. Gay and bi men were not the first and will not be the last to use sexuality that way. Men in general have been socialized to be turned on primarily by physical attributes, gay and bi men did not escape the training, but merely applied the principles to each other.

Sex with no relationship, intimacy or concern for the other can be a trap as much as it can be liberating. What turns many gay men on sexually has been based primarily on physical attributes and the physical aspects of sexual behavior. Physical elements of the sexual experience—like excitement, intensity, and euphoria—are all natural parts of healthy sexual functioning. The issue for gay and bi men is the degree to which these aspects have been emphasized and the degree to which intimacy, closeness, nurturing, emotion and love have been minimized or excluded. It has been very easy for some of us to continue to get a variety of psychological and emotional needs met by focusing on sexuality and ignoring the development of closeness and relationships. In some instances, the amount and type of sex that we have engaged in for two decades has caused us to have some degree of addictive or compulsive sexuality.

Given the amount of sexual repression and heterosexism out of which gay liberation emerged, its early course was inevitable. It is important to recognize, however, that it reinforced typical male patterns of relating both in and out of the bedroom. That period has often been referred to as the "candy store" or our gay adolescence. Adolescence, a natural stage in human development, has its pluses and minuses. It is about self definition, separation, autonomy, grandiosity and omnipotence. It is also a time of defiance, anger, self-indulgence, recklessness and, occasionally, self-destructiveness. In a time of AIDS safe and responsible sex is essential. It is important to look at closely when our sexual expression is a self-destructive act of defiance, and when it nurtures us and brings us closer to one another.

Our liberation and coming-out are on-going processes. As we continue to evolve and re-define positive identities as gay and bi men, we are freeing ourselves from the restrictive and dysfunctional aspects of male gender role training. Most men have almost no training in developing intimacy or building relationships, but both can be learned.

Is There Hope?

Is there hope for Joe, so strongly socialized by rigid male gender and sex role training? Will he be able to overcome his male socialization, and his ten years of liberated gay sexuality? Will he be able to be intimate with another man, have a healthy sexual life and not be obsessed with sex, inside or outside of the relationship? Will he and his lover have the option of being sexually exclusive, if that's the lifestyle they prefer?

There is hope for Joe. And there are many methods of help available, some of which will be discussed briefly at the end of this article. There are several critical areas Joe will need to address to move beyond his early gender and sex role training, and to move beyond the sex and relationships patterns he established during his early years in the gay movement.

Beliefs About Self and Relationships With Men

Because of his early training, Joe believes that his value and worth come from what he does in the world. If his male socialization was delivered harshly and rigidly, or if the family was dysfunctional, he may think he is worthwhile only if he takes care of his partner. Having never seen emotional closeness between men, Joe thinks it just does not exist. Boyhood tells him not to trust other men. His early gay experiences tell him that gay and bi men get close by being sexual. He may have learned from early gay lib that long-term relationships are not desirable or possible, or that sexual exclusivity is not viable because "that's just the way men are."

Sexuality

From his adolescence, Joe has learned that sex has little to do with closeness, which was reinforced by the gay male community in the seventies. From both youth and early gay lib Joe learned that sex was primarily about pleasure and that it was based primarily on looks, bodies, faces, etc., and in order to be liberated one had to be "sexually free." It was an easy shift from "Playboy" as a teen to "Playgirl" as a young adult. Through adolescence and young adulthood, Joe has used sex to fight depression, to end isolation and to bolster his low esteem.

The intense and chronic pain of being gay in a heterosexist and homophobic culture, no one to talk with about it, and feeling ashamed of who he was led Joe to lots of sex during his early years as a gay man in his twenties. Joe is not to blame here. He merely participated in a community of men who celebrated their newfound freedom and liberation through lots of sex with lots of partners in lots of settings. The dilemma Joe is faced with now, however, is that he's an expert in sex without relationship, but knows little about closeness, dating or sex within a relationship. Because of the amount and types of sex he has had, Joe has become somewhat sexually compulsive. Even currently sex is heavily emphasized in the gay male community. He can't open a gay periodical without being faced with images of muscled men, 976 numbers, and pages of personal ads that are primarily sexual in nature. All of this reinforces his male training and early gay sexual experiences. What was once freeing and liberating is now a habit or pattern which he is having difficulty changing.

Joe has also noticed that when he does start dating or getting close to another man his sexual attraction lessens. He's not used to being with one partner for more than a couple of months and gets bored with his steady partner. He misses the constant hunt and variety which now seem integral to his being turned on sexually. These factors prevent him from establishing the close, sexually fulfilling relationships he wants with a single partner.

Internalized Homophobia and Heterosexism

Another area that Joe needs to address in order to have closeness with men and from relationships is internalized homophobia and heterosexism. Getting close to another gay man serves as a mirror for Joe, one that he is often not comfortable looking into. As the relationship develops, Joe feels himself shutting down inside and closing himself off to his partner. He's not able to talk about it, because men are supposed to be able to work things out on their own and not need help.

Joe is "out" to his gay and lesbian friends, but not to his family or co-workers. Dating serves as a constant reminder that he is in fact a gay man, which he is uncomfortable about at times. At work he talks about his weekend dates, but changes the gender out of shame and fear. Not only does this create stress for Joe, but it prevents him from being himself—another essential ingredient for healthy relationships.

Communication

Knowing who he is, working on his esteem, recognizing his issues around sexuality and being gay are all essential ingredients to building intimacy. But unless he can overcome his early training about not expressing his feelings, not asking for help, having to take care of himself, and the larger than life self-importance that most men are taught, Joe is going to have trouble with closeness and relationships. The ability to say what he is feeling (hurt, angry, sad, scared), and what he wants from his partner (more attention, more communication, more distance) are basic elements of any healthy relationship.

No one comes to a relationship feeling wonderful about themselves all of the time. Everyone brings elements of their history into their present—often gender role training, low self-esteem, fear of being smothered or abandoned by the other, or internalized homophobia. Essential for relationship survival is each individual's awareness of what his issues are and a willingness to talk about them.

Growth and Change Are Natural

By nature human beings are curious and growth oriented. Most of us enjoy the company of others and want some form of intimacy in our lives. Sexuality provides pleasure and is one means of express- ing love and closeness. In a perfect world, these aspects of human nature would have developed easily and naturally during youth and young adulthood. Because our world is imperfect most of us did not receive the love, attention, and affection we deserved growing up. Sexism, racism, heterosexism and homophobia have shaped and wounded all of us. Trusting others and getting close to them is difficult for almost everyone. But because we are growth oriented by nature, most of us seek to heal ourselves and become fully human. There are more methods of achieving those ends than I could possibly enumerate here. Healing and becoming fully human are somewhat new directions for men as a group to pursue. Here are some of the essential elements of personal growth and change for men, and the types of activities that provide them:

Healing, Growth and Change for Men

Elements of empowering men to establish identities that are positive and self-defined include:
- increasing awareness of what one is thinking, feeling, or doing at any point in time, and having the choice to continue or dis- continue it
- encouraging men to end their isolation by making contact with others, and learning how to be physically and emotion- ally close with each other
- challenging beliefs and behaviors that discourage closeness and intimacy between men and learning new ways of relating
- encouraging beliefs and behaviors that promote reaching out for help
- learning to confront in ourselves and each other dysfunctional behaviors such as dishonesty about feelings, isolation, and sexually compulsive behavior.

For many years gay and bisexual men have sought help, healing and growth for themselves through a variety of activities. In their own way these activities have facilitated men to feel good about themselves as individuals, as men, and as gay or bisexual. These activities have helped men move beyond early gender and sex role training and specific effects of sexual patterns learned during early gay liberation. Re-evaluating our dysfunctional patterns can be a lifelong process, but one that can be fulfilling in and of itself. Some methods bring immediate results and others are more far reaching. This is a partial list of activities that provide growthful opportunities for men:

1. Gay affirmative individual and group psychotherapy
2. National men and masculinity conferences
3. California men's gatherings
4. Gay consciousness raising groups
5. 12 step programs for—alcoholics, adult children of alcoholics, narcotics users, sexual compulsives, sex and love addicts, and co-dependents
6. The Experience Weekend
7. Co-counseling workshops
8. Radical fairy gatherings and a variety of other groups, workshops, or courses.

Our socialization as males was inescapable. Gay liberation was an essential component of personal and social change for millions of men and women. Some aspects of its early course however, reinforced dysfunctional patterns of relationships and specific forms of sexual expression for men. Change and choice are possible. Many gay and bisexual men are seeking it. Some out of choice and some out of fear that sexual addiction and compulsive sex which is not safe can be deadly.

It is increasingly important in a time of AIDS that we contradict our male programming by seeking help and support. Internalized homophobia is emerging in deeper and different forms. Many gay and bi men have sought help for themselves and in the process have become wonderful teachers, healers, and sources of support for others. We provide hope, encouragement and specific tools for growth and change. We are growing rapidly beyond our male socialization and the notion that "boys will be boys." We are evolving into loving, sensitive, nurturing, intelligent men whose strength and power come from choiceful self-definition and our concern for the well-being of others.

My Sexual Odyssey: A Father's Reflections

H.J. Randolph

It was the summer of 1973. On the living room rug of my lover's house, at age 23, I lost my virginity in the community I called home for most of my life. I was ecstatic, joyful, relieved. It's embarrassing for a man in this culture to admit to late sexual blooming! Seven years after that summer I married a hometown girl. In 1982, my son Zachary was born. At 37 I was divorced and became a joint custody father.

Since that time, with unbounded delight and periodic apprehension, I have watched Zack grow into a beautiful, bright, rollicking child. Luckily, he shares his father's quick wit, indelicate sense of humor, and modesty. Once when he asserted, "Daddy, you are in another dimension," I felt constrained to retort, "You could be right." On another occasion Zack claimed I was in need of "sensibility." The pedestrian "Alvin Show" theme song we hear on television is transformed into the rousing "Bullshit Show" when Zachary belts it out in my car. During a conversation about food one day I asked, "Zack, do you like curry?" The impish reply: "Who's he?"

Then there's the metaphysical Zack, who, upon removing a candy bar wrapper, muses about having "ripped open a dimensional window." I can only gaze in wonderment at a son who tells me, "My memory goes on and on and when it ends, I shall die." The tender Zack worries that my leg is a "little bit broken" when I experience some pain there, or pleads during my nightly lie-down, "Oh, my sensitive daddy, won't you stay in bed two more minutes?"

Whether hurling a football, eating dim sum, playing Nintendo (he always crushes me), or concocting a shaving cream and spices "potion" together, there is a closeness between us that deeply enriches my life.

Like all parents, I want my child to benefit from what I have learned along the way, to impart whatever wisdom I can, to advise him as he makes choices in life. My own sexual history has featured its share of frustration and disappointment amid its pleasures. Now, at 39, I ponder that history in an effort to make Zack's sexual odyssey smoother than mine has been. What was I taught about sex, what were my sexual experiences, and what lessons about a healthy sexuality can I teach my son?

I grew up in a small town in southeast Iowa. Like most children of my generation, I received no useful sex education from my parents. I remember telling a story at the supper table one night that I had heard at school about some boy being busy "on Cherry Hill." Cherry Hill, as it turns out, was a girl in his class. Relating this tale led to a brief after-dinner lecture from my father about "being careful" with girls, whatever that was supposed to mean. Regrettably, that is the only memory I have of any discussion of sexuality with my parents.

They never told me about masturbation, "how babies were made," or contraception. They never explained what it took to create a caring, loving relationship between two people. I wasn't encouraged to ask questions about such things or referred to a book that would enlighten me. A product of their time, my parents were not alone in their discomfort. Feeling ill-equipped or awkward about discussing sex with children was common, and is still a challenge today. Nevertheless, I believe the lack of information I received from my parents retarded my sexual development.

Even if my father never breathed a word to me about sex, he still subscribed to *Playboy*. I remember pulling the issues down from the closet shelf in my parents' bedroom and furtively flipping through the pages with a high school friend. It was exciting to look at the naked bodies, wondering what mysteries of the flesh awaited me in the future. Although I may have pored over issues of *Playboy*, I don't recall talking to friends about sex and I had no older brother who might pique my interest about sexual matters or to whom I could turn for guidance.

As a boy, I was shy around girls, and I'm still somewhat uneasy when approaching women as an adult. I either lacked curiosity as a young man or repressed most sexual feelings. When I was about 12, I did "play doctor" with a neighbor girl in the bushes. Once I was caught playing strip poker in a car with a male pal, but I don't remember either experience as being overtly sexual. I had occasional wet dreams as a teenager and recall times when I lay in bed for hours at night, alone with fantasies of female classmates. Still, I only dated a few times in high school and was never sexually intimate. Moreover, I have no memory of ever masturbating during those years.

Tentative and unsure of myself in the sexual arena, I missed out on potential sexual activity because I wasn't aggressive enough. Susan, Laura, and Bernice remain part of my fantasy life, and I still sometimes wonder where they are now and if they would be surprised by my memories of desire and fleeting pleasure. When, at 16, I sang the Rolling Stones' lyrics "So don't play with me cause you're playin' with fire," my mother thought it was a joke. Who could argue with her? As a teenager, I wasn't a hot sexual property. Not until my freshman year of college did I passionately kiss a woman for the first time. I still vividly recall us thrashing about on a dusty fraternity couch in the darkness.

I was on a Greyhound bus en route to Chicago for a Rolling Stones concert in the early '70s the first time I remember masturbating. In the back of the bus I started touching myself in this marvelous way and was a little embarrassed yet thrilled by the electric feelings that surged through my penis—and whole body—when I climaxed. I immediately concluded that this wonderful event merited further deliberation. I guess the Stones and I have some sort of history.

A passion for cunnilingus was kindled in the summer of 1971, when I would linger for hours beneath my girlfriend's billowing dresses on her porch on sultry summer evenings. I am intoxicated by its wonderful, heady, sensual delights. An inherently tender, loving act, I think cunnilingus is as sexually intimate as one can be with a woman. I've always known that "real sex" in our culture is not simply intercourse. Though that can be deeply fulfilling, I'm a man who has never equated sexual pleasure with just "getting laid." I believe I've satisfied most of my lovers—perhaps more with my tongue than with my penis, cunning linguist that I am.

My first experience of intercourse catapulted me into an intense period of fascination about everything sexual. I composed "Awakening," my dewy-eyed poem to lost innocence. I became conversant with Johnny Wadd, Marc Stevens, and Marilyn Chambers—marquee names of leading porn stars. I bought a vibrator and a dildo (and once even an outrageous rubber "vagina"). When my first two-year romance ended, I began a period of sexual experimentation that was more feasible in pre-AIDS America. This included several lovers, as well as group sex dalliances with both women and men. Though I had the desire, I never attended a full-fledged orgy. I did, however, have an unusual encounter with a man on a bus once (I guess I had a thing about buses, too).

Although to this day I enjoy sexually explicit magazines and movies, I have often felt that it was wrong to be attracted to them, that it was politically indefensible. Though I am repulsed by images of women or men being hurt or humiliated, certain pornographic materials do arouse me. Even when I'm involved in a sexual relationship, I still masturbate on occasion to pornographic stimuli. And I've enjoyed situations where I could observe the sexual frolics of others. I just wish more high-quality sexually explicit images were available. David Steinberg's *Erotic by Nature* is one place to start.

I'm no Tom Selleck, so I don't hold women to impossibly high standards of physical attractiveness. Nevertheless, I remain unduly influenced by pornographic images of what women's bodies are "supposed" to look like. I sometimes feel I'm an unwilling prisoner of these images, which prevent me from beginning liaisons with women with "imperfect" bodies or cause my sexual interest to disappear if their ability to arouse me cannot match my fantasies. Am I always in tune with my real-life lover or do I measure her against an unrealistic ideal?

The end of my first serious romantic relationship in my 20s and of my marriage two and a half years ago can be attributed in part to waning sexual desire. This has caused me considerable pain and regret, because I feel I am a sensitive and imaginative lover. Eventually dissatisfaction with my first lover's boyish body was one factor in our break-up, however, and I suppose I never fully appreciated her sensuality. Similarly, my former wife and I never found a way to bridge the sexual gulf that developed between us. We did a miserable job of communicating about our sexual problems and, even when we did, we were unable to resolve them. Those problems were ultimately symptomatic of other troubles that eventually led to our divorce.

Though the notion of a "normal" sex life is illusive, it seems that too much of my adulthood has been characterized by relationships with either little or unsatisfying sex, punctuated by dispiriting interludes of celibacy. I have contemplated the sexual relationships in my life that have been gratifying in an attempt to understand what too often has been lacking. My hope is that in future relationships I can confront sexual issues directly when they arise and remove the shroud of silence that has often concealed them.

I have been single for over two and a half years. The age of AIDS and other sexually transmitted diseases has altered the nature of sex. Although I am willing to use them, my penis has never met a condom it really liked (or could stand up to) particularly well. After an unexpected exchange of "bodily fluids" a year and a half ago with my last lover, I insisted that we undergo AIDS tests despite our being at extremely low risk. Though the results were negative, it was a scary experience that reaffirms the prudence of my current search for one special lover.

My life as a joint custody father has also changed the context of romance. I have the impression that some—maybe most—women are reluctant to date a single father, are hesitant to become involved in the life of a child even if, as in my case, the father is not acrimoniously entangled with his former spouse. Though my son is accustomed to the notion of his mom or dad being in bed with another person, a lover may understandably not wish to sleep overnight when your child is with you. Remember that embarrassing moment in the movie *Kramer vs. Kramer* when the child and his father's lover meet unexpectedly on the way to the bathroom in the middle of the night?

And is one's lover receiving enough attention or instead feeling neglected when we focus so much energy on our children? Ministering to our children's needs—as it has been historically for single mothers—is paramount for single and joint custody fathers. Though we need the freedom to create satisfying sexual relationships separate from our lives as parents, potential lovers must understand how important our children are to us.

My last lover and I dealt with all of these issues. Though we were never "in love," our fourteen months together featured a stimulating, sometimes rapturous sex life. She always respected the amount of time I needed to dedicate to my son and enjoyed his company on the infrequent occasions we all shared together. Yet she never stayed overnight with me when Zack was in the bedroom down the hall. In retrospect, this simply reflected her awareness that the uncertainty of our relationship didn't merit creating unrealistic expectations in my son that I was involved with a potential stepmom.

Living in a society more supportive of parents providing sexual information to their children than in my parents' generation, I wonder how I can do a better job teaching Zachary about sex. I want to be able to talk to him in an informed and intelligent way. I have tried to answer his questions about sex directly (there haven't been many yet) without foisting too much on him before he's ready. Although I am open to his questions, and will try to help him make wise choices, I realize that I'm not going to be perfect in my efforts, just as my parents weren't. Informative books on explaining sex to children can be invaluable. Peter Mayle's *Where Did I Come From?*, which explains the facts of life in a way that children can understand and parents can enjoy, has been informative. Zack chose it for his bedtime story just the other night. Wardell Pomeroy's *Boys and Sex* is another excellent resource for boys and their parents.

I haven't sent negative messages to Zack about touching his genitals or being curious about other children's. A fascination with penises seems perfectly natural for boys. Zack's penchant for backrubs from Dad at bedtime shows his appreciation of the importance of touch. Massage has been a satisfying part of my sensual experiences and I hope Zack is similarly blessed.

My son already exhibits his father's erotic curiosity. Not long ago he asked me if I liked movies that had sex in them. "Sometimes," I replied. "Then you ought to see *My Stepmother Is an Alien*," he suggested. He's also asked me why I have so many books about sex in my apartment (actually, he had simply stumbled upon that particular section of my library). Just recently he informed me of the little-known anatomical fact that "the penis bone is connected to the bladder bone."

A couple months ago I discovered that a late '80s version of the "Cherry Hill" joke of my youth still retains its vitality. A generation later, the girl's name is "Blackberry Hill." I hope my response was more meaningful than the one I was offered in my youth. Occasionally, to be provocative, Zack feigns revulsion at the notion of a penis and vagina uniting. I resist the provocation and submit that some day he'll love the idea. Though uncertain about how to respond in all of these situations, I feel quite comfortable broaching sexual matters, speaking as I am from the heart to my son.

At some point we will need to discuss intercourse and other forms of sexual intimacy in detail, as well as pregnancy and contraception. There's so much ahead to talk about! How do I bring up the subject of masturbation and orgasms? We have to deal with the bodily changes of puberty (we shared a few words about pubic hair not long ago), wet dreams, preadolescent sexual exploration, and the challenges of the dating world. We've already addressed the issue of homosexuality once already. And when is the right time to consider these topics?

I want Zack to feel comfortable with his sexuality and to understand the changes his body will be undergoing. At an appropriate time, I would hope that sharing my sexual growth (or lack thereof) as a boy would prove instructive for my son. In learning how to bring pleasure to sexual partners, I want him to remember that he has a right to be assertive about his desires, too. Though he will surely come to appreciate how enjoyable sex can be, I also want him to understand the responsibilities of being a sexually active person.

Though unfettered sexual exploration may never again be possible in our society, I will encourage Zack to act intelligently whatever the form of his sexual encounters. I want to teach him not to feel pressured into sex—in the name of masculinity—before he is ready. I will caution him to love carefully in the age of AIDS. As for his inevitable exposure to pornography, I will explain its impact on my life and try to help him sort out what it all means. I don't want Zack's impressions of women to be influenced to the degree mine have been by pornographic images.

Though as adults we continue to ponder this, I will have to address the emotional side of relationships with Zachary—the interplay between sex and love—and what I have learned and am still learning. One thing I'll be sure to discuss is the importance of direct and honest communication, a lesson I unfortunately failed to learn in my marriage.

As a child of divorce, he has lived through the deterioration of a loving relationship. Still, I don't think he will grow up cynical about marriage or the permanence of relationships. *Dinosaur's Divorce: A Guide for Changing Families*, by Laurene Krasny Brown and Marc Brown, has been a valuable resource in helping my son better understand why parents divorce, what kinds of feelings children experience after divorce, what it's like to live in two homes, with a single parent, or with a stepparent (Zack's life the past two and a half years), and other pertinent issues about divorce and its aftermath.

Zack knows his parents still love him dearly. He has seen his mother become romantically committed to another man, quite fond of Zack, whom she will soon marry. I hope my involvement with women since the divorce can provide a positive role model for Zack to emulate in his future romantic life. Bearing in mind Dorothy Sayers' observation that "the only sin passion can commit is to be joyless," I will remind him that sex—whether passionate and intense or tender and languorous—can be a joyful and enriching part of being alive. That is the finest legacy I could leave my son.

Coming Together in the Baths

Craig G. Harris

Last year I had the dubious pleasure of addressing the congregation of a Roman Catholic Church in Harlem on the disproportionate incidence of AIDS among Black gay men, and the related topic of homophobia in the Black community. The assembly was attentive and supportive overall—showing a willingness to discuss issues lurking in the shadows. At one point, however, a physician not possessing the reputation of a homophile, asked, "If you're so concerned about Black gays dying, what are you—what are we as a community—going to do about the Mount Morris Baths?" This woman's tone, subtly suggesting that the establishment be closed, seemed based more on the community's desire to keep Black gay men invisible than on genuine concern for the patrons of the bath house. All eyes turned to focus on my reaction.

I explained that AIDS prevention precautions involve *how* one has sex rather than *where* one has sex, and said that representatives from several public and private health agencies discussed and would investigate methods of using this bath house to disseminate AIDS prevention information. I added that it is easier to reach a population at risk when interventions are performed in the milieu of the targeted population.

While I was confident that this was an adequate response for a church-based audience, the question of the Mount Morris Baths remained unresolved in my mind. Having lived outside of New York for several years, I was surprised to come home and find that this Harlem bath house, which is frequented by Black men, is one of four which escaped the bath house siege during the early days of the epidemic. I opposed the policy of bath house closure because I saw it not as an effective means of preventing the spread of HIV, but rather as a means of calling public attention to the perceived sexual deviance of gay men. Still, I couldn't help question the motives that allow the Mount Morris Baths to remain open while so many similar baths have been shut down.

The relationship between racism, genocide and AIDS must be carefully scrutinized. If health officials are convinced that the closure of bath houses is in the best interest of gay men, does the unwilling-ness to enforce such a policy on the Mount Morris Baths, a family business whose third generation management is both white and heterosexual, indicate a distinterest in the lives of Black gay men, or worse, a conscious desire to eradicate them?

A few months after the physician posed her question, I found myself again searching for answers. I had been requested to go to the baths to investigate, in order to suggest feasible AIDS prevention interventions. My naiveté was probably obvious as I rented a room for the evening, listened carefully to the instructions of the kindly, elderly attendant, changed into my towel and unpacked my bag to ready my pen and legal pad. I was intrigued by the amount of traffic on a weeknight, and by the types and attitudes of the men who came to this place.

I saw men who ranged from their early twenties to their eighties, professionals to block boys, those who proudly strutted their nudity to one who self-consciously wore a long-sleeved sport shirt with his towel. Some came with a burning urgency for sexual release and others came to use the steam room and sauna, and to watch the parade of bodies. The common denominator was that these were Black men who enjoyed the company of other Black men. This realization was striking against the backdrop of a society which pits Black men against each other.

I found that the incidence of anonymous sex was not as pro-nounced as I'd expected. Men asked each other's names, what they did for a living, what their interests were, far more often than one would presume. Rather than a monotonous chant of lustful moans and groans, I heard the chatter of multiple conversations in all parts of the bath house, occasionally drowned out by the sounds of orgasm. It seemed, in fact, that there was more social bonding taking place than physical bonding.

For many of the men that I had seen, my double brothers, the ability to name themselves—to declare their sexual attractions for other men—was neither a priority nor a probability. For these men, the manifestations of racial oppression far outweigh the injustices they experience solely on the basis of affectional preference. In addition, the gay liberation movement's failure to address the needs of gay people of color and economically and educationally disadvan-taged lesbians and gay men has limited the social outlets of Black men who have sex with men.

White gay men can choose from a number of well-advertised gay-oriented social clubs, political organizations and sports collectives. If Black men opt to join such groups, they find themselves in an overwhelming minority, and the recipients of racially insensitive treatment. In addition to community and political groups, the white gay middle class has established businesses which cater to their public accommodation and recreational needs.While the list is by no means extensive, there's a roster of bookstores, gyms, bars, restaurants, dance clubs, theaters and resorts which are gay-owned, operated and identified. But the Black gay man patronizing such facilities will only have one facet of his identity served, in a manner which may not be consistent with his tastes.

In the last few years, there has been a growth of autonomous Black gay organizations to fill this gap. Groups such as Gay Men of African Descent, Other Countries, and Rainbow Repertory Theater which respectively contribute to political, literary and artistic development within the Black gay community have been established. For the many Black men who have chosen to remain in the closet, these organizations and support services have limited appeal.

For these men, there has long been a network reminiscent of secret societies—Black gay social support groups whose memberships are soliticited by invitation or advertised by word of mouth. I will not name any of these groups because their primary feature, and their appeal to many members, is the assurance of anonymity and confidentiality. To an overwhelming extent, these groups provide their memberships with recreational outlets such as parties, boat rides and banquets, but rarely participate in political activities which would prescribe public disclosure of one's sexual/affectional proclivities.

Any time two or more Black gay men gather together, it is indeed a political act. Their mere willingness to share their mutual secret is a pivotal step toward self-empowerment through group identification. These are thoughts which came to mind during my visit to the Mount Morris Baths. From the Harlem Renaissance, through the more repressive Civil Rights and Black Power Movements, to the post-Stonewall era, this bath house, in business since 1927, has served as as refuge for Black men whose ability to connect with other men-loving men in public places was severely limited. There is something affirming about this historical continuity I would hate to see lost.

I can not negate the problematic implications of white heterosexuals targeting Black gay men in an attempt to sell them their birthright of sexual expression. Neither can I ignore the negative reinforcement coming from the overall society, and a paucity of recreational and sociopolitical outlets within the Black, gay community. I can, however, see the political potential inherent in the gathering of members of any oppressed class regardless of the intent and motivation of that coming together.

Because I am concerned about Black gays dying—and living—I would assert that what we need to do, as individuals and as a community, is to go where our alienated double brothers are—whether it be the Mount Morris Baths, the parks, the pier or porn theaters—offering informational resources and tangible support in a continuing process of creating environments which address the needs of Black gay men. If we accomplish this task, the fate of establishments such as the Mount Morris Baths might be left in the hands of its clientele rather than in those of government officials or of reactionary, conservative Black homophobes.

Making Love in Spanish Differs

Shepherd Bliss

"Where are you staying?" the cinnamon-shaded Spanish nurse inquires. "In a hotel in Las Ramblas," I answer, referring to Barcelona's promenade, down which everyone strolls, night and day. "Puedes quedar en mis casa (You're welcome to stay in my home)," she offers.

Hospitality to strangers remains strong in Spain and other Mediterranean cultures. Thinking she probably lives with a large family, I feel her invitation to be gracious and probably not sexual. After all, we had just met a couple of days before at a conference. But, I wonder, what is the message in her invitation? And what do I feel in response to her initiative? And what do I do?

I decline. After all, I am here in Barcelona—beautifully suspended between the Mediterranean Sea and two majestic mountains—for professional, rather than romantic, reasons. I had been invited to the Eighth European Congress of Humanistic Psychology to offer workshops on the men's movement; men and women from over a dozen countries attended my presentation.

Assumpta smiles at my hesitation, then suggests dinner together, which I gratefully accept, basking in the golden glow of her skin and her radiant, outgoing presence. Barcelona exudes beauty—human and panoramic. Its air is charged with the sea's connective moisture, its views incredible, and its art among the best in the world. The streets bristle with activity; people live outside, invite you on *paseos* (strolls), or to the musical fountain. The afternoon meal is quite social and can take hours, followed by a *siesta* (nap), during which the entire city closes down. With its Catalan culture, Barcelona has long been a European crossroads where people gather.

As Assumpta and I walk to my hotel after dinner, she takes my hand and holds it tenderly. "Another Latin custom," I think to my Anglo self, noticing that many are holding hands and gently touching each other. The first verbal initiative had been hers, then physical initiative. Now she is looking—deep black eyes—at me very warmly: visual initiative. I love it when women take initiative.

We hear the sad and florid strains of *cante jondo*—deep song—which is part Moorish, part Oriental, part Gregorian, part Jewish, and very gypsy. It evokes my longing. Assumpta is also very *gitano* (gypsy); she crackles with irrepressible enthusiam. Assumpta was literally clicking castanets when I first met her, adding high notes to the low tones I was playing on my drums.

Still not fully understanding what is happening, I remember those typical Anglo-Latin conversations—where the Latin moves closer, to feel comfortable, and the Anglo backs off, also to feel comfortable. I have prided myself in not being a typical Anglo, but am I backing off? Or is she really coming forward? Something mysterious, beyond my comprehension, seems to be happening.

A part of me melts by the attention. I also keep some professional (Anglo?) distance. Where are my defenses? Perhaps back home in California. What are the rules here? Assumpta reaches up, extends herself, gives me a light kiss, in the middle of my confusion, and departs, "Hasta mañana (see you tomorrow)."

I stand for a while as she walks off, alone, down Las Ramblas. It is past midnight. We have just finished dinner, which began at 10 p.m., the typical dinner time here. The streets are full of people; it is a Wednesday night. This culture is quite distinct. Who will I be here? Self-exploration in a new place or at a new time in one's life can be enhanced by sexual exploration, which can embody and ground the self-exploration. Sexual exploration can help break patterns and habits which restrain growth.

This all happened slightly over a year ago. I wonder how Assumpta's version of the story might differ. "How did you meet?" is a question I enjoy asking lovers. The spontaneous answers often differ, reminding me that we each bring our life experiences and subjectivities to any new experience.

I took the risk of sending this essay to Assumpta. Her response was immediate, strong, thoughtful and full of the passion which drew us together originally. "A beautiful declaration of love—a public statement of what we have expressed privately," was how she described the essay. She was so moved that we arranged to meet again, after not having seen each other for half a year.

Assumpta's memory of our first evening together was amazingly similar to mine. She added (in my rough translation from her Spanish), "The gaze which we exchanged made me feel very close to you—so much in the eyes. Simply looking was a deep experience of rich emotion for me. In those first moments I did not feel as much sexual attraction as tenderness and the desire for fusion."

Assumpta's main addition to the story of how we met was the important role of Ramon—an elder to whom she was quite close. I had met Ramon, a former military officer like my father, at the Congress. Assumpta and I both confided in him our mutual attraction. So he introduced us—quite properly, conforming to Spanish tradition. He was our *tio* (uncle), the respected container of our emotions, facilitating our connection.

Childhood Experiences of Otherness

Looking into Assumpta's eyes, holding her hand, my mind goes back 40 years to Panama and my childhood. I remember the black panthers, boa constrictors, and three-clawed sloths in the jungle outside our backyard. During Panama's rainy season it pours almost every day, usually at the same time. A sensual naturalness and wholeness exists to the trees and wild creatures which I miss in urban America's more artificial environment. In Latin Ameria's rural areas people are more a part of the scene of animals and plants, rather than separate from nature. I remember Panama's dark, attractive people. Their melodic Spanish language entered my soul forever.

"Don't ever go into that jungle again," my stern military father loudly commands, restraining me from the lush expanse which comes up to the fence in our back yard. I remember the Panama Canal Zone, where I was raised, as a moist, dark place full of tropical plants and wild animals. My little friend Gordie and I would crawl through the bamboo in search of excitement. Something ancient was fulfilled as we penetrated the opening reeds.

Full of four-year-old boldness, I curiousy respond to my towering father, "Why can't I go into the jungle?" My giant, khaki-clad father seems to get even bigger, "Because the wild animals might eat you alive." He adds, "Or the head hunters might get you." My eyes get wider as he goes into his room, returning with a bag from which he deliberately pulls out a sight I will never forget—a shrunken head, "You'll end up like this."

Gordie and I never returned to that wilderness beyond the fence, except in our imaginations. The sight of that ugly, tiny head terrorized me and remains embedded in my memory.

Years later I returned to Panama and asked a Panamanian historian, "How are your head hunters doing?" He laughed, "You must have been raised in the Canal Zone." I marveled, "How can you tell?" He noted, "Because the head hunter fiction is what military parents use to control their children's natural curiosity. We are a dark people and the jungle is a wilderness, but our people are not head hunters."

Fear of the wilderness (including sexual wilderness), as well as racism, were what my controlled military family was teaching me by the head hunters fabrication. "Stay away from animals and wild things," was their message, including that vital, refreshing animal instinct within this boy—which so frightened my adult parents, "You might get hurt." Deep inside me there is a story which seeks to block my natural impulse of going toward the otherness of dark, and the beckoning rainforest.

I had been lured by the moist Latin jungle, and restrained by my cautious Anglo parents. Today I echo the lament of that great Spanish poet Federico Garcia Lorca, "Give me back/ the soul I had as a boy,/ matured by fairy tales,/ with its hat of feathers/ and its wooden sword . . . "

My ears continued to incline toward the beauty and otherness of Spanish and my eyes towards olive-colored skin. That darkness and otherness have become part of my erotic preferences. My adult passions include "the life of the mind" (the motto of the University of Chicago, where I did my doctoral studies) and relating to dark women. My desire reaches equally toward the eros of books and women, seeking connections with both.

When it came time to choose a doctoral advisor, I chose the only Black person in my department—Charles Long, an historian of religion who wrote *Alpha: The Myths of Creation*, and emphasized the "otherness" of distinct people and cultures. When it came time in my 20s to choose a *fiance* (a *novia* in Spanish) I chose a South American who spoke only Spanish. My childhood was influencing my choices, as it inevitably does, especially in sexual matters. The fascination with otherness which drew my desire emerged again in my 43rd year in Barcelona.

Spain's Emergence, Spanish Women, and Soul

Spain has long intrigued me—the connecting link between Africa and Europe, Latin America's ancestor, its mysticism, its poetry. Spain has soul, as the great British psychologist and sexologist Havelock Ellis asserts in his 1920 book *The Soul of Spain*, "Spain represents, above all, the supreme manifestation of a certain primitive and eternal attitude of the human spirit, an attitude of energy, of spiritual exaltation." *Alma*, the Spanish word for soul, is a full word with vital meaning. Soul and sexuality; following their paths can help get us beyond contemporary facades to more ancient places.

Spaniards are famous for their passion and hot blood (*sangre*). Two factors have contained Spain's soul and energy—its strong Catholic tradition and General Franco's fascism. Franco's oppressive military rule ended with his death in 1975 and Catholicism's stranglehold simultaneously began to diminish. After forty years of fascist rule and centuries of Catholic domination, Spain is emerging as one of Europe's most dynamic cultures, releasing political, artistic and sexual energies which were long blocked.

Sexual expression flourishes in Spain today, after centuries of containment. During Franco's time it was the outside women, "*Las Suecas*" (the Swedes), who harvested the passion of Spanish men. Now Spanish women are more free to express their own sexuality. As Spanish women emerge from years of oppression, they are adding boldness to their traditional charm and grace. Spain now has a strong women's movement which is demanding equality in a variety of political, economic, and sexual areas.

Spain's current women's movement rests on a spirit which Ellis described 90 years ago in his chapter, "The Women of Spain." He notes the "qualities of energy, independence, and courage—the firm resolve to lead one's own life and possess one's own soul—that seem to me to mark Spanish women in an unusually high degree." The traditional importance of the Spanish woman is indicated by the fact that Spaniards often use the last names of both parents. The greatest of Spanish painters before Picasso is known by the name of his mother—Velazquez. After marriage some Spanish women continue with their maiden name.

Assumpta

Assumpta is not really my "type"—young, not well enough organized, short—let me count the many ways I can talk myself out of a deep connection. But there she is, standing in front of me, looking at me with such open eyes. Then touching me . . . hugging me . . . kissing me. I love the ways in which she takes initiative. Her shamelessness. "*Me de las ganas,*" (I have the desire), she would say. Responding to her opens me to places which I have not felt for years.

Assumpta's earthiness, a characteristic of Spanish women, draws me to her. She is both exuberant and introspective. She carries Spain's *sol* and its *sombra*—sun and shade. She is bright and deep. Spain is Western Europe's wildest country, and Assumpta is one of its daughters. Spain's bread—rough and unrefined—is symbolic of the qualities its people retain and is some of the best bread I have ever tasted. "My initial feelings toward you were very primitive," Assumpta revealed. "They had no logic or room for reason. I was very impulsive—driven by an instinct of great pleasure and affection with a mixture of feelings."

"Trust your body," I whisper to myself. "Trust your heart," I add. "You'll not be hurt," I reassure myself, "And if you are, you can mend."

I'm out of my element. I don't know where I am. Who I am. What I'm saying. It comes from my mouth—but such strange sounds—this Spanish. So many ways to speak of love—*amor, carino, te amo, te gusto, te quiero.* In Spain people are forever giving each other *besos* (kisses) on both cheeks and *abrazos* (embraces). I don't know where I am. Who I am. I don't even know how to get anywhere from here. I feel goal-less. Yet not rootless or without ground.

As I recall Assumpta's *abrazos* I associate them with the embrace of another Latin friend—Gilberto Madrid, a Chicano elder with our men's drumming group The Sons of Orpheus. A big man, he has a special way of drawing some of the younger men in our group—such as Guillermo Ortiz and myself—into his elder's *abrazo.* My capacity to connect with Assumpta, as well as with other women, is aided by the men's movement. My brothers support me in my explorations of male models of feeling and being—beyond shame and judgement. I played one of Assumpta's songs to members of the Sons—who responded by making a tape of our drumming, singing, and playing around for her in various languages. We invited her to visit in California, which for various reasons has not yet happened. Living in California, I realize how fortunate I am to be in a multi-cultural and multi-lingual environment, which engages various distinct parts of me. There are certain feelings, as well as gestures, which I have only in Spanish, aspects of me which emerge only when I am in the Spanish language or a Spanish culture.

Making love in Spanish is different than in English. It differs by approach, sound, pause, memory, expectation, and body closeness. Spanish words often end in vowels, which merge, whereas English words conclude frequently in consonants, which end. Spanish has a romantic legacy which has infused its words with passion less available in the more precise and logical English. Spanish and American modes of love-making are quite distinct. Spanish flows like a river, whereas English tends to be more orderly. Spain absorbed many cultures, some of which conquered her, whereas England dominated many peoples and lands. Their respective languages bear the imprints of those economic and political differences.

Yet part of what Assumpta says to me has a ring of female universality, "The woman will ask the man many times if he needs her, desires her, loves her. The woman wants proof of love to confirm the man's love feelings; the man expresses his love at times in ways which the woman does not understand. Women want evidence that the love is reciprocal and at the same level. At times the codes of communication between men and women are so distinct that lovers believe that the love does not exist and that it was all a marvelous illusion, a desire, a dream." She later adds, "The masculine message does not always conform to the feminine form and desire for communication."

Hearing this, I relax, knowing that Assumpta understands something which is essential to better relations between the sexes, which could be described not in terms of "the opposite sex" but as "the other sex." When women expect men to communicate like and be like women, they are bound to be disappointed, and vice-versa. The differences, especially in modes of communicating, can be quite significant, as well as interesting. A radical otherness distinguishes the sexes—which can bring us much pleasure, confusion, and sometimes pain and even misery.

One of the things Assumpta and I struggle about—sometimes playfully—is closing doors, both literally and metaphorically. I like the boundaries which closed doors provide, such as on bathrooms. Then I can have my privacy and not hear the sounds which can interrupt my writing. Assumpta does not like such boundaries—which can block her feminine flow. So she tends to go around opening doors; I tend to go around closing them. We are sometimes like a comic act—the European, Latin woman with her customs and the Anglo, American man with his, following each other around. People must wonder about us. At times our differences draw us together; at other times they separate us; often they are just comic; which sometimes we are able to perceive. She opens, perhaps inviting me in, which sometimes I accept, other times closing, retaining my boundaries, which have served me long—for better or worse.

The dance continues—sometimes with joy, other times with unmet longing and even sadness. Is this enough? I feel she wants more—an introvert's eternal dilemma: people always seem to want more than we offer. "These are my limits," I often feel. I am not always proud of them; but I have survived. They have protected me.

Thinking/feeling about sexuality, that pleasure gives way to longing. I left—Chile, Barcelona, and many other sides of sexual pleasure. All left behind, though somehow kept inside as well. Will I ever touch again, as deeply? I remember Barcelona's streets—

narrow, loud and full of people. Cars rushing by. And Assumpta's tiny, clean apartment at the top of the hill. Moments of deep relaxation and profound communication. Touching, and being touched.

Assumpta tells me that I have a fear of pleasure, which I must acknowledge, even as I move toward it. My Puritan Protestant and militantly military upbringing has not assisted me to receive it. The barriers of guilt and shame continue to harness me from a more full reception of physical and other pleasures.

After Barcelona

Something shifted in Barcelona. I did not know what the rules were. I did not dominate the language, felt more vulnerable. A spontaneity returned. I felt a deep abandon—following her, in her bed, at her home, in her language. She was in control, though not fully. I never felt my will invaded or smothered. I had no choice but to surrender, or so it seemed. The otherness of the female body, mind and feelings draw me. I like the mystery, though sometimes it can be frustrating. The sexual spontaneity which I had lost—being middle aged and living in the Age of AIDS—began to return in Barcelona. There was no familar pattern to follow.

When Assumpta and I met again, in Boston on my turf, it did not go so well. I was anonymous in Barcelona, known in Boston to many students, colleagues, and ghosts from many years of living there. I was more in control—of myself, of the language, of what we would do, where we would go—hence out of contact with a spontaneous and sexual (connective) part of myself. That control which I have worked so hard to get and maintain seems to block sexual exploration. "You were very open in Barcelona," Assumpta recently commented by phone, "but in Boston you had closed the door. I could not get to you. The Shepherd I met in Barcelona seemed absent."

Later we met in Montreal—French, her third language, I unable to understand a word. We re-connected. In the year since we met Assumpta and I have seen each other three times now, for about a week each time—Barcelona, Boston, and Montreal—three magical cities. Barcelona by the Mediterranean, Boston by the Atlantic, and Montreal that beautiful blend of cultures—all romantic cities. I've invited Assumpta to California, another unique blend of cultures, where I live most of the time. I wonder what it might be like for us here? Place can affect feelings, romance and sexuality.

Reflecting back on my time in Barcelona, I am struck by how relatively open I was to receive Assumpta. My usual body and mind hesitations were not "protecting" me. The stimulation of travel had reduced them. The distance from my own home and its inhibitions had further eroded my defenses. Speaking Spanish, I was not as fully conscious as when I speak English. The deepest sexuality seems to come from unconscious places. Being thousands of miles from home and in a foreign culture and language seemed to unburden me from my customary patterns of holding back. Distance can enhance intimacy. Distance can provide a freedom.

Overcoming Sexual Shame

"Why divulge your sexual experiences in Barcelona?" a close, dark Indian friend inquires upon reading a draft of this essay. "You leave yourself too personally and professionally vulnerable," he cautions. I listen to his wise counsel and pause, for months, remembering awkward and even damaging experiences when sexuality has been a factor.

When I speak to my men's group about my connection with Assumpta—giving voice to my fears, doubts, and joys—I realize that I am overcoming a barrier of sexual shame. Re-experiencing my relationship to Assumpta by talking and writing about it brings me joy. Being able to talk openly of it and even write about that experience has helped me process it, understand it and delight further in it. Story-telling can have healing power.

Another member of my men's group reported a contrary experience of being shamed for his longing for a physical connection. "When I was seventeen years old," Kevin revealed, "I was drawn to this girl. There was something special about being with her. I was too shy to say anything to her, but some of my friends knew. Word got to the nuns, our teachers. One day Sister Mary called me to the front of the class. 'So you want to be with Anne do you,' she humiliated me. Then she put a dress on me, and ordered me to sit with the girls, to everyone's laughter. Though this was over 30 years ago now, I can see it as clearly in my mind as if it were yesterday. I was mortified. I wished I could die. Anne never spoke to me again. I felt terrible about myself and my feelings. I have not had such deep love feelings for a female since then."

Something died in Kevin that day—something having to do with love and its connection to physical feelings for another. A love was killed—by a Catholic nun—not the first time a religious leader has terrified someone away from a human connection by shaming that person. Hearing the utter cruelty of this story stunned the multi-cultural men's group where it was told.

The weapon used by the religious authorities to murder Kevin's longing for connection to the girl was shame. In *Healing the Shame That Binds You* John Bradshaw distinguishes between two forms of shame: "It is a healthy human power which can become a true sickness of the soul. There are two forms of shame: nourishing shame and toxic/life-destroying shame. In toxic shame, we disown ourselves" (p.3). Much deeper than guilt, shame is the feeling not that we have done something wrong but that we are in our essence wrong and bad. Religious authorities have been key in projecting toxic shame, as Bradshaw notes, "Religion has been a major source of shaming. Moral shoulds, oughts and musts have been sanctioned by subjective interpretation of religious revelation" (p.66).

Catholic priests and nuns vow to renounce sexual activity—celibacy. Much of Christianity is body- and sex-negative. This shame does not reign in the Old Testament, with Solomon's gloriously sensual *Song of Songs*. Jesus himself seems to have followed a more open approach, allowing a notorious "sinner" to wash his feet with her tears and hair. Some research indicates that he was involved with that "sinner"—Mary Magdalene. Paul, the main author of the New Testament, had great problems with women, which became institutionalized in the celibacy of priests. St. Augustine in the fourth century deepened that shame; he had at least two love affairs, one of which produced a child. When St. Benedict in the sixth century was tempted by the vision of a woman, he threw himself into briars and nettles until he bled. Sexual passion can threaten order, which both the church and the state seem to feel they need; surrendering to desire can take one into the unknown.

One approach to dealing with shame is to break the silence barrier, which is what I seek in this article. Shame, including sexual shame, is rampant in American men today; it leads to many forms of violence against others and the self, including passivity. Too many men are ashamed of being a man and of having male sexual longings. Taking sex positive stands in a sex negative culture can be dangerous. Being sexual in an anti-sexual context is difficult.

The Intimacy/Distance Dance

I spoke to Assumpta recently by phone—California to Quebec—talking about this essay. We will continue to see each other. Ours is a contemporary connection—one without a model of which I am aware. We are not sure what we are doing—the Anglo writer and the Spanish nurse: bicultural explorations. When we meet, the body connection is strong. When I think about our relationship, it is easy to talk myself out of it. When I feel it—beyond judgement—it feels right.

With my faulty Spanish, I reach toward Assumpta. From my flawed childhood, I reach toward Assumpta. At other times, I want to be alone, to myself, solitary. I long for an intimacy which I can manage. Can I have both my distance, necessary for creation, and intimacy? Must distance and intimacy be contrary, or can they be compatible?

My connection with Assumpta reawakened desire in me. And not just sexual desire, or merely desire for her. She quickened my life force—in response to her initiative, her body, her being, her love. My incompleteness unfolded toward her—with both my assets and liabilities. Our relationship has become a form in which I can more fully emerge. Yet that desire did not become attachment. A joy rises as I reflect on our time together. That joy is not dependent upon being in immediate proximity to her. It is not Assumpta as an object which I desire but something transcendent that happened between us.

Desire can degenerate into delusion, attachment, entanglement. Distance can nourish desire and inhibit its degeneration. Desire can surely be the gateway to hell—described in the Hindu's spiritual text the *Bhagavad Gita* as "an insatiable fire" and "the eternal foe of knowledge." The Hindu deity Krishna speaks of desire as the soul's ultimate peril. Many religious traditions are skeptical of desire—including Christianity, Buddhism, and Hinduism. Of these three perennial wisdoms, perhaps only Hinduism celebrates desire (*kama*) for its central role in creation.

A member of a neighboring men's lodge got married recently, to a member of a women's lodge. Over one hundred of us attended, including many members of men's and women's groups. It was a unique all day manifestation of the gender reconciliation toward which many of us are working. The man and woman are in their 50s, already grandparents. Their children, rather than their parents, gave them away.

At the wedding I recited Robert Bly's poem "In the Month of May," which includes the following: "I love you with what in me is unfinished. / I love you with what in me is still/ changing, what has no head or arms or legs . . . " I love Assumpta for her otherness—as a woman, as a Spaniard. The unfinished and unfolding parts of me reach toward her in ways which I do not understand. It is not a constant flow. But it is hot when it connects. And it feels like it will endure. Ours is a unique love—as any true love is. From her home by the Mediterranean Assumpta expresses our connection as follows, "The union which we maintain is like the sea . . . it has waves which come and go . . . even sea-sickness which flows and ebbs . . . also tempestuousness . . . silences . . . and much mystery."

This essay has drawn Assumpta and I into another level of communication—writing about being together and taking the risk of sharing our experiences with others. As I write this in my living room in my second home in Boston, she is typing in the kitchen in Spanish, from which I am translating and quoting. This second visit here has gone quite well. We have had this common project of reflecting and writing to draw us together and to recall pleasant memories of being together. This writing has given me a way to express some of my feelings—which at times are more difficult for me to express in conversation or face-to-face. As a writer I am more comfortable with hand-to-paper expression. As a nurse, Assumpta does wonderfully with hand-to-body expression, giving great massages.

Men and women are often quite distinct in our modes and codes of communication—even when we appear to be speaking the same language.

As we enter the 1990s and the twenty-first century, the patterns and models which have guided relations between the sexes no longer function adequately. A whole world exists out there—with all its pleasures and dangers—which has never been as available as it is today with contemporary means of communication and travel. We need to discover new paradigms of how to love. Weddings between older people, for example, may become more common. Cross cultural relationships can also become more common. Love comes in many forms—if we would move beyond the shame, fear and judgement which hold us back. If one responds to his (or her) desire, he opens up the option of expanding his soul, for the soul is made by what we do and how we are on this earth. Blessed be!

Loving Without Limits

Bob Vance

1.

The second night it rained again. That day they have traveled throughout the state, found waterfalls draped over slick greygreen rocks, followed twisted roads through narrow green valleys. The clouds were low and full and fingered down the sides of the mountains. The organic smell, the damp fertile air and the undulating land itself became projections of the sexual tension between them. He had a hard-on nearly the entire day. She would notice and laugh, just acknowledge, or they might stop for a while to play.

They would sleep in a lean-to shelter that night, the inside of the small tent too wet from the night before. In the lantern glow, deep in the trees, they made love again. She slid down over him, moved slow and steady in excruciating ecstasy that he could have held on to forever. He had never felt anything like it. She said later that some men didn't like to make love that way. He couldn't imagine why not—had always been frustrated by the expectation that *he* be the mover.

Their first night together was just his second sexual experience that included insertion. The first, with a woman at home, had been initially exciting, but finally frightening as they were both virgins and she bled quite a bit. He felt he had "done it" wrong, had hurt her, and so he left rather quickly, feeling failure and ineptness at his own inability to understand what he should do in this situation. This, in the mountains of Vermont, was different. They were both happy, infatuated, wanted to share this feeling with everyone they met and were able to in small ways the entire time they spent together. The Vermonters and other tourists smiled and greeted them warmly with knowing looks and good-natured humor. Their sex felt like the most natural relationship possible between two people. He thought: this must be what love is about, comfort and intertwining ecstasy.

2.

Sitting in the teacher's classroom had become a disturbing exercise in nearly ecstatic learning mixed with intoxicating fantasies; a nearly hypnotic connection with the teacher that he could never determine the source of. Was it just a trick? A product of his infatuation? It seemed too electric, like plugging into and completing the circuit for some advanced mental power tool. He had never thought so clearly, been so aware of his own mental acuity and ability for critical examination. He wrote down everything, took notes voraciously, along with short comments that, more often than not, attributed this, he thought new, ability to understand to his teacher.

He visited the teacher's offer weekly; another exercise in ecstatic torture. The man's eyes were the most incredible green he'd ever seen. And they were not frightened of staying on his own.

"This is it," he thought, "I must be queer." What to do? Well, he surmised that first he ought to tell the woman he was currently sleeping with. Then he would need to tell the teacher (as if the man didn't already know). He would find out if his perceptions were right and they would have, or not have, a relationship. That's what one did if one felt this strongly about someone. You told them. At least that had been his experience with women he loved. Having had no real experience loving other men in this way, he supposed it could not be very different.

So he confessed his infatuation to the teacher. The teacher smiled broadly in acceptance, but openly questioned the student's conclusion that he must be homosexual. Apparently the teacher had a roommate once who had decided he was homosexual in much the same way the student had, but then changed his mind very soon after. Perhaps, the teacher suggested, he was bisexual.

Though this meeting went well, a definite beginning, things got more confusing and painful from then on. He became very conscious of the necessary secrecy surrounding such a love. The teacher seemed to want to put off an after class meeting until after the term ended. He took that as some rejection, and doubted the wisdom of having told the teacher his feelings in the first place. His love grew stronger, more fierce for expression than ever.

Then he flunked the midterm exam, an event that sent him crashing. Other things in his life had taken a decidedly unbalanced turn. He impulsively quit his job (because he felt he was applying the ideals he was learning in the class), had gotten a woman he slept with once pregnant. There was an abortion. The midterm was the final straw. The teacher told him not to worry about it, but none of anything he was hearing, feeling or experiencing made any sense. He doubted the reality of everything and there was no new reality that he could find to take its place.

He dropped the class. Luckily the teacher was with someone when he brought in the drop slip, so there was no discussion: just a horrible cracking of the teacher's otherwise beautiful face. His life continued to fall apart, but with a strength he felt at the time must be superhuman, he rebuilt it. A year and a half later he left that city for another. He heard through a friend that the teacher quit teaching at the same time. He thought this must be what love is about: devastating passion and chaos.

3.

Everything in me resists packaging my sexuality in a word and using that word as a part of my identity. This does not mean I do not believe sexuality to be a part of one's identity, but rather that the words used for such definitions seem arbitrarily assigned and ultimately harmful. Choosing one or another and relying on it exclusively to define a very important part of me seems stifling, a serious understatement about a part of me that is always in flux and too mysterious and integral to be named (i.e.: the Tao that can be named is not the eternal Tao).

I chose the stories that precede this essay as a personal example of what has been my experience of sexuality with women and men. That is not to say that I haven't had experiences with women I have loved that seemed to threaten annihilation and overwhelming passion, or that I haven't had warm and comforting relations with men I have loved. I have, but I think the point is that, because passion and physical expression of love between a man and a woman is expected and reinforced in our culture, I've been able in most cases to follow my instincts toward sensual/sexual connection with women easily and without the blocks one encounters in a budding same sex relationship. My long term relationship with my female partner (a nearly ten year linking, at this writing) has often taken on the sometimes frighteningly passionate aura of love's chaotic side. But we have been born in a world that is safe for most heterosexual expressions of love, healthy or no, and the process of healing and affirmation of our love is embraced and given direction and assistance through freely exchanged and inherited cultural myths and stories about loving one another. This is hardly so for male/male love.

For one thing I think men in general are not taught to love anyone very well. We are raised as warriors to the detriment of our other psychic parts. Warriors do not love. They fight, they fuck, they follow directions unerringly. That our culture chooses to ignore the sensual/sexual side of male/male bonding, that it has censored all or large parts of our culture's rich heritage of same sex love stories has damaged our ability to form healthy attachments to each other and resulted in a fearfully homophobic population of men who can only subvert their natural feelings for bonding and cause them to react superficially or violently toward each other even while, in reality, loving one another deeply. Because our natural urge is to love and care for each other, parts of our cultural story that might teach us how to do this have been chopped out in order to serve the sickest of us who want to direct and subvert that urge and use it to produce soldiers who will fight for their petty and selfish goals of conquest and ownership.

My favorite story in literature that, I think, comments on the inability of two men to find direction or expression for the passion they feel toward each other is in a short story by D.H. Lawrence called *The Prussian Officer*. In this story the two men who feel strong passion for each other eventually create a situation that kills them both. Although this is an extreme example, and not what has to happen, it is what can happen on both an individual and societal level, unless we, as men, actively stop denying ourselves access to each other's natural inborn abilities to love and comfort others we are drawn to. We need to rediscover, unbury, and reinvent our myths and our history of loving one another. Different people can choose to do this in different ways. I have chosen to be, as others define it, bisexual. I believe it may be the best way for me to proceed on my quest toward learning how to love others.

This does not mean I will be, or will want to be, sexual with everyone I love. It means I am committed to being open to the possibilities that shared sensuality and sexuality present to me. I will not limit myself to those few physical experiences deemed appropriate because of artificial barriers that serve no useful purpose but to prevent unity among people and engender fear and warfare between peoples.

I could never believe physical attraction to others can only be considered for purposes of eventual reproduction. As generally furless creatures, we have had to depend on each other to stay warm and safe in a sometimes cold and hostile world. It is our heritage, our birthright, to want to be physically involved with others of our species that we love. I refuse to deny this for purposes of conforming to unproductive and artificial concepts of normal human behavior. I will try to approach it honestly and without subverting its potentially cooperative, peace-making, ecstatic and spiritualizing nature.

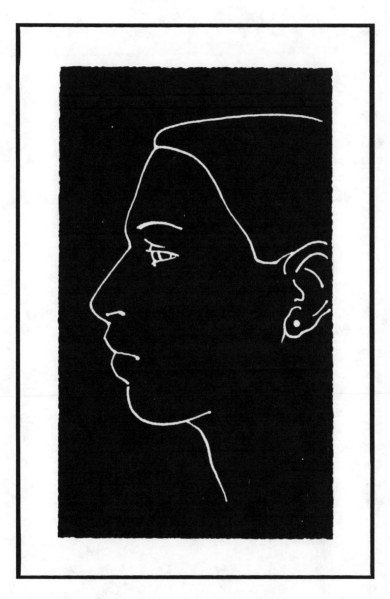

Part III: *On Our Own*

Changing Men

Cary Alan Johnson

living life
in the cracks that things
fall through
dark has never
known this color
this hue
this total
void

time falls off
a man's life
and he is left wondering
am i a job, a wife,
a children?

am i nothing?
do i nothing?
is my singleness a punishment?
was my coupling a crime?

time falls off
a man's head
and he is left
bald shining
what wise wide thoughts
what wisdom
does it hold
that i cannot see
this man's head
this many years
this single radiant life.

Rite of Passage

Gordon Murray

This is a story about coming to manhood, or at least about coming to mine, which happened yesterday. It's a sad story, about trading in trust for mistrust, to put it simply. I know people who've been men all their lives, and others who never arrived. When I arrived yesterday, I took one look and cried.

It was still dark out, and Stephen and I were in the kitchen making coffee. We poured two mugs and went outdoors—the dark morning air was surprisingly cool. Crossing the highway, cupping the warm coffee, we walked up the service road. A high voltage electric tower emerged against the dark sky, then another, and another. They straddled the Maine countryside like silent dark giants holding hands.

Climbing the tower to watch the sunrise had become our morning ritual. The challenge was to avoid spilling the coffee while you climbed the cold steel rungs of the ladder. At the top we made ourselves as comfortable as possible nestled among steel girders wet with dew; thick wires hummed faintly just above our heads, and below, valleys heavy with mist stretched to the pale horizon. We warmed ourselves with the precious coffee, and waited for the sun to appear.

Stephen had been a classmate at school. We'd done a lot of playful, boyish stuff together: played a lot of frisbee, hitched across New York to study Zen for a weekend, broken into the new science building to climb around the elevator shaft. I loved Stephen, and he loved me. Today we are mostly silent. Stephen was going into town with his girlfriend Debby to see if she was pregnant. They hoped she wasn't; there was little more we could say. But that was all right; to feel close it was enough to be on an adventure, to be alone together high above the sleeping world, watching each other's face turn gold with the rising sun.

Stephen and Debby drove off to town. I was sitting in the front room, which was already filled with sun, when Shadrack began to bark. Looking out the window, I saw Ed driving up in his old green telephone truck.

Instantly I was nervous. How is it that men make me nervous, I thought? This particular nervousness took the form of feeling like I mustn't let Ed see me just sitting here doing nothing, so I busied myself at the record-player, and by the time he came into the room I had my arms full of records, looking purposeful. He asked if Bob were up the hill; I said I didn't know. He asked if Bob had come down off the hill; I said no, I didn't think so. So he turned and set off up the hill, without worrying about those questions that were bothering me. That's because Ed was a Scientologist, I thought, and pretty good about just getting what he needs and moving on.

Ed had come and gone when Phoenix entered. By that time I'd put a Ravi Shankar record on and the room was awash in sound and sunlight. Phoenix just appeared, silent as a cat, and I remember feeling proud that the record was playing so nice, because it fit the sunny day just right, and I wanted to make a good impression on Phoenix because I liked him. He walked in fragile, on the balls of his feet, looking bony and hunched up and smiling a thin smile. He lives in Portland, where he has a small bookshop of what you might call occult books, really nothing more than Wilhelm Reich and Carlos Castenada. I'd always felt he was a bit different, which meant perhaps we could understand each other.

I'd never told Phoenix I liked him. I guess that's my biggest fault, maybe the biggest fault of the whole world, or at least the men: not telling how we love each other. I liked Phoenix and knew he'd like the music and he looked happy just sharing this sunny space without words, for Phoenix rarely used words—he seemed to prefer reading them. He sat and listened for a while in his fragile quiet way. Once he opened his mouth to say, "You know, they say Confucius was very fond of music." After a while he stepped quietly out.

• • •

When the raga was over, I decided to go outdoors. The day was warm now, even in my cut-off Levis and yellow T-shirt. I started up the path toward the top of Haystack Mountain, enjoying the feel of nature: the soggy path under my bare feet where the stream passes through the grass, the smell of the manure pile, the feel of tall grass between my outstretched fingers.

I got to the steep part where you can begin to see the upper field which stretches up towards Bob's cabin, and remembered Ed and Phoenix had passed this way. Feeling that nervous feeling again, I shied away, and took the lower trail where I could be alone. At the edge of the lower field I lay down in the shade and watched the clouds, the tall grass growing up all around me. There was one wisp of cloud that kept changing, never achieving any fixed shape, and that was how I felt. I kept changing every day. What little I knew about me I didn't know how to tell others. Ed and Phoenix seemed to know who they were. How did it happen, how do you grow up? How does the cloud ever stop and say, this is me, I'm a cloud?

I sat up and looked around at the grass, how it had been bent over where I lay on it, hurting, I supposed. I must seem like some enormous monster to the grass, crushing a pathway as I walk, wounding a whole circle as I lie down. I stood up, suddenly sad for hurting the grass, and looking around at the tall grass swaying gently in the breeze, I realized the absurdity of my situation: anywhere I went I'd be killing more grass. I rely so much on killing things to move about, or on having others do it, like paving a road. The only thing to do would be to stay in that spot without ever moving, like a monk, but I didn't feel I could do that. I'd lain in fields before, a carefree boy staring at clouds, yet today I felt the suffering and death of the bent grass, and I knew it was silly of me to feel sad, but just the same I did.

I followed the path along the top edge of the lower field, looking over the tall grass swaying in the breeze, looking out to the twin ponds, Steven's and True's, set like jewels in the green forest below, and I started to sing. It was my regular mountain-climbing song, which I called Ramesh's song.

I'd met Ramesh my first week in Asia. He'd invited me over to his house, and when it grew late and was still raining, he invited me to stay the night. We fell asleep side-by-side on the floor, along with numerous family members, all in the same small room. In the middle of the night Ramesh sat up, lit a smoky kerosene lamp, opened a book of Hindi film songs and began singing. He sang in a soft, excited voice, cracking on the high notes. Then he put the book down, threw his arms around me, and kissed me on the lips. "This is Nepali love" he said. The next morning as the sun rose pink on the Himalayas the world had a different feel to it: I'd come halfway around the planet to discover love.

All that and more came back to me as I sang Ramesh's song, for we'd spent a good six months together, and his song makes my chest ache. It was a sad song, the way I sang it; it would have been happier if Ramesh had been there to share it.

• • •

The path came to the old rock wall, and I climbed over it, into the garden. I stopped and sat at the three rows of bush beans I'd planted a couple of weeks earlier. The beans pushed and twisted their way out of the soil, leaves folded neatly down like a bird's wings.

Every so often I'd hear the buzz of a chainsaw coming from up at Bob's cabin, an angry sound. I'd always felt Bob had some hex about him, some dark secret man-magic, something dangerous. I wondered what unmentionable sacrifice was going on: Phoenix gaunt and silent in a black robe, Ed conversing with the higher spirits, while Bob held the chainsaw, dripping with blood.

Eventually I left the garden to head across the upper field, toward the sounds. When I got close I could see Bob's girlfriend Kathy out front, rising and falling, as she worked in the garden, where they'd dug up the field-sod and a row of poles waited for the beans to come. She said "Hi" and I complimented her on the neat garden and asked about what she was planting. She asked me where I was going and all I could do was smile and shrug.

I turned to watch the men working on the cabin. The sun streamed through empty window frames. There was Ed with saws and hammers, working with a steady, self-contained rhythm. Phoenix lounged in an overstuffed chair, his white legs extended, surveying the scene and, I supposed, dropping cosmic comments from time to time. Then looking up among the new rafters I saw Bob, the sun filtering through the trees, lighting up his powerful hairy chest, his face twinkling from behind his mammoth beard. He had a big, sly face, with quick eyes easy to anger, which spoke of a wild fearlessness. The Big Bad Wolf.

I was afraid of Bob. Not the way I was afraid of other people, sort of nervous and insecure; no, really scared, scared of his violence. He was the most violent man I'd ever been up close to. I'd watched him do little violent things, small unpredictable cruelties; he was powerful, raw, impulsive, explosive, and I avoided being alone with him.

I greeted Bob and complimented his cabin, and said I thought it was coming along nicely, and got a nice lot of sunshine; he answered that there was too much sun in the summertime. Then Kathy was by my side and was asking Bob some questions, and then he told us to watch out as he pushed a bunch of boards with ugly bent nails in them off the edge of the rafters. I jumped back as the lumber thundered to the ground in front of us, feeling all of Bob's violence in that small act, which seemed all the more significant because at that moment Kathy had been at my side. Kathy returned to the garden plot, Bob glanced at me with a tiny glint in his eye and a faint smile, and I tried to pretend that nothing at all unusual was going on. I took this as my cue to leave, and said goodbye.

• • •

I headed up the path—the long path that winds around the mountain—stopping here and there to think. At the old rock wall marking the beginning of Stuart's Blueberry Company, with its sign about no trespassing and no snowmobiles, I decided I wasn't a trespasser, just a passer-by, so I climbed over the wall and had a lunch of wild blueberries and then lay down and dozed.

The sun was already pretty far into the west when I awoke, got up, and turned toward the summit of Haystack. I sang Ramesh's song again, now that I was out of earshot. It struck me as odd to wait to sing a pretty song till no one can hear you. Ramesh hadn't been afraid, singing out like that in a room full of sleeping people in the dead of night. But he was another one of these men who seemed to know who he was. I didn't have any way of telling anyone who I was, so I wasn't so sure myself.

There was a breeze at the top, and a fine view all around, for miles and miles over green forest. There was big Lake St. George to the southwest, shimmering silver in the late afternoon sun, and there were a few houses on the outskirts of Liberty to the South, but the main town with the gas station and the store was blocked from view. I walked around the top for a while, my body feeling alive and full of a nice glowing energy. I felt like a lone wolf, scaling and prancing, alone on the mountaintop.

There was one spot of grass that grew in a rough circle, maybe ten feet across, in the middle of a large slab of rock, and I sat down. My body felt a nice animal energy glowing out all over, a sexual energy that wanted to flow out through my whole body, lying naked in the grass under the sun as the wind blew, lying naked in the grass with anyone else who wanted to climb this mountain and lie naked in the grass. This sexuality had nothing to do with male and female, and hardly even with anatomy at all. It had to do rather with trust and love. Who would you trust to roll naked with in the grass? Who would you lie next to in the night as you sleep? I stood up; life seemed wonderful and simple, I was a young man, at the top of a mountain with a long, long view and everywhere to go.

I looked out over the woods, saw the cabins and shelters and houses that people had built for that time when the sun, which was slowly sinking now into the west, would be gone, and the person they'd chosen to lie beside naked in the dark would come and they would roll around on white sheets and thick mattresses in rooms with closed doors and beamed ceilings, windows with curtains, and doors with locks, and at some point they would have orgasms which would drain them of energy so they could sleep and let the energy flow slowly back into them. And it seemed that all nature was cyclic like that, filling and emptying and waiting to fill again, and that everything people did was a round-about way of finding someone to exchange this sexual energy with, and that this was so important that as soon as you find someone you begin to set up a territory that's all yours, you make a bed in a private room to lie naked together, you make a kitchen to cook food to give you the energy to lie naked together, you plant a garden or plough a field or get a job or somehow acquire the money that will allow you to set up this fortress around your need. You discover you have to guard against your neighbor because you've found your person to lie naked together with and he might want to take over, so you argue and wrangle over your territory, and eventually men build fences and then quarrel over them, and fight wars and kill people and learn to hate them out of their fear that they'll overrun the palace they've built so carefully in which to lie naked together. As a result of all this lying naked together children are born, and so bright metal swings are built, schools and barbers and station wagons come into existence, and being a child is a brief period of innocent fun, and being a man is realizing it all.

I felt for the first time I understood what it meant to be a man. Perhaps this was the hex Bob laid on me, for he was the archetypal man, who had found a woman and was building his cabin and now guarding his territory with a ferocity that frightened me away. If Kathy were to come up to the circle of grass I could not lie naked with her without fighting Bob: it was so simple and so strange. For the first time I felt the shock of realizing that men act as if they possessed women, and that I could not participate in that game. I knew at that moment sitting in that circle of grass at the top of the mountain that it was all right with me whoever came up and lay naked in the grass beside me, it didn't make any difference if it were a male or a female, but that if it were Kathy I would be afraid of Bob, and if it were Phoenix I would feel safe. I knew some people say homosexuality is a fear of women, but I could see it wasn't that. I was afraid of men, but that, I knew, is what they call civilization.

I felt an immense sadness, the sadness of being a man, an adult, a mature animal in nature who knew the secret now: a man's role is the filling and emptying of desire, around which he had spun the elaborate hoax he called civilization. I couldn't see any point to this everlasting exchange of energy, of growing and decaying, sowing and reaping, day and night, desire and satisfaction: it all seemed trapped in itself, inevitable and meaningless. The everlasting ebbing and flowing of need, of hunger and horniness and heat and cold, of the seasons and centuries, ultimately defeats time itself, for time only has meaning in rhythm, and this rhythm was endless. Monks must understand this, I thought, and so they've chosen to live away from this struggle. But the rest of the world mostly ignores monks.

The sun was almost to the horizon when Phoenix appeared. It had gotten cool, and I was sitting with my knees up to my chin, staring at the orange-red sky. He sat down next to me, wordless. When the last speck of sun was snuffed out by the horizon he said, "You know, the Egyptians say Ra, the Sun, created people and all other living creatures from his tears." Yes, I could believe that. I turned to Phoenix—his eyes were moist, his pale face glowing with the sky. I put my arm around him, kissed his cheek; he turned his face and we kissed, then lay together in a bittersweet embrace. We lay like that till it was almost too dark to find the path down the mountain.

• • •

As I approached the house I could see Stephen and Debby through the window in the front room, and I could tell Debby was pregnant. They sat huddled at the table, Stephen staring blankly at the floor. This child was one of Ra's tears that wouldn't be born. And you know, I had a similar feeling about my manhood that I'd just conceived: I thought I might consider an abortion, and go on being a boy. Frisbees and hitchhiking, climbing the electric tower to watch the sunrise.

Later, saying goodnight to Stephen, he was a new person for me. We held each other at arm's length. There was sadness in my look, but not as much as I felt. Then we hugged and held onto each other, wishing it were as easy as it had been that morning, but knowing it wasn't. When we pulled apart, Stephen's face had a wisp of a smile on it, expressing a faint memory of our morning's closeness, and the sad irony of being a man.

Fertility and Virility: A Meditation on Sperm

Richard Newman

Any serious consideration by men of the right of women to reproductive choice, a right which eliminates the traditional power with which patriarchy invests biological fatherhood [see R. Newman, "His Sexuality, Her Reproductive Rights," Changing Men, no. 19], should leave us with a question: what are—or even are there—male reproductive rights? While the existence of male reproductive rights may seem self-evident, most discussion I have heard or read on this topic begins precisely where it should end: after the egg has been fertilized. Certainly men are justified in our concern over how women's reproductive rights will affect our relationship to biological fatherhood. However, to express that concern in terms which negate women's reproductive rights—namely, that the presence of our sperm in their bodies gives us rights over those bodies—is to deceptively relabel patriarchal power as "Male Reproductive Rights."

Biologically speaking, men provide the sperm which fertilizes the egg. Nothing more, nothing less. Therefore, it seems to me that our reproductive rights lie in the control we can responsibly exercise over our sperm, in our right to say to the women with whom we have sex: "This is my sperm. If I do not believe that you will do with it what I want to be done with it, I will not agree to put it in your body." However, to arrive at the place where this statement is more than a platitude, more than just a defensive response to women's reproductive choice, we must rethink male sexuality in order to redefine what it means to be a man.

Traditionally, women have had too much of men giving them our sperm. The conventional patriarchal view of childbirth as evidence of male virility (as opposed to fertility, a distinction which will become important later), coupled with the image of motherhood as that which would absolutely fulfill every woman's life, meant that sperm—from the male perspective—was a "gift" which every woman should be glad to receive again and again. The gift, however, was also a danger. If a man wanted to have sex with a woman, he had somehow to convince her that, should she get pregnant, he would not abandon her. His patriarchal privilege to her sexual availability carried with it, for him, the specter of just about the only "power" which she could have over him: that, should she get pregnant, she and the child she carried were his responsibility. The social meaning of sperm, then, has hardly been a benign one. Both genders have had, within the context of patriarchy's sexual "ethic," good reason to fear the consequencs of "unprotected" sex. Artificial birth control has certainly made it easier for men and women to have sex without worrying so much about pregnancy. But not even the pill with its nearly 100 percent effectiveness has done much to alter our basic perception of sperm as, at worst, dangerous, and at best, an inconvenient residue of male sexual desire.

The Sexuality of Virility

But what are the consequences for men of this perception of sperm? Because such a perception relates our sperm only to the ova they fertilize and not to ourselves, it means that we live out our sexual lives, which means our entire lives,without any awareness of ourselves as biologically fertile, as beings inherently able to reproduce. Women, of course, carry and give birth to children, but children would not be possible without our sperm. Still, that does not prevent women from feeling their reproductive *capability* as a source of power. It is a power which derives from within themselves, which is defined by their bodies and so requires no other to dominate.

Fertility lies as much in the potential as in the fact of reproduction. Virility lies only in having reproduced. Men, by privileging virility, by investing our sense of sexual validity in the effect our bodies can have on the bodies of women, have created a situation in which our feelings of sexual self-worth *depend* upon the presence of women. Only when they give birth, or in the precautions they, and we, must take to neutralize our sperm can we see ourselves as fully sexual, fully human beings. Once women refuse to be present for us—as the women's movement has encouraged them to do—once they step outside the boundary of the authority we have claimed as ours, our power dissolves, our world seems empty, and we feel helpless to do anything about it.

And boundaries are precisely what I am talking about here. The fertilizing nature of sperm is dangerous—as opposed to simply a fact—only as long as no one sets a limit beyond which the sperm's potency is meaningless. The military aspect of our phallic symbolism grows directly out of the patriarchal concept that male sexual power transcends all boundaries, and that the places into which our power reaches become extensions of ourselves. Traditionally, women have functioned as sexual extensions of men, as objects for our use. However, with women's victory in claiming their right to reproductive choice, *to draw a physical line beyond which men have no power*, we have been faced with the loss not simply of the object that made possible our virility, but of the sexuality which depended on both.

Reclaiming Our Fertility

Since you can only lose something that is not yours to begin with, and since the fact remains that human beings are sexual by definition, men cannot lose that sexuality which inheres in our bodies, which is our birthright and which depends on no other for its existence. It is a sexuality rooted in the facts of our biology, in the rhythms of the penis, the fertility of our sperm, the fact that each hard-on, each orgasm, expresses the power of the male body to reproduce itself. It is a sexuality limited by the reality that our bodies end, both in space and in time. Therefore, it is a sexuality over which we have certain rights, one of those being the right to demand that anyone with whom we choose to share it must respect how we want the consequences of that sharing to be dealt with.

And so we return to the statement with which I began: "This is my sperm. If I do not believe that you will do with it what I want to be done with it, I will not agree to put in your body." As a reproductive right, this statement does not seem to amount to much. After all, what keeps a woman from agreeing and then going back on her word? That people are human, that the reality of being pregnant might actually, and for very legitimate reasons, change a woman's mind about what she intends to do with her pregnancy, is something no one can change. All that men *can* do is impress upon women how seriously we take our biological fertility, and how potentially dehumanizing of us is any decision on their part that does not respect our wishes. (If you think about it, this is the position women have always been in: What keeps a man from failing to take his responsibility should she get pregnant?) It does seem to me that a pregnant woman who knew her partner's feelings about having children before they had sex, who chooses against his wishes to have the child they both conceived, forfeits any right to hold that man accountable for that child; the decision to have the baby will have been hers alone. It is her absolute right to make that decision; but, in the situation I have outlined above, the right to sue him for support does not follow, since he would not have had sex with her if he had known she would choose to have the baby. (I also think that the man should *voluntarily* assume some responsibility for the child, not for sentimental reasons, but simply because no child should go in any way unprovided for.) In the case of a woman who chooses to abort a pregnancy she originally said she would carry to term, once men stop thinking of childbirth as proof of virility we may find that the fate of each individual sperm no longer carries the entire weight of validating ourselves as men: abortion threatens virility, not fertility.

Living Our Manhood

Sperm is not only the genetic product of our bodies, it is also the physical product of our masculinity. Just as patriarchal power enables men to deny the biological specificity of pregnancy and childbirth, and so deny women their womanhood, a woman who does not respect a man's feelings about his sperm denies him his manhood. And just as women have asserted the self-evident validity of their womanhood by reclaiming their sexual biology and the right to determine its meaning, men too can begin to redefine our manhood. We can consciously claim our sperm and give it significance congruent with the limits of *our* lives, thereby changing the patriarchal meaning we have, until now, given it. The point is not to play tit for tat with social/sexual power, nor to look for ways of blaming women for the same kind of power strategies of which men have been guilty. The point is to learn how to live our manhood in such a way that a statement like the one with which I began, because it grows from our deepest convictions about ourselves, will bespeak our own self-respect and, therefore, leave our female lovers no choice but to take us seriously.

But what does it mean to "live our manhood?"

It means to live fully *in* our bodies, to commit our lives first to what we can know *of and with* our bodies. Just like a woman's body, ours also has a reproductive cycle, and we go through it, whether alone or with a partner, every time we orgasm. Nor does it matter that we do not ejaculate inside a vagina. For men, biologically speaking, there is no difference between erotic and reproductive sex. To accept this, to live it, to make a part of the rhythm of our lives, is to alter irrevocably what it means to be a man; is to assert that men, simply by living consciously aware of the biological limits our nature imposes on us, are masculine. Masculinity becomes, then, not something we must prove *with* our bodies, but the perpetual condition *of* our bodies.

For example, men often feel threatened by lesbians. What lesbians themselves would probably call a simple lack of sexual interest is felt by some men as an active assault on our sexuality. To the degree that we allow ourselves to define our sexuality in patriarchal terms, the threat is real. Female homosexuality is a boundary which patriarchal power cannot cross except by force. However, once men begin to live our manhood as an inherent, self-evident quality, once we see ourselves as fully and reflexively sexual, someone else's lack of sexual interest—be they male or female—cannot threaten us because the *meaning* of our sex resides within ourselves, not in how another person sees us.

A sexuality so deeply grounded in a physical masculinity contains the potential for a new phallic symbolism, non-violent and non-hierarchical. Rather than a representation of sex as power, as existing within the dichotomy of potency and impotence, the positive-negative polarity of the hard vs. the soft penis, we might instead develop a symbolism of the continuum between dormancy and activity, of sexuality as an embodied process. Such a sexuality, because it would be self-contained, would not be predatory, would not require the subservience of another for its fulfillment. It would recognize that we are all embodied individuals; it would form its community with others who also live embodied lives; and it would always insist first on its own integrity, on being faithful to the body which shapes it and to which it, in turn, gives form.

(This essay is a work in process and, as such, it is flawed. To some, the flaws will be glaring: the implicit assumption that my white, middle-class masculinity can be used for all masculinities; the failure to deal with the fact that the statement I propose as a way to begin thinking about male reproductive rights assumes a vulnerability on the part of men that male privilege renders inaccessible to us—unless we first deal effectively with that privilege; and there are others. Still, the main ideas about the boundlessness of male sexuality and the need for men to accept the limitations of our bodies are, I think, sound. R.N.)

Masturbation: Touching Oneself Anew

David Goff

One afternoon in early spring two years ago, I touched myself in a new way. Looking back on that afternoon I am now amused to realize that despite having masturbated since I was five or six years of age this was like the very first time. Through the magically transformative power of emotional crisis I had the opportunity to rediscover and re-possess my self through the simple act of making love to, and pleasing, myself. This simple hour I spent in bed exploring my own passionate longing, erogenous zones, and expanding sensitivity to love, changed my love-life totally.

What I experienced that day, and in the months that followed, was a unique and powerful sense of love and caring for and from "something" in myself that fulfilled and healed me. After two years of examining this ongoing intra-psychic, erotic, love affair, I have come to believe that masturbation contains the potential for something of greater significance to well-being than simple sexual release. I believe that auto-erotic love provides an opportunity for the inner feminine and masculine to merge in an act of harmony that dimin-ishes the emotional charge associated with projecting the Beloved upon men and women in our external lives. This creates a freer internal atmosphere from which to express ourselves and engage others. I want to share with you how this process came about in me, and why I think it meaningful, and replicable, for those who might be seeking greater fulfillment in their relationships and love lives.

I started "playing with myself" consciously around the age of six. By eight years of age it became part of morning and evening rituals. Somehow, I had already developed the good sense to keep this delicious activity to myself. I found great solace in the warm tickling sensations that both excited and relaxed me, and assured me that wherever I was, I always had a secret friend with whom I could play. By the time my mother and the church began their urgent warnings about the dangers and corruption of self abuse, I was already addicted to myself. They never succeeded in getting me to abandon my first lover. But, they did succeed in making me feel guilty, dirty, and very paranoid that anyone (especially my mother) should find out about my "disgusting" habit. The pleasure, however, got ever so slightly more delicious.

I have masturbated more or less regularly ever since those early years. Touching myself provided a necessary pressure release valve that helped me survive adolescence. Later it got me through times of loneliness and complemented the times of plenty in my life. The guilt remained, but declined significantly after I darted out from the heavy-handed wing of the church. I remember one priest telling me in confessional that no woman would ever want to marry me if I continued.

In my early adulthood I kept my auto-erotic activity a closely guarded secret. As I became capable of deeper and more intimate relationships with women I found that they were often open-minded about masturbation as a phenomenon, but none too pleased to know that I practiced it despite the quality of our relationship. My observation was that it was cool to acknowledge that we "normal" people did it, as long as there was no discussion about the hows, whys, and the frequency. It seemed that what one did with one's self was much more private and taboo than what one did with others. I have since come to wonder why in a sexually liberated age, masturbation, now considered a normal behavior, still carries the stigma of being associated with unsatisfied passion, sexual insatiability, and self-absorption?

Having reflected on that question for some time, it occurred to me that masturbating always provided the physical release from sexual frustration that I wanted, but it frequently left me feeling empty and lonely. This feeling of emptiness seemed inherent in the experience and resulted in my feeling less than complete. This feeling of being incomplete translated into unwholesomeness, and contributed directly to my unwillingness to openly and freely discuss masturbation and its attendant rituals. As a man acknowledging my feelings of being less than whole remains a difficult task. Despite all that I know about my self, admitting that I am missing something still seemingly threatens the self-image that permits me to function as a man in the world.

I am reluctant to generalize from my own early experiences a widely held male belief system around masturbation. In the last two years, male friends willing to discuss their experiences with masturbation have reiterated my experience. I have no doubt the popular euphemisms, "jerking off" and "whacking off" are indicative of attitudes that are widespread. There is an aura of derision and inauthenticity surrounding masculine self-love. References to people as "jerk-offs" or to experiences of being "stroked" by untrustworthy neighbors or manipulative business associates are consistent with such attitudes. The hand motions associated with masturbation occasionally crop up as a means of putdown, implying someone is inferior. I believe that for men, masturbating, something we almost all do, still too frequently is experienced as a failure of our manhood, and as a testimony to our unwholesome sexuality.

My experience with women suggests that their attitudes are similar but perhaps less virulent. The women's movement, and the relatively new (last twenty years) demand for sexual satisfaction and orgasmic fulfillment has tended to bring women into a more endearing relationship with their bodies. Women are encouraged by sex therapists and popular women's magazines to touch themselves, to get to know their bodies, and their erogenous zones. For many women the road to becoming orgasmic includes a great deal of self-love. Still, by and large, the women with whom I have discussed masturbation admit to infrequent practice and solely as a means of release.

So it is with some wonder that I look back on my experience two years ago, and marvel at the circumstances which constellated a whole new approach to, and deeper respect for self-loving. I was two months into a very painful separation from my wife. I was experiencing agonizing feelings of being rejected and abandoned. Our twelve year relationship had totally capsized. Emotionally, I was deeply wounded and enduring incredible doubt about my self. Additionally, for the first time in my life I was suffering from prostitus, an inflammation of the prostate gland that can result in painfully swollen testicles. The urologist I consulted suggested regular intercourse as the best available treatment for what was essentially a stress-related ailment. Sexual intimacy with another was impossible. The pain and discomfort could only be relieved by regular masturbation. The only sexual fantasies I had were about my wife and these were emotionally painful. Arousal itself was intensely painful physically. I was faced with an incredible dilemma. I had to masturbate, but I could not do so, as I always had. My initial attempts were so painful and difficult that I simply could not continue. I was very unhappy.

I persevered through those difficult days thanks to the support of some loving and nurturing men friends, and a real determination to accept and be transformed by this experience. Without my wife to love, I soon wisely chose to give that love to myself and to explore new ways of loving my self. A man friend told me of a feminist adage he had heard. "A woman should become the man she wants to marry." I decided that made sense for me as a man, and that I could become the woman I wanted to love. The desire to heal myself physically and emotionally, combined with the stimulus of thinking about, and experiencing the feminine I embodied, culminated in my creating a whole new masturbatory ritual, organized more around my need to love and be loved than around sexual release.

At last I arrived, that spring afternoon, in my bed with time to be with myself. I created an environment rich with textures, music, incense, and massage oil that would stimulate and please the one I chose to be with. Very slowly I began to touch and explore my body, as if I were the woman I had longed for, loved, and now had the opportunity to experience and express those feelings with. With the excitement of discovery I ventured into my erogenous zones and found feelings and sensations that were sometimes familiar and sometimes new. I became quickly aroused and anxious. It was painful, but instead of driving myself over the threshold of orgasm, I slowed my breathing and pace and re-explored my body, connecting all of myself with the excitement I felt. For nearly an hour I repeated this drama of approaching release and retreating. My body sang to me in ways that I had known only in my most incredible moments with a lover. As I let myself slip over that threshold I was released into a full-bodied orgasm that washed away all my fears of lost and un-recoverable love. In the afterglow I knew myself as well-loved and as complete as I had ever felt.

With this experience I noticed that I felt loved as if I had been with my beloved. I found that I was a lot less obsessive in thinking about my wife. I needed to masturbate less frequently as time went along because my physical condition improved. I got greater satisfaction out of the times I did touch myself. And, surprisingly, I needed to put less energy into creating a fantasy to catalyze my excitement. The care-full touching and loving attention I gave my self seemed quite enough.

This experience of self-love seems to encapsulate the real and virtually undiscussed potential that masturbation carries for each of us. I do not believe masturbation must remain an experience needlessly encumbered by connotations of dirtiness, self-absorption, and empty longing. I believe my experience calls into question the attitudes and rituals that we men perpetuate in our self-love. What do our goal oriented and abbreviated auto-erotic rituals say about our relationships with our own bodies, our internal lovers?

And how do we play these attitudes out in our relationships? I believe the quality of masturbatory rituals is indicative of the love we hold for ourselves.

There is much talk these days about the importance of our inner relationship between our masculine and feminine sides. Much has been written about how our healthy development depends upon the success of this inner merging. Elaborate theories about this inner courtship and its impact upon our relationships in the world have emerged from psychotherapists and spiritual teachers alike. I believe conscious masturbatory rituals that align the erotic power of our instinctual sexuality with a desire to explore, know, and love our total being can help increase our well-being and self-fulfillment. By focusing a greater degree of regard upon our intra-psychic opposite we access and reinforce communication of the most healing, nurturing, and intimate sort.

The equation of love that seems to govern and regulate our capacities for unconditional relatedness remains "Love Thy Neighbor as Thyself." A conscious, passionate, and full-bodied experience of self-love then becomes an affirmation of love for all. The quality of relatedness within is reflected without. The richness of my internal marriage enlarges the spectrum of experiences and emotions I can embrace in my relationships with others. I am much more capable of loving and supporting the emergence of masculine and feminine attributes in others.

In one sense it seems almost trite to say that masturbation is self-love. We see it unfold unselfconsciously in children and then it goes underground. When it re-emerges in adulthood it is understood as normal and quasi-acceptable but is framed in mechanistic terms of providing release of pent-up instinctual energy. And, it is precisely this reason that the gift we give ourselves sexually, remains so unsatisfying. It fulfills our physical criteria for satisfaction but usually ignores the psycho-spiritual instinctive urge to merge. When I followed that instinctive urge to merge it led me to internalizing an I-Thou relationship with my beloved. What had been intuited and understood now became dynamic and soul-satisfyingly real. Masturbation became procreative. What is born of this intra-psychic coupling? Love has its own chemistry in each of us. My guess is that when it takes, what emerges is a deeply individuated and authentic manifestation of our truest sexual identity. I offer that possibility as incentive enough for considering and recreating masturbation and its attendant rituals.

Why Do Men Wear Earrings on One Ear?

Trinidad Sanchez

Sepa yo!
Maybe por costumbre, maybe porqué es la moda
or they have made promesas, maybe for some vieja
for cosmetics or because some women love it
because they were on sale
because they are egocentric cabrons y buscan la atención
because la chica selling them was sooooo mamacita
and they could not refuse
maybe to tell you they are free, innovative, avant-garde
and liberated, maybe because of the full moon
maybe because one earring is cheaper than two
maybe to keep the women guessing and the men on their toes
maybe they are gay caballeros
maybe as a reminder de algo que no querien olvidar—
like the last time they had sex or to be sexy looking
maybe they are sexually confused
maybe to let *you* know they are very easily sexually aroused
maybe to separate themselves from lo mas macho
maybe they are poets, writers y la literatura is their thing!

Why do men wear earrings on one ear?
Sepa yo! Maybe baby . . . .
they are reincarnated pirutos of yesteryears
maybe they lost the other one
maybe they are looking for someone good at cooking
maybe it makes them look like something is cooking
maybe to send signals—the left ear is right
and the right ear is wrong
maybe it depends on which coast you are on.

Why do men wear earrings on one ear?
Who knows . . . . maybe it looks much better than the nose, the toes
maybe to remind others which ear is deaf
maybe to distinguish them from those who don't and
those who won't, maybe to separate them from the women
maybe because as women say: Men can only do things half right
maybe to be imitators of the superior sex—half way
maybe they are undercover policia trying to be *real* cool
maybe they are Republicans trying to be progressively liberal
maybe they are Democrats disguising their conservatism
or leftists telling you they are in the right party

Maybe they are revolutionaries—
looking for a peace—P E A C E!

maybe they are undecided
maybe to be cute
maybe because life is short

Why do men wear earrings on one ear?
Sepa yo!

Loyalty

Essex Hemphill

For my so-called sins against nature and the race, I gain the burdensome knowledge of carnal secrets. It rivals rituals of sacrifice and worship, and conjures the same glassy-eyed results—with less bloodshed. A knowledge disquieting and liberating inhabits my soul. It often comforts me, or at times, is miserably intoxicating with requisite hangovers and regrets. At other moments it is sacred communion, causing me to moan and tremble and talk dirty as the Holy Ghost fucks me. It is a knowledge of fire and consumption that I will carry beyond the grave. When I sit in God's final judgment, I will wager this knowledge against my entrance into the Holy Kingdom. There was no other way for me to know the beauty of Earth except through the sexual love of men, men who were often more terrified than I, even as they posed before me, behind the learned constrictions of manhood, mocking me with muscles, erections, and wives.

I discovered any man can be seduced—even if the price is humiliation or death for the seducer. Late nights and desperate hours teach us to approach loneliness unarmed, or risk provoking it to torture us with endless living sorrows we believe only the dead can endure.

But who are these dead, able to withstand the constant attack of merciless loneliness with its intense weapons, clever trickery and deceit? Many of them are men like me, born of common stock and ordinary dreamers. Men who vaguely answer to "American," or exhibit visible apprehension when American is defined and celebrated to their exclusion. Men who more often than not are simply called "nigga" if no one remembers their name.

We constitute the invisible brothers in our communities, those of us who live "in the life"; the choir boys with secrets, the uncle living in an impeccable flat with a roommate who sleeps down the hall when family visits. Men of power and humble peasantry, reduced to silence and invisibility of not speaking out, rendered mute by the middle-class aspirations of a people trying hard to forget the shame and cruelties of slavery and ghettos. Through denials and abbreviated histories riddled with omissions, the middle-class sets about whitewashing and fixing-up the race to impress each other *and* the rednecks that could give a damn, the lethal ones who believe the only good nigga is a dead nigga.

I speak for thousands, perhaps hundreds of thousands of men who live and die in the shadow of secrets, unable to speak of the love that helps them endure and contribute to the race. Their ordinary kisses, stolen or shared behind facades of heroic achievement, their kisses of sweet spit and loyalty are scrubbed away by the propaganda makers of the race, who would just as soon have us believe black people can fly, rather than reveal that black men have been longing to kiss one another, and have done so, for centuries.

Surely the "Talented Tenth" are among the most destructive and deadly members of our race. Some are misguided watchdogs aspiring to a mythical white perfection through emulation. They busy themselves classifying black culture into celebrations, lectures and symposia that wrongly present black people as sexually, culturally and politically monolithic. Black homosexuals are unacknowledged or ridiculed. Our love of our race is attacked as suspect. Our love of each other, man for man, is often deemed a pathological expression of racism. This has justified accusing us of being race traitors or victims of matriarchy.

The black homosexual is hard pressed to gain audience among his heterosexual brothers—even if he is more talented, he is inhibited by his silence or his admissions. This is what the race has depended on to erase homosexuality from our recorded history. The "chosen" history. But these constructions of silence are futile exercises in denial. We are not going to go away with our issues of sexuality. We are coming home. Black homosexuals are demanding that self-appointed proprietors of history release our brothers (and sisters) from psychosexual fears and ignorance.

It is not enough to say that one was a brilliant poet, scientist, educator or rebel. Who did he love? It makes a difference. I cannot become a whole man simply on what you feed me: watered down versions of black life in America. I need the ass-splitting truth to be told, so I will have something pure to emulate, a reason to remain loyal.

Rabbit, An Interview

Allan Troxler

On Route 48 the directions blow out the window. I call R. from a
McDonald's somewhere. I'm late so he tells me about a shortcut. Take
the second or third Summerton exit. Turn back under the highway;
there may be a sign. After so far, turn right. Cross fishing creek twice.
Eight to ten miles. Top of hill. Pecan trees. No, no landmarks. Everybody knows me, if you get lost.

Tobacco's turning bright yellow. Flowers spangle the cotton fields.
The heavy air smells like grape Nehi—kudzu must be blooming. His
vague instructions, the haphazardous distances, would apply in most
any direction. He could be thirty miles back the other way by now.

Justus Seed Farm Road. Half Acre School Road. A worn farm
town at a crossroads. A jumble of dusty rockers and pitchforks fills
one window of the general store. Seems like he could have mentioned road names, or towns. Somebody's lettered a sign that says
"RABBITS" in a yard where bottle-gourd birdhouses hang way up on
crooked crossbranches.

Ahead something black unfolds, spreads out, lifts off and soars.
Buzzard. The grinding sound from the left front wheel's getting worse.
Down a hill. Across some creek.

"Godforsaken wildernesse!" bellows a European adventurer as
his horse sinks up to the saddlebags. I imagine R. sitting at home,
smiling slightly. What, after all, are transitory towns and road signs
when your people have been here since time began? "Everybody
knows me," he says as I pass houses where brown, impassive
families sit in the shade.

At the top of a long rise, a colonnade of pecan trees watches over
an old house. I holler through the screen door: my voice hangs in the
dark parlor. Here and there are signs, finally. This is his place after all.

Next door, an old sprightly Indian woman, R.'s mother, chats at the
kitchen table with a big rough-hewn black woman. We exchange

pleasantries and they resume their talk of family in voices strange to my ear. R. and I put together a lunch—fried chicken, thick soup, butter beans, sweet potato pie, watermelon, iced tea—and then we walk back through the pecan grove and settle in his parlor.

"Whooooooeeeeee!" he squeals, tasting the soup. "Take somebody mean to grow peppers that hot!" I start with the pie myself, and surmise that his mamma must be infinitely kind.

"There were all sorts of landmarks, and those roads do have names."

"Why confuse you with details?" he asks loftily over a chicken leg. His dark eyes are laughing.

This afternoon we aim to record R.'s stories as a gay man, native to this place. Where shall we begin?

Naming. That seems a good place to start. Straightaway R. chooses Rabbit. "I'll be Rabbit!" he laughs, raring back in his sawed-off straightback chair. Rabbit the trickster, the sly joker. And I'll be the credulous European in a new and ancient world.

Rabbit's people will be the Birds. Through all the open windows come their soft chirps and sweet whistling.

Very few people can say, "I am where my ancestors have been before the memory of man runneth to the contrary." We get all these white theories about the Bering Straits, Polynesia, the Vikings, all that silliness, but we know we've been here forever.

Being nature and a part of nature—a natural spirituality, a natural harmony—that's what is essentially Indian for me. And also it's about family. There's an immediate, present sense of your own identity because everybody else in the family and in the tribe is a clone of yourself. So you look at yourself, everywhere you go, you look at yourself.

There's a drawing that John White did around 1585. It's called "The Flyer"—probably a conjurer, a shaman, homoerotic. He's almost naked, with a dried bluebird attached to the side of his head, and he's literally in the air, dancing, flying. An Algonquian ancestor. He looks just like a boy up in the community, a cousin. Every time I see him I tease him about being the flyer or the conjurer.

One thing about pre-Columbian America was the virgin forest—climax-formation forest. The sweetgum and pines are the first trees to come back after a fire. Then the oaks force the pines out and form a canopy over the forest floor, and you get the dogwoods and hollies and ferns. It's nothing like the savage wilderness that the white folks described when they came here. The oak trees are a cathedral with the sun shafting down through them.

So it was a Sunday night. I took some acid maybe around seven o'clock and I finally got out of the house around ten. I went to Elora; there was nothing happening there. And I drove to Mayhew, it was a little bigger, but there was nothing happening there so I decided to come back to the disco in Pleasant Hill, where the families are. My great-great-grandfather's house is on one side, and my uncle's house is on that side, and my granddaddy's house on this side. It's on a knoll right in the middle of the community, on top of ancestral ground.

The two brothers who run the place were closing up. I mentioned to one of them I wanted some firewood. He said, "Well, hang around. We can talk about it." There were about six or seven guys still there. The older brother was high and when he realized I was tripping he went and turned the sound system back on, and when he did the light system came on too, and the spotlights came beaming down through the dark of the empty dance hall.

I was halfway conscious of the song he kept playing over and over—"You so fine. You got style, you got grace . . . " Over and over, so I get up and start dancing, in the semidarkness. Suddenly I flip into the world of the virgin forest, with the sun shafting down through the oak trees. Climax-formation forest. I strip naked and I'm dancing native. "You so fine. You got grace." Naked, dancing. Ancestral ground. And then everybody else was naked, and we were having an orgy!

Here in the community people know that I'm Indian, of course; but I go anywhere else, they assume I'm black. You see it just all goes to show we all niggers in America, unless you're white.

In the early '60s, when I first went to college, there were nine of us. We were these nine "others," these nine niggers, right? There was a restaurant outside of town that wouldn't let black folk in. It didn't matter whether you Indian or black, they wouldn't let niggers in. So we go out there—nonviolence, right? "Go limp." So we going limp and this big white woman pulls up her dress and starts to piss on me, saying, "This, nigger, is the closest you gonna get to white pussy!" And I look at her—it's such an irony because I'm a faggot, and I don't want no white pussy!

Years later, up north, this dark man automatically assumes that I'm a mulatto. He don't know that I've been pissed on in civil rights, protesting a segregated restaurant. He spits in my face! Says, "You probably love having all that white blood." And you know, I'm speechless! Now I'd sock the shit out of him first, but I say, "Goddamn, I been out there fighting for your ass and you've got the stupidity to spit in my face!"

You get a lot of that still—how homosexuality is a form of genocide against blacks, and that the only reason you find black guys sleeping with faggots is that they were trying to make some money to survive, to get bread for their babies. They said that AIDS is something that the white boy put on black folk, right?

Rabbit slumps down in his chair. The room is quiet, except for the ice in a glass of tea. We look away from each other. Bird songs embroider the late afternoon.

The curing season . . . Hear that?

I hear a machine's persistent hum from across the road.

That is a gas-fired, bulk tobacco-burning barn. Ruins the night. You be out there listening to the cicadas and the crickets, the stars like moons, so bright and beautiful, and then there's this fucking bulk-barn blower.

When I was a kid, the tobacco barn had one of these mole-hill furnaces, and you had to cut firewood to feed up into the stone furnace, which cured the tobacco inside. You had a hammock and you had to sleep down there, to stoke the fire every hour. You'd go down with your daddy and you'd just sit and watch the fire, not saying a word. Listening to the night. Curing. And the wonderful smell of tobacco in the air. That's how you knew the curing season was on.

When he was a boy, my uncle came up unawares on my great-granddaddy one night. My great-grandma happened to be down there in the hammock with my great-grandaddy and they were fucking. So my uncle just stayed in the dark and listened and watched. My family has always been educated and propertied and *very* respectable, but there is Great-Granddaddy in the hammock fucking Great-Grandma! And she's saying, "Oh, Mr. Bird! It's so good, Mr. Bird! Ohh, ohhh, OHHH, Mr. Bird! Mr. Bird! Mr. Bird!" *And Rabbit hunkers back and howls in ecstasy and claps his hands.* Aah, the curing season.

This was a dirt road when I was growing up, and on a lazy day, this time of afternoon, you'd sit on the front porch and all you'd do is watch a few cars come by. You'd watch the dust rise and then you'd watch the dust settle. That was our excitement—to watch the dust rise and fall.

Did I ever tell you the story about my uncle and this white boy who had the local grocery store, where they sold on credit, and at the end of the year you had such a bill you never could pay up and then you started the whole shit over again the next year. He and this white boy would sit around the store joking about who had the biggest dick. So finally one day he say, "I'm getting sick of you telling them lies about your tiny white dick!" "And I'm sick of you, nigger, telling about your big dick!" "All right, let's have a contest!"

So the white boy says, "Go bring me a gallon fruit jar! I'll show you my dick is so big it won't fit into the mouth of a gallon fruit jar!" So my uncle says, "Go bring me a pickle jar! Show you *my* dick is so big it won't get into the mouth of a pickle jar!"

Well, years later my uncle's in the hospital and he's lying there in one of those hospital gowns, a big-boned, beautiful man with straight black hair. I had wanted to do this all my life, because when I was a child he would come and he would grab my knee, and he would squeeze it real hard, and look me right in the eye, and I was like a deer flashlighted at night, mesmerized—and being the faggot that I was, loving it!

So to get back at him for squeezing my knee all those years, I grabbed his dick and squeezed it! It was a shock! If it had been a heart problem he would have had a heart attack. And then he burst out grinning! He grinned and he grinned, and I grinned. I shook that thing! It was like squeezing a big Coke bottle!

I was a sharecropper's son. We'd start in January, clearing the tobacco bed, preparing it to plant. Then we'd break land as soon as the rains stopped. And then once you got the tobacco growing, you plowed and chopped and plowed again. I walked a hundred miles a day behind those two mules, traipsing down the furrow mile after mile after mile after mile, day after day after day.

I'd go to school maybe the first couple of days, register and get my books, and then I'd stay out and help finish priming the tobacco, and tying it up at night to get it to the market.

But there was time for pleasure, too. Rabbit enjoyed the company of the older boy across the road, and two cousins. They carried on "with impunity" in the back of the neighbor's daddy's car, circle-jerking and sucking. From age 10 or 11 on, though, his true love was Jimmy, the son of a black lumberjack who worked for his father occasionally. Their family lived a feral existence far from the road. The hulking lumberjack skirted through the pasture, dreading Rabbit's grandmother's chickens, and the littlest boy would take off for the woods running when Rabbit approached.

Jimmy was always around. I don't think he ever had gone to school. I don't know if he could read or write. I still remember the first time we made love, on the north slope below the tobacco barn, in the woods. I can go there now and get a hard on. We made love everywhere. Even in the curing barn one time, with the furnaces going and maybe a hundred and thirty degrees heat. You loop the tobacco on sticks and you hang them in tiers, eight up to the top. You'd leave the middle tier, the bottom of it, free so you could look up to see how the leaves were curing up above. I was thirteen or fourteen, hanging from the rafters, and we were fucking and sweating and every time we come together we be sloshing and the sweat would fly everywhere and you'd hear this deep "slush" sound. Whap! Whap! Whap!

My daddy had a '59 Impala Chevrolet, and I just hated that goddamned car because I had to learn to drive on it. I'm a country boy, right, and they make you parallel park. You know how big a 1959 Impala Chevrolet is? Took me five or six times to get my license. So, I'd be sitting in there, playing like I'm shifting the gears. And he'd be standing outside and he'd get a hard-on that would go down his pants. And he'd take it out, and we'd play with one another, and the family would be sitting right there on the porch, unaware.

It was what got me through adolescence really, that friendship. After that I suppressed everything, sublimated into studying and trying to get away from the farm, being valedictorian and getting a scholarship and getting off the farm. I be damned if I was going to be a sharecropper.

During my sophomore year in college, I was home and Jimmy's little brother came to visit. "How's Jimmy?" I asked him.

"Haven't you heard?"

"Heard what?"

"Well, his woman shot him."

He was married and had kids, but it turned out he was living with this other woman. I think she lived with her mother, and he was staying there with them. He had made some comment at dinner about her mother, and then he went to take a bath. She came in and said, "Do you still mean what you said about my ma?" He said, "You damn right!" And she shot him, dead.

In the backyard, a little brown rabbit watches while I pee. Then, all weightless nerve and muscle, ear and whisker, it arcs away. Rabbit dreams sometimes of Indian youths setting off on vision quests in emblematic quilts. I ask him, what of his own experience?

Well, there was the quilt his grandmother made when he left for college, and there were epiphanies along the way, as he became student, poet, lawyer, art collector. Far away, in a three-piece suit, he found himself walking down 5th Avenue after lunch, playing spoons. Clickety clickety click. *Waiting for "wait" to change to "walk."*

Clickety click. *The next day he told the office he had another job, somewhere else. Soon he was home. All his aunts gave him quilts for his new life, on ancestral ground. At first he lived in the cabin down through the woods, by the farm pond.*

I'd be lying down on the pier with the rim of trees around me and the bowl of the sky above. Sometimes I'd be masturbating and the sky would descend, would come in on me, would rapture me. The sky, the sun, the clouds would be right on me. One time I was out on the pier, moaning and groaning, and a young deer came down the steps, right down the embankment, out onto the pier. It came toward me, making the same sounds. Perhaps it had gotten lost from its mother. I continued beating, baaing, and it came toward me, along the pier, this baby deer!

Later he moved into the house where his grandmother had raised his father, and then him. "Sometimes I'm totally baffled by the way life jerks you around, brings you back around. That's one of my biggest ironies, that I'm back, in the house I grew up in."

Rabbit has never told his family he's gay. "I don't think it's necessary," he says, "because it's understood." He's sure his daddy knows because he rescued Rabbit once from a couple of men he'd brought home—rough trade who were getting mean. And his mother doesn't pressure him to get married or to find a woman. "You need a friend," she suggested a while back. Rabbit shook his head and said, "You damn right I need a friend."

What of his search for friendship? And what about Indianness and blackness along the way?

"I'm an Indian," Rabbit says. "I deal with blacks. I deal with Indians. I don't deal with whites. Is that what you mean?"

In its blunt way, I reckon it is.

By happenstance, Rabbit's early partners for sex were black. In an apartheid world which reinforced the closeness of blacks and Indians—Rabbit's birth certificate reads "Colored" rather than "Indian"—Rabbit's light skin was sometimes a sign of the sissy, while "the real men, the athletes, were these black guys, the so-called 'mandingo' types."

I started first grade in a four-room schoolhouse. "The Pleasant Hill Julius Rosenwald School" it said above the portico. It had pot-bellied stoves, and of course it had an outdoor john. The students when they took a leak stood around this circular well-casing and pissed in front of one another. And I loved it.

In retrospect you wonder, how did you get away with all these things that you now know were connected with your sexuality and sexual interest? Like raising your hand, saying "Teacher, may I be excused?" to go every hour on the hour to check out the pissoir. At the time there were poor boys who had to stay out to work, sixteen, eighteen years old. They'd come the first day and then they'd come back when it snowed or rained. And I loved it, these huge mandingos, mature farm men, pissing right in front of me!

In my sixth-grade year, after integration, the county said, "We don't want you, but we gonna give y'all the best facilities so y'all can't say that you not equal." So we got brick schools and central heat and indoor toilets! And they tore the pissoir down!

"Anthrophilologist." That's what Rabbit calls himself. And a significant part of his fieldwork has been conducted in and around the pool halls nearby. Watching, listening, "trying to absorb the scene."

It's the only thing in town, right? A funky jukebox, a couple of pool tables, guys standing around the wall watching. Too broke to play or to buy beer. Just hanging out because there ain't nowhere else to go. You have to learn the signals: "You can wink at me and I can follow you out, but you better not speak to me, and I definitely ain't gonna speak to you."

But if you get them around the corner, then you can deal. You say, "Hey! What's happening? Want to smoke a joint?"

"I know what the deal is," he'll say. Which means he understands that we can get together and have sex. And the second aspect of that is, "The deal is that we can deal. You make me an offer and I'll think about it." There's a *quid pro quo*. It's not hard and fast, but there has to be something.

It could be, "Why don't you buy me a pack of cigarettes, man. Yeah, we can deal." Or, "Hey man, you know, I need a couple of bucks to get me a haircut. You know what the deal is."

Or it can be more outrageous. "Hey man, I need a new pair of sneakers. I can't come see you if I can't get no sneakers to walk on, man. You know the deal."

And part of that deal in a third sense is, "You're the sissy, and I'm the man. I fuck you, you suck my dick, but I ain't gonna do none of that shit. You know the deal." It's a way of doing what you want to do, maybe getting something out of it in a financial sense, and preserving your macho.

Or, "Hey man, I got a wife, I got a girlfriend. What am I gonna get out of this deal? I'm not gonna enjoy this. If I wanted to get off, I'd go and fuck my old lady!" And I say to myself, "Well shit, why ain't you at home fucking your old lady?" He probably doesn't even have an old lady, which is also part of the deal, right?

It may be that people have to sell their bodies out of economic circumstances, but I think that's *de minimis* in terms of the attraction of men to one another. There has to be a homoerotic element to that turn-on.

Now the AIDS epidemic, that's had a major impact on this kind of activity. Now the thing is, "Hey man, you know the deal. You got any rubbers?" I'm reminded of this recent news story, from prison, how the administration couldn't figure out why the plastic covering the chickens in the kitchen was disappearing, why the plastic in the stockroom was disappearing, why all this plastic from different things was disappearing. And finally they figured out that the inmates were making homemade condoms! God I'd hate to get fucked with a piece of chicken plastic!

Well, anyway, it was March 1985, and this man walked up to me at the pool hall and he says, "Hey, how did those pictures come out?"

(For years Rabbit has used his camera as a lure, introducing himself as an amateur photographer and asking guys to model for him.)

I just looked at him. Didn't know who he was. I said, "What? What?" And then I remembered him.

About six months earlier I had been riding from Pleasant Hill to Wisdom and I saw him walking down the highway in nothing but a pair of cutoff jeans. I was zooming to get to someplace, and then as I got down far enough to where he was in my rear view mirror, I picked up that he was standing in the middle of the road, looking, facing in the direction I was going, which was the opposite he was going. So I said, "Well, damn! I should go back." So, I had my camera and I went back and said, "Let me take a picture of you." He said, "Sure." So he stood there in the middle of the road while I took a couple of shots, and I moved on.

At the pool hall, I thought he must be trying to cause trouble. He said, "What's happening? Let's do something." I said, "I'm just hanging out. Just needed to get out of the house and have me a beer." But he wouldn't be put off, so finally I said, "Look, let me finish my beer and I'll think about it, maybe."

So he wanders off and I forget about it and maybe a half an hour later he comes back around. "Haven't you finished that beer yet?" I thought, Damn I need to deal with this man and see what he's about. So we walk out of the place together, and everybody knows. I had been going there for years. He knew what the deal was.

He says, "Of course this is going to cost you." I said, "I'll take you home. Where do you live?" And he said, "All right, I'll treat you tonight." I said, "Whatever you want. Because I can take you home." He said, "No. Go on."

And so we get out here, and we spend the night, and it's wonderful.

His name was Anthony and Rabbit didn't see him again for several months. Then one Sunday afternoon he came back.

He wandered around the house and he saw a chessboard that a friend of mine had given me 20 years ago. He spread it out on the daybed, set it up as a checkers game and said, "Come on man, let's play checkers." So we played checkers with my chess set all afternoon, and the more and more we played, the more I fell in love with this man.

I had had this fantasy since childhood, since playing with the black dude across the road, of having a local, farm black man as a lover. I felt like this fantasy had just walked up to me.

At first, as Rabbit and Anthony negotiated this quid pro quo, there were steak dinners on Tuesdays and Thursdays at a steakhouse decorated with a mural of the Matterhorn, Saturday afternoons getting high, naked, watching the baseball game, and trips to the beach.

We used to ride around the country at sunset and there was this dirt road that went for maybe fifteen miles and there wasn't one house on the whole road. We first went down it because he wanted to learn to drive my stick-shift. There was a one-lane bridge over this little branch, and in the swamp along the creek there were these wonderful yellow flowers. They were maybe two feet high, and covered with tiny yellow pentacles. I called them the Anthony flowers.

Every year I go back around the first of summer and the Anthony flowers are there.

Then the deal escalated. "He was less and less giving, and I was totally in love." Rabbit sold his art collection, so they dined at the Rainbow Room and the Top of the World, and they discoed all night. "It was the only place that he would dance with me, in New York."

At sea, on the fishing boat he rented just for the two of them, Rabbit vomited for four hours and Anthony caught two sharks. Rabbit shows me a snapshot from that outing. A dark, young, powerful head stares off to the horizon. Blue-green ocean, blood-red tee shirt.

"In January of '87 he tells me, 'Hey man, my girlfriend just had a baby.' Turns out the boy's 16 years old and he's got a girlfriend and a baby! Triple shock!"

The girlfriend dropped out of school, moved into Anthony's bedroom, and they were man and wife. "I would call and the baby would be crying in the background. Or she would take the phone and demand, 'Who's this? Who's this?'"

One phone call, Anthony told him, "Hey man, I'm about to get on the bus for New York to go live with this dude."

When I called back, I got his mother. I always felt terrible in terms of the mother, because if I were a parent and I had some man calling there for my 16, 17-year-old son, I would want to shoot him.

So I said, "May I speak to Anthony?"

"He's not here."

"You expect him?"

"No."

"I understand he went to New York."

"Yes."

So I said goodbye.

I ask him about rabbits, what he recalls. As "a child of nature" he would come upon their nests in the fields, filled with tiny balls of fur. Then he pauses.

You know what a rabbit gun is? It's like a long wooden box with a trap door. You lure the rabbit in with onion or apple inside. And once he gets in deep enough, he trips a little stick that's in the middle of the gun, and the door collapses on him.

I'm sure it's native. What they did was they burned out logs to use, before boards and European tools. My daddy still sets out four or five of them.

In the gathering dark, downhill from Rabbit's place where the road crosses a creek, I breach the vines and enter an open forest. High up, the cicadas chatter and keen, and cardinals chirp. The creek is up from yesterday's storm and its deep splash draws me. The trough of an ancient roadbed, with giant beeches shoring up its banks, leads down to the water—earth-colored and urgent—and continues on the other side. Elm and maple branches float above the creek as the night settles in. I listen to the voices of close and distant insects, the rushing water's voice, and Rabbit's.

My grandmother's room off the parlor was a quiet reserve, and in the evening she would usually be sitting there in her large armchair, reading her Bible.

We didn't talk that much. Sometimes, when I was younger, I might ask some silly kid question, but when you grow up in an extended family, before long you know everything. She wore her long grey hair in a chignon, and at night she would pull the tortoise-shell combs out and let her hair down to her waist. Then, with a dramatic gesture, she would bend over, put her hands behind her neck, and flip her hair over her head. She looked ghostly with her long hair covering her head, when she bent over like that.

She would brush it over and over again, from the back to the front. Such a laborious thing to do, to keep brushing and brushing her long hair.

In her room there was a sense that time really didn't change. The present was no different from the past, and the future, more than likely, wouldn't be different either.

That was what her room was like. Timeless. Outside of the house. It was this eternal world where you suspended disbelief. The world where art exists.

She was an untouchable fairy godmother, and I said, "I can go into this world. I'm coming in."

I've always taken risks.

Afterword

The warm March breeze riffles the funeral home awning, in the circle of bare white oaks. In front of me a woman in high heels teeters in the red clay.

"The smell of fresh-turned earth in the spring—it's a transporting smell," Robert had said. "The deep earth that's turned over in the springtime when you break the land, there's nothing like that smell."

My friend Robert Lynch—"Rabbit"—died last week of AIDS. At the funeral in a country church filled with his aunts and uncles and his double-first and double-second cousins, an old woman rose up behind the vast bank of chrysanthemums and carnations and said, emphasizing each word, "Robert was different. Robert was special. *We* march to a different drummer. *Robert* marched to a drummer of his own making."

Indeed, among the gaits and cadences of his various people—the native tribal family, the big-city gay scene, rural black communities, the art and dance worlds, the Southern left—he conjured up a rhythm all his own. And he would prance back and forth, paradoxical and stubborn, throwing folks out of step and laughing. Rabbit, the Trickster.

The Image and the Act: Men, Sex and Love

Franklin Abbott

My father, as most fathers of my generation did, abjured his role as sex educator. For Dad, like a lot of people now in their sixties, sex wasn't much talked about especially with their children. I guess I was lucky in one sense, I'd rather it that way than the other: fathers and mothers who wouldn't let their children alone with their sexual energy. His parents were more taciturn than he. They were part of a tradition passed with little variation for hundreds of years—Protestant Puritanism. Sex was of the body: dirty unlike the spiritual cleanliness one could achieve washed in the blood of the Lamb. An interesting exploration of our dis-ease with our corporeal nature is to be found in Stephen Kern's *Anatomy and Destiny: A Cultural History of the Human Body*. Professor Kern explores in detail the anxiety induced morality which until very lately made the body and its functions, especially its sexual functions, a topic off limits to most and unclear to the few professionals who dared study and comment.

I found a key of my own when I was just 19. I was living free, high in the Adirondack Mountains near Indian Lake, New York. My friends and I had rented an old farm house that had been closed up for years previous. There was an antique secretary in my room. When I opened it, I found several nests of pink, eyeless baby mice. I also found some old, old books. One was a guide to health and vigor for young men. Young man that I was I perused the old tome. One chapter I recall from my vivid interest in its topic: The Secret Sickness.

It was all about the vice of self-pollution nowadays known as masturbation. In a most stern tone this turn of the last century author warned young men that self-pollution led to moral and physical deterioration. He held out hope for those, like myself, already victims of the secret sickness: cold showers, hard beds, brown bread. Did you know that graham crackers were originally invented to remedy this problem? Did you know Freud once concurred with his physician friend Wilhelm Fliess that masturbation caused insanity and that people who masturbate excessively have an extra bone in their nose that needs surgical attention?

All that to say we often expect our fathers to know things that no one ever taught them. My father did take me to a film at the Jewish Community Center in Buffalo. You may have seen it. It's the one where in cartoon diagrams the sperm unites with the ovum. I was thirteen and street-wise, my friends had already spilled the beans. Still the diagram lingers to this day. On the way home my father said he, ah, hoped that I didn't, ah, you know what, with myself. Poised on the brink of adolescence I'd been lying for almost a decade and could do it well. Of course not, I assured him. We've never spoken again on the subject.

When I was growing up in the '50s there was a strong taboo on being naked. My family were all very modest in undress and they passed that on to me. The habit took me twenty years to shake and then only partially. When I was a kid I heard stories of other children who ran outside naked and was assured by my mother that such children were spanked upon apprehension and in a better position for spanking because no britches had to be removed. The worst I did, rather got caught doing, was swimming in my underwear with other kids in a neighbor's play pool. I wasn't spanked but warned that next time I'd come home for my swimsuit or else . . . I was then four or five and thought "underwear" was a dirty word.

Not only was there a taboo against nakedness but a greater taboo against looking on another's nakedness. You could chance it in the locker room but as a teenager I was very concerned my attraction for other boys go unnoticed. If you were ever labeled queer that was it. Your life would be pure hell until you graduated or killed yourself. So I looked sparingly, furtively and from afar. Alone at home I'd turn the pages of the high school yearbook to look at faces of other boys I couldn't look at squarely in person. It was thus I charged my erotic fantasies and stayed safe in my little straightjacket until I graduated.

Still the fear of being thought queer followed me like a ghost. After college I self-exiled into rural south Georgia for a much needed respite from the urban gay scene. In the mid-'70s there was no trace of gay life south of Macon or north of Jacksonville. For my images I found few in the white redneck men around me and had no way of knowing many Blacks as the line between races was taut. I was terrified to look at teenagers not yet jowly and crude like their elders. From time to time I drove to the little town of Tifton where I'd buy a *Playgirl* magazine in an isolated convenience store. I was too afraid even to subscribe.

I kept "the fellows" under the bed and would pull them out at will. The glory of most of these guys faded quickly as what was foreground became background as it always does. This would necessitate another trip to Tifton always worried would the clerk in the convenience store raise an eyebrow or chance a remark. Still I was determined to look at those pictures. It is unreasonable for us gay men to be expected to know what we want until we've looked around. Looking around in public can be lethal. So I was grateful for *Playgirl*, a limited catalogue of pecs and buns and penises. There were no older men, few Blacks or Asians, no one on crutches or in a wheelchair. I didn't find them either when I switched to *Blueboy*, my first gay porn fix, and I lost in the transition something that I came to miss and later long for: the men in *Playgirl* smiled while the blueboys feigned sleep or indifference.

In retrospect I think "sleep" was on the bottom and "indifference" on top, subtle indoctrination to the cultural more of dominance and submission. A man I picked up at a bar when I was twenty-three told me, "You better make up your mind what you want." I had wanted to make love and sabotaged that once again by trying with a stranger, in a stupor bought drink by drink in a dirty bar. I don't remember whether or not he looked like one of the guys in my erotic archives. He was older and drunk as I was. I didn't trust him. Like so many others I never saw him again and have no regret. Straight people, if they want to, get you one way. Your own kind, key to your house in hand, can hurt you far worse. More than a few lonely gay men have fallen victim to another man more confused, even crazy, and the axe they have to grind can be real. As gay men we take incredible chances just to get a closer look. What position we choose to view our lovers in is another matter entirely.

I hold with whoever it was that said there are as many sexual preferences as there are people and while "genetic altruism" may account for the ten percent of us who are gay and lesbian, the variations on those themes are as multitudinous as we are. As a psychotherapist I believe our basic training in the politics of pleasure and pain came early on. Maybe your mother wiped you sweetly and crowed in delight over the perfect tiny rose of your asshole. Maybe mommy was afraid of shit. Some of us fed from the breast, others from the bottle. Some breasts dripped sour milk and others flowed honey.

Thus the source of one's pleasure can be another's degradation. Part of the way first encounters are so awkward is in the figuring out of this very thing. Some gay men have developed a system of signals, keys on which hip, different colored hankies in different pockets, a leather jacket, sweet perfume. Little clues that will hopefully translate in shorthand what are our likes when it comes time for sex. The system is marginally effective and its continued use signals more how much we don't know each other. Too often we masquerade behind "sleep" and "indifference" hiding our terror of our deeper vulnerabilities. One of those vulnerable places is the deep, abiding need to love another man and be loved by him in return. We may want to do that passionately or very slowly. In our chosen positions, sometimes watching and sometimes, eyes closed, deep in the ecstasy that is a human birthright.

I confess ambivalence about pornography. Part of it is that I don't know quite what is pornographic and what is not. The pornography that I look at is made of men by men and for men. I'm sure there is exploitation and I wonder to myself about the occupational risk many of these models run who sexed with so many others before the advent of safe sex and after the dawn of AIDS. I know how unerotic (perhaps ultimately unerotic best defines pornography) life in the city can be, and as I've mentioned, hiding one's homosexual orientation can be wearing, tiring. Are the magazines I archive good for a little erotic pick-me-up like a cocktail or a joint? If I look do I betray my lover? Will my spilled seed be wasted? Will anyone notice and if I'm caught make me humble with their silence or their laughter? Masturbation is often better than two aspirin or a sleeping pill and so what if I look at pictures to make it more interesting?

When I was in college I took a class in modern art. It was taught in the dark, the instructor talking over the whir of a slide projector. Part of our exam was to identify slides and special slide show tutorials were offered. I memorized the images as I suppose I once memorized the alphabet. I had those pictures in my brain.

I know pictures can come back to haunt you. More needs to be made, a lot more, of how women have suffered on account of pornography. Men suffer, too. It limits our range of response and fetters our imaginations. It can train a man to hate his partner or himself or both. Pornography does not have a sexual preference and when it is unerotic can sow sad dreams deep in the mind that burn like a fire, hard to extinguish. (I complained to my therapist once I'd had bad dreams after seeing the movie *Alien*. He said, "I wouldn't put that in my unconscious.") Perhaps for at least some, if not all, gay pornography a little warning like the Surgeon General puts on cigarettes is in order. It might read: USER BEWARE. LOOK IF YOU WISH BUT REMEMBER TO DREAM YOUR OWN DREAMS. WHAT YOU SEE IN THE PICTURE MAY LOOK VERY DIFFERENT SHOULD YOU

TOUCH THAT MAN IN THE FLESH.

• • •

When I was in Thailand in the fall of '86 I was chaperoned in Bangkok by a very proper and hospitable Chinese family. They were ever in attendance and I was never alone except as I slept or showered. I travelled on by myself to Chaing Mai in the north, known not (as Bangkok was) as the sex capital of Asia, but for its very ancient Buddhist temples. Even so I was always suspected, a western man by myself, of wanting female companionship. I disappointed one cab driver after the next. Finally one of them looked at me coyly and said, "I like boys too." He was a cute, tiny man; shook my hand, told me he was Tony and 19 years old. I would not buy his company, but bought him a beer. He came from a village not too far away, knew where to go to catch fish. He knew a place we could go and he would give me a real good massage. I meditated hard on the face of my lover. It gave me the courage of no thank you and the safety of my hotel to return to.

The next day I'm on foot wandering the little city, map in hand, seeing the temples. Usually I am spoken to by a young man or taxi driver who wants to be my guide. I kept to myself until finally walking in the ruins of an ancient Buddhist temple. As I circled the central ruin for a second time a saffron robed Buddhist monk who was sitting on a bench with a book and a cigarette spoke to me, "Are you in a hurry up?" I wasn't. He motioned me to sit down so he could practice his English. He offered me a cigarette, Krong Tip, a Thai variety. They taste alot like Lucky Strikes. It was the first of many times we sat and smoked and talked. There were no sexual innuendos but over the next few days there was in our connection a growing reverberation of affection that stayed simple and immediate. Head shaven and bespectacled, the monk, Ruangvit, was a wise old twenty-six. There was a lightness and gentleness about him especially in his eyes and in his laughter I will never, I hope, forget.

His story was simple. He came from a poor family, mother, father, sisters and water buffalo lived on a farm in northeast Thailand. School for poor children stopped at 14 so his father took him to the monks at a temple deep in the forest, the only way he knew to further educate his very intelligent son. Ruangvit ran away. After awhile his father took him to the less austere monks at a temple in town. Ruangvit stayed as a novice and became a monk. At twenty-six he had been a monk almost half his life. Of course, I wanted to know what that was like and was told of the early rising to chant, begging for food, no intoxicants, nothing to eat after noon. "What about sex?" I asked this vigorous young man. "If you have sex in your dreams that's okay because it's not your fault," he said. He went on to tell me of one of the strangest disciplines of celibacy I'd ever heard of. With other novices, all in their teens, he'd be taken by the over-monks to meditate in front of decomposing corpses in the local morgue. I expressed my horror, Ruangvit flashed a smile and laughed. "Really," he said, "it's quite effective."

When I think of that mortification I think of what I and many of my gay male friends have witnessed as AIDS has cast its pall over our community. Beautiful men we once knew and loved have withered away and died, most long, long before a natural death would have come. The face of someone you love sick to death before his time, either in the hospital suffering or in state at a mortuary, is seared in the brain with sadness and high anxiety. A plague is a terrible thing to behold, and a plague transmitted by an act of love the cruelest joke the Divine Trickster has chosen to perpetuate in my lifetime.

Gay men have done a remarkable job educating each other about safer sexual practices that preclude contact with the AIDS virus. And yet there is reluctance and resistance on the part of some to alter their behavior even if that means the simple dispatch of a condom. Heterosexuals are even more ignorant and unwilling to avail themselves of this urgent new common sense. The heirs to the Puritans still hold sway, individual choices denigrated to two: get married or don't do it. It is time for our national denial to end. But the truth about human beings is we are stubborn: we defend our games often to the death. To talk about safe sex is to talk about sex, something dirty like dirty underwear. Only when we are more mortified of something else, like a plague, are we willing to consider changing our ways.

● ● ●

Most men that I know are homoemotional. This has nothing to do with sexual preference although curiously, many more gay men than straight are heteroemotional, preferring the friendship of women. It only further illustrates the taboo for men against getting your love and your sex in the same place with the same person. Intimacy always complicates autonomy. Did cowboy John Wayne have a nagging wife? Did 007 alternate espionage and weekends at home with his lover? We've got these pictures in our minds and they say no. The call to adventure, the call of the road, these are things men do alone by themselves or alone with other men, but alone. It's a sadly destructive pattern called competition practiced as the art of winning. So far, as best as I can see, no one's found the Golden Fleece or the Holy Grail. Winning is always temporary and when you're not winning, you become the Loser, the Lesser and if you don't watch out the Least.

Andrea Dworkin, an astute observer of the sexes in battle, likens heterosexual intercourse to enemy occupation. Even if we find her view extreme it makes more poignant the question how are we to be safely sexual with each other. One clue may come from that ancient, modern paradox called Japan.

My friend Takafumi took me to my first Japanese gay bar, the Bonzai Pipeline. It's down three narrow lanes off a side street near the center of Osaka's night district. I could never have found my way alone. On first glance the bar looked similar to those in the states except 95 percent of its clientele were well dressed Japanese gay men. Sitting at the bar with a scotch and a cigarette is as boring in Osaka as it is in Atlanta, so I asked Takafumi to show me the dance floor. It was small, darkened except for flashing lights and fronted by mirrors. I asked Takafumi to dance; he declined. Later I asked again and he declined again. Was he feeling protective of his absent lover? I didn't think so. Like a lot of things in Japan I couldn't quite figure this one out. Then as if a fog had parted I saw something remarkable that I hadn't seen before. None of the men were dancing with each other. Each was dancing alone facing the wall of mirrors. I learned later it was the custom.

In my collection of slides I took in Japan is one I would later have made into a photo I have hanging in my office. I took it in Kyoto and it was of the very simple altar in a little Shinto temple I had found in a park. Central among its ritual objects arranged sparsely in the Japanese way was a mirror. When you come to this holy place to nourish your spirit and make your offerings who you see looking back from the altar is yourself. Now I'm not saying that the mirror dancers at the Bonzai Pipeline were in any way aping old Shinto tradition. These images lodge together in my mind, a mirror that mirrors a mirror.

It seems to me that too often we run from the mirror of our own inner wisdom to look in another's in a futile search for a missing and longed for piece of ourselves. Whether, as Jung thought, it's a man looking for his feminine anima in the person of a woman or a woman doing the reverse with a man, whether it's two men or two women looking to the other in search of a piece of a personal puzzle, it is dangerous. It can and often does render sex and love a painful, sometimes "fatal" attraction. Recently a retired Air Force man killed his family and several others until he had in his own words gotten everyone who could hurt him. A New York attorney beat his wife for years and finally beat to death his six-year-old adopted daughter. Safety in sex and love is not simply a matter of wearing a condom or knowing what not to touch and when not to swallow. If we could reason together perhaps we might call a truce for a day or a month or a year and each of us repair full speed to the mirror in our own little temple, polish the glass with our prayers and wait for our own soul-deep revelations.

Scott Peck, a Christian psychotherapist, has written a perplexing book called *The People of the Lie.* In it he tries to understand the nature of human evil. It is a common obsession. Hitler is a cult figure. People pay millions to see demons writhe in Hollywood exorcism. TV evangelists make big money exploiting the devil. The Irish have a gentler version of the demon, one I much prefer. You meet him at twilight at the crossroads, a lone dark figure. When he fixes his fiery eyes on you you know you're done for. He tosses you on his back and like a wild stallion carries you this way and that over cliff and vale til morning scaring you half to death. Then he throws you in a ditch and, howling with laughter, vanishes into the morning mist. When you return to your, by then frantic, family and they see you disheveled, mud on your face, grass in your hair, to say, "Last night at the crossroads I met a man who was really the Pooka," is the only explanation required.

In the lack of safety in sex and in loving I do not find the culprit evil but ignorance. A college professor of mine used to claim a "studied ignorance" of economics. By that he meant he knew little on the subject and would be content knowing less. I think more than a few of us, especially the men in power, have a studied ignorance of our own hearts. It's not that they/we are totally at blame. You can't get a Ph.D. in compassion. Therapy helps but ignorance is essential in the evolution of human consciousness. Of course there are things we do not yet know. Once upon a time we did not know there was a virus colonizing our blood supply. Even when we finally found it we didn't know for a time how to stop its spread. The victims of AIDS are, at least in part, victims of ignorance. And as I said earlier we cannot blame our fathers (or our doctors) for not teaching us what they did not know themselves.

• • •

If you were to disrobe and stand yourself in front of a mirror and look down and slowly raise your gaze you'd see feet under legs, between your legs your sex and wonder where under your torso is your heart. If you continue watching upward over the horizon of your shoulders you'll find atop your neck, up above your mouth and nose, your eyes. Hold at that place and see if you can let your look go loving. Perhaps he or she would like to dance and if you can learn to dance well with each other perhaps it is safe to dance with another. It's a simple place to begin to learn about safety in sex and love and it's a place, call it what you will, self-pollution, self-love, narcissism, masturbation, it's a place we are all in secret familiar with. I prefer it to its all too contemporary alternatives: another ride on the back of the Pooka's North American cousin, a poisonous demon who breaks bones and hearts as he goes for the soul or sitting, saffron robed, meditating on corpses until I lose the will any longer with my body to desire another. Making love is a rite hard won in this culture and I wish not to give it up—not yet, not now and I hope not ever.

Contributors

FRANKIN ABBOTT is a poet, activist and psychotherapist who lives in Atlanta. He has worked with the editorial collectives of *Changing Men* and *RFD*, edited *New Men, Men Minds: Breaking Male Tradition* (Crossing, 1987) and this anthology. He coordinates The Circle of Healing at the First Existentialist Congregation in Atlanta, and co-hosts "Soundings" on WRFG-FM.

ANONYMOUS is a social worker who counsels with men who batter their wives or women friends and leads men's support groups.

JEFF BEANE is a certified gestalt therapist in private practice in West Hollywood. He has been active in the lesbian and gay movement for 18 years and has been a leader in the feminist men's movement for 15 years.

SHEPHERD BLISS is a pioneer in the mythopoetic men's movement. He helps direct the Sons of Orpheus, a men's drumming troupe, and teaches men's studies and psychology at J.F.K. University and workshops in the U.S., Canada and Europe. A contributor to eight books, he lives in Berkeley.

CHARLIE R. BRAXTON is a poet, playwright and activist from McComb, Mississippi. His first book is a volume of poetry entitled *Ascension From The Ashes*.

BILLY RAY BOYD is a teacher and writer who co-founded The Victims Speak, a group of men, friends and loved ones hurt by circumcision, for the purpose of bringing nonviolent direct action to the Intact Baby Movement.

TOM CAHILL, a long-time activist for disadvantaged people, is himself a victim of prison rape and has been director of People Organized to Stop Rape of Incarcerated Persons (POSRIP), since 1984.

LAWRENCE J. COHEN is a clinical psychologist in Madison, Wisconsin. He has been active in research and clinical work in the areas of sexual assault and incest.

EDWARD FIELD's books include *Stand Up, Friend, With Me* (Grove Press, 1963), winner of the Lamont Award, and *New and Selected Poems*

(Sheep Meadow Press, 1987). He has also published an anthology, *A Geography of Poets* (Bantam, 1979) and a book of translations from the Eskimo.

DAVID GOFF lives in the San Francisco Bay area where he works as a transpersonal therapist with men and pursues doctoral studies on existential community. His articles have appeared in a number of men's journals.

CRAIG G. HARRIS has been published in *In the Life*, *Gay Life* and *New Men, New Minds*. He is presently working on a poetry manuscript. He works as Coordinator of AIDS Prevention Program Development for the Gay Men's Health Crisis in New York City.

ESSEX HEMPHILL is a poet and activist living in Washington, D.C. His books include *Earth Life* and *Conditions* (BeBop Books, 1985 and 1986). His poems are included in *In The Life: A Black Gay Anthology* (Alyson, 1986) and *Tongues United* (GMP, 1987) and are featured in the film, *Looking for Langston* (1989).

CARY ALAN JOHNSON is a writer, activist and Africanist who lives in Washington, D.C. His work has appeared in *Changing Men, RFD, Blackheart, Blackout, Christopher Street*, and the *New York Native*. He is managing editor of *Other Countries: Black Gay Voices*. His screenplay, *Seven Days*, was produced by Third World Newsreel.

GUS KAUFMAN, JR. and DICK BATHRICK founded Men Stopping Violence in 1982. They co-lead groups and classes for men who batter. In their public speaking, training and independent practices Dick and Gus struggle to confront the abuse of power as it occurs in legal, religious, medical, therapeutic and marital hierarchies.

MICHAEL KIMMEL and MARTIN P. LEVINE: Dr. Kimmel is in the Department of Sociology at SUNY at Stoney Brook. He is editor of *Changing Men* (Sage, 1987), *Men's Lives* (Sage, 1989), *Men Confront Pornography* (Crown, 1990), is currently completing *Against The Tide: a Documentary History of Pro-Feminist Men in America* and is writing *Gender and Desire* with John Gagnon. Dr. Levine is an associate professor of Sociology at Blumfield College in New Jersey. He is widely published on the sociology of AIDS, sexuality and homosexuality and is a research associate on a study on sexual decision making at the Sloan Kettering Cancer Research Center.

BRUCE KOKOPELI and GEORGE LAKEY: Bruce is the father of two daughters and lives in Eatonville, Washington where he works as a general contractor. He has served in the national council of the Fellowship of Reconcilation. George lives in Philadelphia where he combines writing, activism and teaching with being a grandfather. He co-authored *No Turning Back: Lesbian and Gay Liberation in the 80's* and *Powerful Peacemaking*. He has worked as a trainer for Act Up in New York City.

ARTHUR LEVINE lives in Brooklyn, graduated from Brown University and has since published works for both children and adults, including *The Boy Who Drew Cats* and *A Thousand Lights*, two picture books forthcoming from Dial Books. He works as a senior editor at a New York publisher.

JIM LONG is a landscape architect, herbalist and farmer living in Arkansas. He is editor and publisher of *The Ozark Herbalist Newsletter*.

DAVID R. MATTESON is a founding member of both the National Organization for Changing Men and the Campaign to End Homophobia. He teaches family counseling at Governors State University, south of Chicago. He also does research in family dynamics and adolescent identity.

JOHN M. is an AIDS activist who is working to get more honest and to integrate his politics into his career. He believes passion stimulates talent and that we should all be encouraged to nurture and express whatever helps us feel strongly.

THOMAS MOORE practices archetypal psychology in New England. He is the founder and director of the Institute for the Study of Imagination. He is author of *The Planets Within* and an anthology of the writings of James Hillman entitled *Blue Fire*.

DAVID MURA is a *sensei*, a third generation Japanese-American. He is author of a book of poetry, *After We Lost Our Way* (E.P. Dutton) and the chapbook, *A Male Grief: Notes on Pornography and Addiction*. His essays have appeared in *Partisan Review* and *Threepenny Review* and his poetry in *The American Poetry Review* and *The Kyoto Review*.

GORDON MURRAY is a gay man living in San Francisco where he practices psychotherapy and teaches. He is active in the changing men's movement and served on the founding steering committee for The Campaign to End Homophobia.

RICHARD NEWMAN is a poet who began writing essays on gender issues because he found they helped his poetry. His essays have appeared in *Changing Men*.

JOHN NIERENBERG was an activist and writer living in San Francisco before his death from AIDS in 1989. His essays, erotica and poetry were published in a variety of journals.

H.J. RANDOLPH* has been active in the National Organization for Changing Men, is the coparent of a seven year old son and lives in Seattle.

ALEX RODE REDMOUNTAIN is a psychologist in private practice in Atlanta. Long concerned with social change, he founded The National Organization of Psychologists for Social Responsibility.

SY SAFRANSKY is the editor of *The Sun*, a magazine of ideas, 1074 North Roberson St., Chapel Hill, N.C. 27516.

DON SABO studies men's changing roles, exercises regularly but not fanatically, and teaches at D'Youville College, Buffalo, N.Y. He has been involved in men's studies since 1974.

TRINIDAD SANCHEZ, JR. is a Chicano poet and long time activist for peace and justice issues. A book of his poetry, *Why Am I So Brown?* will be published by Inter-American Development, Inc. in 1990. He lives in Detroit where he is active in the Latino Poets Association.

ROBERT STAPLES is a professor of sociology at the University of California, San Francisco. He has written *Black Masculinity* (The Black Scholar Press, 1982). He gave the Simon Bolivar Lecture at the University of Zulia, Maracaibo, Venezuela. He serves on the board of directors for the National Council on Family Relations and the Black World Foundation.

ROBERT J. TIMMS and PATRICK CONNERS: Dr. Timms is a clinical psychologist specializing in treatment of men and women sexually and physically abused in childhood. A member of The American Academy

---

*(Pseudonym)

of Psychotherapists and The American Group Psychotherapy Association, he regularly offers training in group therapy. Mr. Conners is a massage therapist specializing in emotional release work and neuromuscular therapy with abuse survivors. He is Director of Admissions at the Atlanta School of Massage and in private practice with Dr. Timms at the Atlanta Center for Integrative Therapy.

ALLAN TROXLER is an artist and folk dance teacher in Durham, North Carolina.

BOB VANCE writes and publishes poetry in Grand Rapids, Michigan where he works as a social worker with chronically mentally ill patients. He is a charter member of The Twilight Tribe, an activist poetry collective.

CHRISTOPHER WILEY lives in Washington, D.C. His play *Private Quarters*, four scenes in public restrooms, was recently produced by Theater BoBo. He has previously published in *RFD* and *The James White Review*.

SELECT BIBLIOGRAPHY

Part I

"AIDS Education." Editorial, *Washington Post*, 28 February 1987.

"AIDS: The Public Reacts." *Public Opinion*, 8 December 1986.

Altman, Dennis. *AIDS in the Mind of America*. New York: Doubleday, 1986.

Anderson, Jack. "Fear consigns AIDS material to the shelf." *Newark Star Ledger*, 11 November 1985.

Beeson, Diane R., Jane S. Zones and John Nye. "The Social Consequences of AIDS Antibody Testing: Coping with Stigma." Paper presented at annual meetings of the Society for the Study of Social Problems, New York, 1986.

Brandt, Alan. *No Magic Bullet*. New York: Oxford University Press, 1986.

Brannon, Robert. "Introduction" to Robert Brannon and Deborah David, eds. *The Forty-Nine Percent Majority*. Reading, MA: Addison-Wesley, 1976.

Center for Disease Control. "AIDS Surveillance Report." December 1987.

Dalton, Harlon and Scott Burris, eds. *AIDS and the Law: A Guide for the Public*. New Haven: Yale University Press, 1987.

Des Jarlais, Don C., Cathy Casriel and Samuel Friedman. "The New Death Among IV Drug Users." *AIDS: Principles, Practices and Politics*, edited by Inge B. Corless and Mary Pittman-Lindeman. New York: Hemisphere Press, 1988.

Frumkin, Lyn and John Leonard. *Questions and Answers on AIDS*. New York: Avon, 1987.

Gagnon, John and William Simon, *Sexual Conduct*. Chicago: Aldine.

—— and Michael Kimmel, forthcoming. *Gender and Desire*. New York, Basic Books, 1973.

Gostin, Larry. "Traditional Public Health Strategies." (Dalton and Burris, eds.). *AIDS and the Law: A Guide for the Public*. New Haven: Yale University Press,1987.

Gould, Robert. "Measuring Masculinity By The Size of a Paycheck." (Brannon and David, eds.).*The Forty-Nine Percent Majority*. Reading, MA: Addison, Wesley, 1976.

Green, Richard. The Transmission of AIDS. (Dalton and Burris, eds.). *AIDS and the Law: A Guide for the Public*. New Haven: Yale University Press, 1987.

Hall, Lynn and Thomas Modl, eds. *AIDS: Opposing Viewpoints*. St. Paul: Greenhaven Press, 1988.

Harrison, James. "Caution: Masculinity May Be Hazardous to Your Health." *Journal of Social Issues*, 1978.

Helms, Jesse. "Only Morality Will Effectively Prevent AIDS from Spreading." Letter to *The New York Times*, 12 November 1987.

Hughes, John. "The Madness of Separate Spheres: Insanity and Masculinity in Late 19th Century Alabama." Paper presented at conference on

Masculinity in Victorian America, Barnard College, 9 January 1988.

Institute for Advanced Study of Human Sexuality. *Safe Sex in the Age of AIDS*. Secaucus, NJ: Citadel Press, 1986.

Institute of Medicine, National Academy of Sciences. *Confronting AIDS: Directions for Public Health, Health Care and Research*. Washington D.C.: National Academy Press, 1986.

Kimmel, Michael and Jeffrey Fracher. "Hard Issues and Soft Sports: Counseling Men About Sexuality." *Handbook of Counseling and Psychotherapy with Men*. Edited by Murray Scher, et. al. Newbury Park, CA: Sage Publications, 1987.

Kropp, Arthur. "Religious Right Cashing in on AIDS Epidemic." *Houston Texas Post*, 20 July 1987.

Levine, Martin P. " Gay Macho." Ph.D. dissertation, New York University, 1985.

Los Angeles Times. 12 December 1985.

Martin, John L. "The Impact of AIDS on Gay Male Sexual Behavior Patterns in New York City." *American Journal of Public Health* 77 (5) May 1987.

McKusik, Leon, William Hortsman and Thomas J. Coates. "AIDS and Sexual Behavior Reported by Gay Men in San Francisco." *American Journal of Public Health*, May 1985.

New York Post. 24 May 1983.

The New York Times. 15 December 1985; 18 March 1986.

Quinn, Thomas C., Mann, Jonathan M., Curran, James W. and Prot, Peter. "AIDS in Africa: An Epidemiological Paradigm." *Science*, 234. 21 November 1986.

"Sex in the Age of AIDS. A symposium." *The Advocate*. 8 July 1986.

Sullivan, Ronald. "More Women are Seeking Test for AIDS." *The New York Times*, 23 May 1987.

Watney, Simon. *Policing Desire: Pornography, AIDS and the Media*. Minneapolis: University of Minnesota Press, 1987.

Part II

Matteson,D.R. "Bisexual men in marriage: Is a homosexual identity and stable marriage possible?" *Journal of Homosexuality* 11, 149–171 (1985).

McWhirter, D.P. & Mattison, A.M. *The Male Couple: How Relationships Develop*. (Prentice-Hall, 1984).

Latham, J.D. & White, G.D. "Coping with homosexual expression within heterosexual marriages: Five case studies." *Journal of Sex and Marital Therapy* 3, 198–212 (1978).

Matteson, D.R. "Mixed Orientation Marriages: A Six-Year Study." (in process).

Miller, B. "Adult sexual resocialization: Adjustments toward a stigmatized identity." *Alternative Lifestyles* 1, 207–234 (1978).

Coleman, E. "Bisexual women in marriages." *Journal of Homosexuality* 11,

87–100 (1985).

Garbarino, J. *Adolescent Development: An Ecological Perspective.* (Merrill, 1985).

Calderwood, D. "Same Sex Behavior," in *About Your Sexuality.* (Beacon Press, 1971); and A.C. Kinsey, W.B. Pomery, C.E. Martin, & P.H. Gebhard, *Sexual Behavior in the Human Female.* (W.B. Saunders, 1953).

Part III

Abbott, Franklin (ed.) *New Men, New Minds: Breaking Male Tradition,* Freedom, CA: Crossing Press, 1987, is an excellent companion volume to this anthology. It includes articles by thirteen of the authors represented in *Men and Intimacy* and is available at bookstores or may be ordered from The Crossing Press (800/777-1048).

RFD: A Country Journal of Gay Men Everywhere, P.O. Box 68, Liberty, TN 37095, may be of interest to readers of this anthology.